W9-CNU-885

P.W.

869

THE
OUTDOOR COOK'S
BIBLE

THE OUTDOOR COOK'S BIBLE

Joseph D. Bates, Jr.

With Drawings by Jack Murray

DOUBLEDAY & COMPANY, INC.
GARDEN CITY, N.Y.

ISBN: 0-385-02107-0

Library of Congress Catalog Card Number 63–19269
Text Copyright © 1963 by Joseph D. Bates, Jr.
Illustrations Copyright © 1963 by Doubleday & Company, Inc.
All Rights Reserved
Printed in the United States of America
15   14   13   12
Cover photo courtesy Johnson Motors, taken at Cypress Gardens, Florida

CONTENTS

Introduction

OUTDOOR COOKING IS EASY!

Back in the days when lots of families could afford servants, mine imported sight unseen from the Emerald Isle a female who could cook all right, but her main drawback was that she had a few screws loose somewhere. What she lacked mentally was evened up to some extent by her magic with the coal stove and the skillet. She put in dough and she got out doughnuts, or hot bread, or cookies, or cakes and pies, or something else. Whatever came out was hot, fragrant, and delicious, so she stayed with us quite a while.

Those were the days when my dog and I went fishing down by the brook, or even perhaps as far as the river. I didn't realize at the time that the fish I caught mostly were dace or chubs, but Mother cooked them for me anyway, and never complained because they weren't always trout. We lived in what was then the country, and I went to the proverbial little red schoolhouse, which had eight grades in one room and only a couple of dozen kids, some of whom should have been in college. By pooling our knowledge after school and at recess, we learned how to roast potatoes and corn over the coals and how to cook swiped soup in tin cans. We also learned how to make a tin-can stove that would fry bacon and eggs.

By that time I was a Boy Scout and had learned how to bake bread on a stick and how to broil trout on a hot rock, plus several other similar culinary triumphs. But I often wondered how many years you had to go to college to know how to make doughnuts and cookies and pies and cakes like the ones Bridget made at home.

When I got to be a Second Class Scout instead of a Tenderfoot, it suddenly dawned on me that if Bridget could cook that well almost anybody could. (She didn't have all her marbles, if you will remember.) Well, I've been working more or less assiduously at it ever since. The main thing I pinned in my hat late in my teens was that cooking—either indoors or outdoors—really is fairly easy, if you are content not to try to compete with the chefs who have been decorated with the Cordon Bleu. I learned that you could cook pretty good food without fancy equipment and scarce ingredients and complicated methods. I learned that you could make things like reflector-bakers and stovepipe stoves and pothooks and forks and tongs all by yourself. If you wanted a good wire grid to cook on, you probably could find it at the town dump. These, of course, were the days before aluminum foil and camp stoves and portable iceboxes and other things that make outdoor cooking even easier nowadays.

When I got older and out of college and could afford such luxuries as canoe trips and guides and expensive guns and tackle I learned how easy it was to make bean-hole beans and fish chowders and blueberry muffins and Brunswick stew and lots of other viands that would stick to your ribs and that seemed like a considerable improvement over what they serve at the Ritz. But most cookbooks seemed unusually complicated—and I decided that one day I would try to write one that made outdoor cooking really easy. There's not much sense in wading through recipes only to find that you haven't got some of the unusual ingredients. There's not much sense in trying to decipher a formidable formula when your buddies are screaming for chow. Why

Whether it's a snack or a feast, food always tastes better outdoors. (Abercrombie)

didn't someone write a cookbook that called for simple ingredients and told you that if you were out of one thing you could substitute another?

Then there's the matter of equipment. I learned about outdoor cooking before the days of hundred-dollar grills, and my allowance in the Boy Scout era was such that I had to improvise most of the cooking paraphernalia we used. Why didn't someone write a cookbook that explained how to improvise the essentials—if you couldn't afford to buy them, or if you happened to be in a spot where they were unavailable?

Then the war came, and I got stuck in some far-off places. We had the usual attrition in mess sergeants and cooks and bakers, but it seemed that this was no excuse for letting the boys murder the grub—whatever there was of it. Sometimes the mess sergeants got the notion that the battalion commander couldn't cook either, and one thing that is very annoying is to tell somebody something, only to get a wise look in return.

So the alternative occasionally was to take off my jacket and make a batch of macaroni and cheese myself, or to show them how not to make French toast taste like shoe leather. This, and occasional visits to the company kitchens in the cold gray dawn, usually got matters straightened out. We had good food, and I learned a bit about production-line cooking.

When things got back to normal—or as near normal as things probably ever will get—I became outdoor product marketing consultant for a number of firms. Part of their public services to outdoor-minded people was to have me write some little outdoor cooking booklets telling folks how to do outdoor cooking the easy (and inexpensive) way. It pleased everybody involved in these projects to have these booklets requested in the hundreds of thousands as recommended guides for sportsmen's clubs, scout organizations, and other outdoor-minded groups. The idea that outdoor cooking could be made easy and economical and fun seemed to have considerable appeal. Hundreds of letters came in saying, in essence, "The sample is wonderful. Now why don't you write a full-sized book and give us the complete course?" So, after all these growing pains, this volume is the result, and I hope lots of outdoor-minded people will find it helpful and useful, and that it will help them to greater enjoyment of our beautiful out of doors.

This book, then, is an effort to provide easy, sensible outdoor cooking information for everybody—from the Tenderfoot Boy Scout (which I was once) to the chap who wants to do his own cooking the easy way on a hunting or fishing trip, or in his own back yard on an expensive fireplace or grill—or even on one he makes himself for little or nothing. It covers the plain and the fancy; that is, all but the very fancy! If you want the Cordon Bleu stuff, there are other books that will take care of it. Outdoor cooking, to most of us, is a hobby and an expedient. It is not a profession.

When I started this book, I seriously wondered if I were competent to write it. I've skipped around in preparing chapters—doing each one when the ingredients seemed about ready to jell. This was one of the last parts of the book to be written, and I'm beginning to be hopeful that, whatever it may lack, its readers will get a baker's dozen in exchange for their money.

Obviously I could not have conceived all of the many recipes described herein, although I take the blame for many of them. My thanks go to the thousands of sportsmen (and sports wives) who sent in their favorite outdoor recipes in response to my television programs. The recipes I have selected are the real McCoy—many handed down in families whose old-timers really knew how to cook. As far as is known, these recipes are entirely original, and have never before been reproduced in book form.

My thanks also go to William Hillcourt, National Director of Program Resources of the Boy Scouts of America, for the many instructive photographs his organization has provided. I hope this book will reciprocate, at least to an extent. Included also are outdoor cooking ideas and recipes developed by guides, lumberjacks, trappers, sportsmen, and the hunting and fishing companions with whom I've enjoyed the bounty of the out of doors during the years. To many of these, a knowledge of outdoor cooking is a necessity vital to their existence. To others, it is merely a hobby—an attempt to introduce the gourmet's touch into tasty and properly cooked dishes from very simple ingredients.

My special appreciation also goes to my old friend, the celebrated wild-life artist, Jack Murray, for the drawings that appear in this book (and that have illustrated others with which I have been in labor in the past). Whether it be a simple sketch or a painting for a magazine cover, Jack has the genius to make an animal look as it really is, and to make how-to-do-it drawings precisely understandable.

Outdoor cooking, especially far from home, is much more than merely preparing a good meal with whatever may be on hand. It is the comradeship of men who love the wilderness and who safeguard their heritage of its enjoyment. It is the fragrance of wood smoke drifting invitingly over a rusty chimney in an ancient and well-gnawed cabin shared with various furry creatures, some of which may not be entirely desirable. It is what John Madson, of the Olin Mathieson Chemical Corporation, was thinking of when he wrote *The Palace in the Popple*— which he has given me permission to reproduce, and which goes like this:

It's a smoky, raunchy boars' nest
    With an unswept, drafty floor
And pillowticking curtains
    And knife scars on the door.
The smell of a pine-knot fire
    From a stovepipe that's come loose
Mingles sweetly with the bootgrease
    And the Copenhagen snoose.

There are work-worn .30-30s
    With battered, steel-shod stocks,
And drying lines of longjohns
    And of steaming, pungent socks.
There's a table for the Bloody Four
    And their game of two-card draw,
And there's deep and dreamless sleeping
    On bunk ticks stuffed with straw.

Jerry and Jake stand by the stove,
    Their gun-talk loud and hot.
And Bogie has drawn a pair of kings
    And is raking in the pot.

Frank's been drafted again as cook
　　And is peeling some spuds for stew
While Bruce wanders by in baggy drawers
　　Reciting *Dan McGrew.*

Nowhere on earth is fire so warm
　　Nor coffee so infernal,
Nor whiskers so stiff, jokes so rich,
　　Nor hope blooming so eternal.
A man can live for a solid week
　　In the same old underbritches
And walk like a man and spit when he wants
　　And scratch himself where he itches.

I tell you, boys, there's no place else
　　Where I'd rather be, come fall,
Where I eat like a bear and sing like a wolf
　　And feel like I'm bull-pine tall.
In that raunchy cabin out in the bush
　　In the land of the raven and loon,
With a tracking snow lying new to the ground
　　At the end of the Rutting Moon.

John adds, in a letter, "I doubt if the guys in the poem are really looking forward to that meal. This particular band of deerslayers has endured one man's slumgullion recipe for five days hand running, and no one dares to gripe because the first man to bellyache about the grub will inherit Frank's spoon, spatula and feedsack apron.

"Like many hunters and fishermen who feed themselves in the boondocks, the men in this poem aren't good cooks. They know the deer, the rifle, and the ways of rising trout, but they do not know how to vary and balance their diet with well-prepared grub.

"It's too bad, for no sportsman is any better than the state of his bed and digestion. Give these same men some relief from Frank's slum and canned prunes and they'd all be lighter of foot and sharper of eye tomorrow. Tonight, give them some meat that isn't fried or greasy, with a simple salad and some soup, and some fresh hot bread with Hudson's Bay jam. And then, the Red Gods willing, maybe tomorrow night we'll have broiled deer liver with creamed onions!"

So it seems that this book was written for guys like Frank, and I'm sending a copy to John to give to him. I hope it will help to improve the boys' digestion during deer week, and also when he presides over a dinner cooked for his family and friends on his own back yard grill back home.

THE
OUTDOOR COOK'S
BIBLE

Chapter One

HOW TO BUILD EFFICIENT COOKING FIRES

Many years ago we took a three-week canoe trip into the famous Allagash region of the Maine wilderness to fish for big brook trout. My guide was Ross McKenney, who began his career running logs down river in the old lumbering days, and who had acquired such a profound knowledge of woodcraft that he later taught the subject at Dartmouth College. We pulled the canoe ashore at the campground in the pouring rain. While I started putting the tent up, Ross took his ax into the brush and quickly returned with an armful of wood split from a spruce stump. Bent over the pile to shield it from the rain, he worked some kind of magic that quickly started a fire. A few more trips gained us enough firewood to last through the night.

Ross McKenney's ability to make a fire so quickly under such circumstances made a lasting impression on me. Aside from cooking, the warmth of a fire has saved the lives of a great many people. The lack of one has caused unnecessary deaths and needless suffering, as well.

Since then, I have hunted and fished in countless wilderness regions with guides and companions possessing varying degrees of "savvy" in fire building, in camp cooking, and in the several other arts that make up a woodsman's skill. As far as the really good ones were concerned, some could cook excellently, while others did less well. But all the good ones had one thing in common: they all knew how to build an efficient fire.

Now, building a fire sounds very easy. It is— if the weather is good, and especially if we have charcoal in the grill, along with a fire starter and a match. But building a really good cooking fire under any circumstances is quite another matter. It's something of an art. It separates the men from the boys, as far as outdoor cooking is concerned. It makes all the difference between serving up a delicious meal with ease and comfort —and burning one thing while undercooking another on a fire that may be too hot, too cold, too big, too small, too poppy, too smoky, or may die out almost completely just when we begin to think that everything is going fine!

No matter whether we plan to cook in the back yard, on the trail, in camp, or at a picnic area beside the road, there are many angles in knowing how to build a good cooking fire. Once learned, this knowledge is never forgotten. It's half the battle in learning how to be a good outdoor cook—a cook who can broil, boil, fry, or bake the foods necessary to a complete meal, and do them all easily and "to the queen's taste," outdoors.

So please bear with us if we go into fire building in this chapter with considerable detail. It's important!

Passing by the familiar bags of charcoal and briquettes for the moment, let's start in by discussing wood fires. Let's leave the "fancy stuff" for the end of the chapter, and talk now about the basic problem—how to build a really efficient outdoor cooking fire from the woods that nature provides.

SELECTION OF WOODS

Woods that make good kindling may not make good cooking fires, and vice versa. In general, evergreens are reserved for kindling, as we shall see shortly. They pop too much, are too sooty and smoky, and burn for too short a time to be good for anything but kindling. An exception is the bark from old, dead hemlock stumps—perhaps from ancient trees killed by lightning or by forest fires. Thick bark pulled from such stumps burns well and reduces to good coals, although it is not to be preferred to hardwoods unless it is handier.

In general, standing dead hardwoods make excellent cooking fires, because they reduce to hot, long-lasting coals, without popping and smoking. My favorite of all the hardwoods is hickory; it excels in these qualities and it is fragrant—an ideal wood for broiling meats, birds, and fish. Oak, apple, maple, beech, hornbeam, butternut, ironwood, locust, Osage orange, holly, and several others follow in about that order. Birch, ash, alder, basswood, and aspen make a quick and hot fire but do not last as long. Birch and aspen (among others) can be burned when green on a fire already going well.

Note that *standing* dead hardwoods are preferred for fire building. Leaning hardwood limbs or trees also may be sound and useful. Branches or logs lying on the ground usually are damp, rotting, and generally unsatisfactory for efficient fires.

If we have no ax or hatchet, fair-sized hardwood branches can be broken from dead trees. Wood from the branch tips is broken off first, to aid in kindling the fire. Then the larger section can be broken in pieces by pulling it against one's knee or by hitting it against a rock.

Assemble a good pile of hardwood before collecting the kindling.

TRICKS WITH KINDLING

While dead evergreen branches are unsatisfactory for cooking fires, the wood of evergreens is pitchy, and excellent as a fire starter. Lower branches of many live species of evergreens are dead and brittle, and can be broken into kin-

dling easily. Such branches get a degree of protection from the rain, and thus can be used to start a fire in wet weather.

A favorite fire starter (where available) is the bark peeled from *dead* birch trees. It is pitchy, easily peeled from the trees, and can be broken into tinder quickly. Dead maple twigs also are excellent. So are ash and aspen.

With a pile of hardwood branches handy, and a fistful of shredded bark or tiny evergreen branches available, clear a safe spot, well protected from the wind, and light the tinder.

The next step is to add somewhat larger kindling, without smothering the fire. A way to do it is to stack short pencil-sized or finger-sized branches teepee-fashion over the burning tinder —then add larger pieces in the same manner until the fire is going briskly.

Another method is to light the tinder between two short logs that are spaced five or six inches apart and are three or four inches in diameter. Lay short lengths of fine kindling over these two logs at right angles, and then crisscross others on top, until several crisscrossed layers have been piled on each other.

fuzz or shavings as possible along two inches or so of its length. These shavings should be as large and as bushy as they can be made, leaving one end uncut from the stick. We make at least three prayer sticks and prop them together, tee-pee-fashion. A match held under the teepee should start them burning, after which un-shaved sticks can be stacked against them. Prayer sticks whittled from dead evergreen branches, or split from the inside of a dead ever-green log, light very quickly—even more so than when cut from dry hardwoods. To me, making prayer sticks is a tedious and usually unnecessary procedure, but it is worth remembering when building a fire at times when the branches are wet on the outside.

The idea in both of these methods is to provide air circulation, so we do not smother the fire. A fire needs oxygen to make it burn. If sticks are laid directly on the tinder, the fire will not burn as quickly, and it may put itself out altogether.

Another idea that seems to be a favorite, but which outdoorsmen rarely bother to use, is to start a fire by making a "teepee" from "prayer sticks." A prayer stick, as shown, is a dry, finger-sized stick about four or five inches long that has been whittled with a knife or ax to raise as much

If a fire smokes too much, it is due to a poor choice of firewood. Following is a list of some of the more common woods for various fire-building purposes. It is well to be able to recognize these woods. Two books helpful in doing so are *A Field Guide to Trees and Shrubs*, by George A. Petrides (Houghton, Mifflin Co., Cambridge, Mass., 1958), and *Trees: A Guide to Familiar American Trees*, by Zim and Martin (Golden Press, Inc., New York, 1952, 1956).

TINDER (to use as a fire starter)

Birch bark (avoid removing bark from live trees)
Dead evergreen twigs (from lower branches of trees)
Shredded cedar bark
Dry palmetto fronds
Dry pine needles and evergreen cones
Prayer sticks (as described above)
Dry grass or leaves (a last choice)

KINDLING (for quick, hot fires)

All species of birch (the small, dead branches)
Resinous wood (split from dead evergreen stumps—particularly pine)
Ash   Alder   Aspen   Basswood
Hard Maple   Red Maple   Sage

COOKING FIRES (for long-lasting coals)

Apple	Hornbeam
Ash	Ironwood
Beech	Locust
Birch (logs)	Oak
Butternut	Osage orange
Hemlock (bark only)	Poplar
Hickory	Rock elm
Holly	Rock maple

SLOW FIRES (for long nighttime burning)

Ash	Hickory
Aspen	Maple
Birch	Pitch pine
Elm	Poplar
Green logs from red oak	Sourgum

WOODS TO AVOID (for cooking fires, because these woods pop, spark, or smoke excessively, or because they have an unpleasant odor)

Basswood	Tamarack
Chestnut	Tulip
Box elder	Tupelo
All evergreens (conifers)	White elm
Paloverde	Willow
Sassafras	

Split firewood whenever possible, because split wood burns much better than whole logs.

FIRE STARTERS

While discussing these elementals with which most sportsmen are familiar, it is obvious that it is very easy to start a cooking fire when conditions are favorable. But it may be quite another matter to get a fire going easily when the woods are wet. Efficient fire building under adverse circumstances is a work of the true woodsman. And let's remember that, while these points may be elemental, they can make all the difference between getting a fire going fairly easily in the cold and the rain—and having to admit to failure after using the last match.

So—let's face it. The times when we need a fire the most usually are the times when it is most difficult to start. Matches are useless when they are damp. The safest matches are the old-fashioned, sturdy wooden ones. The safest way to carry them is in one of the little round waterproof metal matchsafes—or in some other type of waterproof container. To be on the safe side, these emergency matches should be dipped in paraffin or, preferably, in varnish to a depth of an inch or so from the head, and allowed to dry. These waterproofed matches, in their waterproof container, are kept for *emergencies*. We carry them all the time, when in the woods, but we carry other matches for ordinary uses. Every month or so we test a match from the emergency container, just to be on the safe side. Many woodsmen carry two such containers, to be even safer.

Being a habitual pipe smoker, I don't bother with matches, except for this emergency supply. Before World War II someone gave me a "Zippo" lighter with some advertising on it. I carried this lighter during action in the Pacific all through the war, and it still is a prized possession. The wilds of New Guinea can be rather dismal in the rainy season, and this little lighter, with a can of fuel and some extra flints, has started many comforting cooking fires. Once I had to pull out some of the cotton to use as tinder, but the lighter never failed me. But there's one thing that must be said about using any lighter in the rain. Don't let a drop of water get on the mechanism, or it won't light until it dries out.

The motto is, When going into the woods, be sure to have a means of fire lighting that is absolutely foolproof. It's better to be safe than sorry.

Many woodsmen I know, including the cow hands who ride the Western ranges, have a fire-starting idea that is well worth copying. They always carry a candle stub or two. When it's wet, it still is easy to light a candle with a single match. When the lighted candle is placed under some tinder, it is almost sure to get a fire going, even if the tinder is damp.

These, though, are emergency measures. The trick under all circumstances is to get a fire going quickly and easily. To do this, one of the commercial fire starters is a great help. You'll find some old-timers who think that such fire starters are "sissy"—but to most of us they are an expedient that makes a great deal of sense.

A non-commercial type that can be made in camp or at home consists merely of rolling a sheet of newspaper into a compact roll almost as thick as a cigar. The roll is tied or sealed, then cut into convenient lengths for immersion in melted paraffin or candle wax. When the candle wax has soaked thoroughly into the paper, the rolls are removed and dried. Then they may be cut into shorter lengths of two inches or so. These light easily with a match, and provide excellent fire starters.

In the commercial category, we find fire starters of many kinds, but there is a great deal of difference between them. Some are little blocks of compressed sheathing board made of paper or ground corn husks impregnated with a hydrocarbon that causes them to light easily. The longer these are kept, the less easily they seem to light, because much of the hydrocarbon evaporates. Another type is inflammable liquids of one sort or another which are sold in containers for pouring or squirting on combustible materials to make them light easily. These work well unless they leak—and if they leak, it may be unfortunate for the duffel with which they are packed.

A third type is the "napalm-like" jelly that comes in tubes, like shaving cream or toothpaste. You squirt an inch or two of the jelly onto whatever you want to light. This works well unless there is a small puncture in the tube. If so, the material inside may evaporate and leave little or nothing in the tube when its contents are needed.

A fourth type consists of fire starters that look like cubes of sugar, or disc-shaped white candies. These are compact, and they light readily. Some types may be toxic for use in confined spaces, and most of them are rather expensive. Their compactness is their best recommendation.

The fifth type is, in my opinion, without peer among fire starters. This is old reliable "Canned Heat," which is a smokeless solidified alcohol product that comes in small cans with covers (like small paint cans). "Canned Heat" never deteriorates when tightly covered, and thus can be stored indefinitely—even for five years or more. A small (2⅜-ounce) can of "Canned Heat" or "Sterno" is easy to carry and equally easy to use. Just remove the cover; dig out a small glob of the jelly with a stick; put it under the tinder and light up! A can will start many cooking fires, with no smoke and no smell, but with a very hot (165°) flame.

Another thing I like about "Sterno" is that it is a multipurpose product. If a hunter's hands are cold, he just sets the can on a stump, lights it, and warms up. Replacing the cover puts out the flame, ready for use again. We use "Sterno" to warm frozen gun actions; to remove fishing rod ferrules or arrowheads; to thaw frozen pipes or locks—and for scores of other uses. The small can burns continuously for about an hour, and larger sizes can be obtained if desired.

The lightness and versatility of the Hudson's Bay-type ax makes it a favorite of campers and outdoor cooks. (Peavey)

AN AX IS VALUABLE

In obtaining wood for outdoor fires, we have spoken of breaking up small pieces, such as limbs from dead hardwood trees. This, of course, is the hard way to do it. The easy way is to carry an ax or a hatchet.

There are as many ideas as to what constitutes a satisfactory ax or hatchet as there are ways to mix a martini. What suits one man may be heresy to another. My feeling is that an ax is far superior to a hatchet, because its length provides more leverage for cutting. In the ax department, for camp woodcutting and for other odd jobs, my favorite is one of the Hudson's Bay type. These are made by the Peavey people, in Brewer, Maine; by the Collins Company, in Collinsville, Connecticut; and by other firms. I've had my little Hudson's Bay ax for twenty-five years or more. It is light to carry, yet sturdy enough to do a good job. The ax is equipped with a sheath that can be fastened on the belt. Along with it, a woodsman should carry a small file (the kind made for sharpening axes) and a whetstone. The stone should have a coarse side and a fine side, and it can be a very small one. With this equipment, it's easy to keep the ax razor sharp. His ax is a woodsman's favorite treasure. No one ever asks to borrow it. It would be safer to run off with his wife!

Along with an ax, a saw of some sort is good secondary woodcutting equipment. A saw is an article for camp rather than for the trail. Of the many kinds, some fold up rather compactly. If there's a large amount of firewood cutting to be done, a saw is necessary but, as far as the outdoor cook is concerned, it should rarely be needed.

WET-WEATHER FIRES

Now that all this has been discussed, let's return to that cold and soggy September afternoon when Ross McKenney so expertly built the fire in the rain—in Maine. How did he do it? Ross merely slipped into the wet woods, where his expert eye quickly located an old dead evergreen stump. A few belts with his ax, and he had knocked into sections the side away from the direction the rain came from. He picked up an armload of these and hurried back, grabbing some bark from an old dead birch as he returned. He dumped this in a sheltered spot and sliced into the resinous wood, knocking the still dry interior into sections. He shredded the bark finely as he knelt over it to keep it as dry as possible, and lighted it. He piled the dry evergreen splinters around the bark, in the teepee fashion we have described, and then pyramided more dry wood around the expanding flame. Despite the wet weather, he had his fire going quickly. He didn't use a fire starter. Except for candle stubs, I don't recall that we had any in those days—but of course they would have made the job easier.

If Ross, or any other good woodsman, had been in any other part of the country under such conditions, he could have done similarly. No matter how hard it rains, the insides of sound, dead hardwood or evergreen stumps remain dry. The barks of birches and many other trees ignite (after a fashion) even when wet. Wet, dead branches can be shaved to get to the dry wood under the bark. During such fire building, a rain shield of some sort always helps—even a jacket held over the fire maker while he does his job. Along this line, carrying a thin sheet of folded plastic often helps—and such need take little more room than a folded handkerchief. If the ground is wet, turning over a flat rock may find us a dry spot—or the fire can be built on some of the dry wood chopped from the stump. A good woodsman quickly estimates the situation and uses whatever limited facilities are available —even if he has to put up his shelter first and build his fire inside it in a frying pan before transferring it outdoors. With waterproofed matches (and especially with a candle or another type of fire lighter), it's not a very hard job for a good woodsman to do.

THE BILLET FIRE

Now let's return home and see how simple it is to prepare an efficient cooking fire amid modern conveniences. After our session in the woods, it will be easy!

Back yard or camp outdoor fireplace or grill fires, of course, are made with charcoal or with briquettes—but excellent ones also are made with wood. Here's my formula for a "billet fire," which broils the best steaks, chops, chicken, and fish we ever tasted.

Some years ago a bow-hunter friend owned a wood lot that was taken over for the route of a superhighway. He drove up one weekend morning. "The bulldozers have wrecked the place," he said, "but there's some excellent hickory lying around. Let's take the station wagons and go and get some before they burn it all up."

We each returned that day with a station wagon loaded with straight hickory logs, each five or six inches in diameter. I cut mine all to six-inch lengths and piled them until they had dried enough to remove the bark. Then I split each short section into pieces nearly as small in diameter as one's finger. I put these into burlap sacks and stored them in the garage to cure.

(Why remove the bark? Because insects may be under it, which could ruin the wood during storage.)

The sawing and splitting of the billets is easy, particularly if there are no knots in the wood. I had six or eight sacks full in less than a day, and have been using hickory billets for broiling fires ever since. Hickory imparts a delicious "hickory smoke" flavor to broiled foods. The dry billets burn to coals almost without smoke. If a smokier flavor is desired, a few can be soaked in a pail of water, and one or two of these wet ones can be added to the coals from time to time.

Preparation of the hickory billet fire is very easy—either in the grill or in the outdoor fireplace. We lay a closely packed layer on the hearth, so that the row of billets are in the form of a square or rectangle. We lay another billet on both ends, at a right angle to the layer below. In the middle of this we put a cube of "Sterno" charcoal lighter (which is pink solidified alcohol fuel about the size of a cherry, available in a glass jar of twenty "cubes"), and we light it. Then we pile a layer on top of the

open layer below and (still piling each layer at a right angle to that below) we add several layers on top of this. When the stack of billets is piled, the fire is burning briskly. When it has burned to coals, and the flame has died down, we tamp the embers flat—and are ready to cook.

This fire is hot for a relatively short time, but it lasts long enough to broil a steak or several chops to perfection. If a larger fire is needed—to cook chicken broilers, for instance—some charcoal or a few briquettes can be added to the pyre of billets after the fire has been started.

When going on a cookout we don't depend on native woods for firewood. We put a sackful of hickory billets and a jar of "Canned Heat" in the car, and have a fire going anywhere in no time. The hickory billets make a hot and fragrant cooking fire—and they are much cleaner to transport than charcoal.

In regions where hickory exists, most farmers who own wood lots can be induced to part with a few hickory logs. One log makes a big pile of billets. If hickory is unobtainable, maple or oak will do almost as well.

CHARCOAL OR BRIQUETTES?

Since these are familiar to all outdoor cooks, we will dwell on them briefly. Charcoal is a fairly standard product, since most of it is made from hardwoods which, when in charcoal form, are about as good when made from one hardwood as from another. Charcoal does not provide as hot or as enduring a fire as briquettes— and thereby lies the chief difference between the two. Charcoal, however, is favored over briquettes by most outdoor cooks who want a bed of coals lasting long enough to do a good job on a steak, some chops, fish fillets—or other foods requiring relatively short cooking time.

Briquettes vary a good deal, depending on who made them. Some have a distasteful odor, while others do not. All burn so hotly that outdoor chefs are cautioned not to use too many. Being more compact than charcoal, they burn longer, and thus are excellent for roasts, whole birds, and other foods needing long cooking time. Also, the chef can use tongs to move burning briquettes from one place to another on the hearth, or can add new briquettes when they are needed to maintain proper heat.

With any of the good fire starters, getting a charcoal or a briquette fire going is simple. Just lay a small bed of the fuel on the hearth; add a little fire starter; light up, and pile more fuel around the flame as needed. One has only to guard against piling fuel on top of a new flame, because of the danger of choking it.

When cooking is done, let's save the remaining fuel for use next time. Charcoal fires can be extinguished by pouring enough water on them to put them out. If the fuel has not dried out when a new fire is needed, merely push it aside and start a new fire with new fuel. The new fire will dry out the old fuel, which probably will

start burning, if not pushed far enough out of the way.

Let's not start cooking until these fuels have burned down to glowing coals that show a little gray ash. The fire will be better—and the food will taste better—if enough time is allowed to let the fire burn down properly.

HOW BIG A FIRE?

Embryo outdoor cooks invariably make their fires too big—much too big. This can ruin the foods completely, can scorch the cook, and perhaps get us in trouble with the fire warden.

I vividly remember a back yard cookout where our hosts proudly remarked that we would have "barbecued spareribs." The ribs had been marinated and prepared with loving care. Our host started a tremendous fire in the charcoal grill and, when it was burning furiously, immediately put on the spareribs. Before making a suggestion, I glanced at my wife, who tossed me that "Don't you dare open your big mouth" look, so I kept still. As a result, the spareribs quickly were reduced to charcoal and bones. We ate them, as far as possible, without comment, and I still think our host thought they should have been cooked that way.

The lesson in this "How Big a Fire?" question is to make a fire no bigger than necessary to do the job at hand—and to let the fire burn down to graying bright coals before starting to cook.

If we're cooking on an outdoor grill or fireplace, usually only a part of the cooking surface will be needed for the fire. Thus, there will be a hot area and an area of lesser heat. Foods can be seared over the hotter part of the fire and then moved to a less hot area where they will keep on cooking even if they are not directly over the fire. Different foods require different degrees of heat. A thick steak may need to remain over the coals during the entire broiling period, particularly if the cook wants to "burn it a little" to give the outside the charcoal flavor that is desired by many people. On the other hand, foods such as broilers need to be cooked much more slowly, because the outside should be a golden brown, rather than charred. Thus we brown them lightly over the coals and then rotate them in the heat away from the coals to allow them to cook through without burning. We'll learn more about this in later chapters.

An iron rod and swinging pothooks or pan holders allow utensils to be raised or lowered over the fire and swung over the fire or away from it, as desired. The rod is driven into the ground beside the fire. The weight of the arms prevents them from sliding down the rod. (Wisconsin Conservation Department)

This close-up of the rig shown in the photos above also shows steel frying pans with detachable handles. Sticks can be inserted in the handles to extend their length. (Wisconsin Conservation Department)

When the fire has burned down to coals, tamper with it as little as possible, because excessive poking, stirring, and tamping interferes with burning and may reduce heat to less than the desired amount.

NOTES ON FIRE SAFETY

No chapter on outdoor fires would be complete without a word of warning that a few minutes of carelessness can disfigure the countryside for years to come.

If the woods are dry, or if it is windy, let's not take chances. If a safe place for an open fire is unavailable, it may be better to do our cooking over one of the handy little camp stoves described in Chapter Six.

If conditions of fire safety seem suitable, open fires should be built in the protection of a large rock, or somewhere else out of the wind, where sparks cannot reach combustible material. A source of water to control the fire (if need be), and to put it out, should be nearby. Fires should never be built against a stump, except possibly in the deep snow. If a fire is built against a stump, even if it seems to have been properly extinguished, the fire may burn down into the roots and smolder along the roots, only to reignite, perhaps several days later.

Fires should not be built on peaty soil for the same reason. They should be built in a protected place, away from the wind, where flying sparks can do no damage. They should be built on dirt or rocks, but never on or near combustible material. For the convenience of the cook, as well as for fire safety, they should be kept as small as possible.

When cooking is done, fires should be extinguished with water—drenched with water—and the embers should be stirred into mud, to be positive that no chance of reignition remains.

Fire safety is a mark of a good woodsman, and the lack of it is the stigma of a goon who should never have been allowed to play with matches in the first place. So—let's conclude this chapter by mentioning a large sign I saw at a crossroads leading into the Maine wilderness. The sign said, "This is God's country. Why set it on fire and make it look like Hell!"

Maine Forest Service Photo

Chapter Two

COOKING METHODS— ON THE GO

In the deep, damp evergreen and hardwood forests of northern Maine and Canada there lives a big, brownish bird as delicious to eat as it is unintelligent. This is the spruce grouse (or partridge)—a near cousin to the similar but wilder and sportier ruffed grouse so dear to upland gunners in woodlands farther to the south.

Coveys of these succulent birds sun themselves along trails and tote roads, barely bothering to move when happened upon by sportsmen traveling from one place to another in the wilderness. Killing them is not a sport, even when one shoots their heads off with a .22-caliber rifle or hand gun while they scuttle in the underbrush or perch dumbly on nearby spruces. I've seen them brought down with sticks, rocks, and even with a sling-shot. But, sporty or no, the spruce grouse is a game bird that is simply delicious when broiled over an open fire.

One day early in October, Ross and I walked from our camp on Haymock Lake through the cathedral-like columns of one of New England's few remaining tracts of virgin forest to Carpenter Pond on our usual quest for the big, pink-fleshed Eastern brook trout that attract so many anglers to the wilderness regions of Maine. On the way, we killed two grouse for lunch, and I collected nearly a hatful of berries as we reached the pond.

Ross selected an open spot in the protection of a big rock and quickly had a small fire going. He dipped water into his battered and blackened coffeepot and hung it on a dingle stick over the fire to boil. He mixed the berries into

bannock dough, molded this into a cake, and put it in a skillet which he propped at an angle toward the heat of the fire. He removed the breasts from the two grouse and impaled each on a long green branch cut from small trees growing beside the water. When the little fire had reduced to hardwood coals and the bannock bread had begun to rise and take on a golden glow, Ross propped the bird breasts over the fire. Then he sat back and contentedly puffed at his pipe, rising occasionally to turn the bannock and to baste the birds with a slice of salt pork impaled on a stick. This was noon; too early to

The author (left) and Ross McKenney on a canoe trip into the Maine wilderness. A carefully prepared check list of foods and equipment is necessary in planning trips far from home.

go fishing—and we were in no hurry. While I eyed progress in the "kitchen," I put my rod together and selected a few flies for the afternoon's fishing.

In less than an hour the meal was cooked. We used a flat rock for a table and enjoyed our lunch of golden-brown grouse, steaming bannock with berries fairly dripping rich juices, and scalding coffee that was as black and delicious as good coffee can be.

"After all," Ross commented, "if you can't float a jackknife in it, it's too damn weak!"

"Weak or strong," I answered, "this is the kind of grub for me. You can have your fancy restaurants. The folks in the city never had it so good!"

Trout were beginning to rise off the point. We soaked our fire, rinsed the cups, pot, and skillet, and spent the afternoon fishing. We killed two gorgeous brook trout weighing between three and four pounds each, and then pinched the barbs off our hooks so we wouldn't hurt the rest. At Carpenter Pond it's either a feast or a famine. We could have filled the canoe with trout—but we took only the two. The fishing would be as good today, if those who have fished this beautiful wilderness since then had done the same.

As the sun began to set, we walked the three or four miles back to Haymock. We picked some more berries on the way, and Ross made a pie in the reflector baker. We had baked beans, fresh from the bean hole, and broiled brook trout. As darkness came, we threw on wood for the night fire and basked in its warmth while a loon far out on the lake called to its mate to say it was time to turn in.

THE DINGLE-STICK FIRE

The little fire we used to cook birds, bannock, and coffee is the simplest and most often used by people traveling on foot—so let's start with it and then go on to more elaborate methods. It is the smallest hardwood fire that can be built to do its job, which usually is merely to "boil the kettle" and toast a sandwich or two—or something equally simple, like the Hot Dinner Package described in Chapter Four. It may or may not be enclosed by rocks or logs, as will be described. Its main purpose is to prepare a hot drink.

To hold the hot-drink container over the little fire, we use a dingle stick, which is a green branch an inch or two in diameter at the larger end and five or six feet long, tapering to around an inch in diameter at the cut-off forward end. The base end usually is pointed, so it can be pushed into the ground, extending at an angle over the fire, as illustrated. Branches cut from the main stick are cut to leave an inch or so on the trunk, to prevent the pot or kettle from sliding down. Sometimes we drive a nail into the stick for this purpose. A rock or log placed on the ground against the base of the stick keeps the stick propped up at a proper angle to hold the pot at the desired distance over the fire.

Usually, in addition to a beverage, the only foods we prepare on this little fire are simple ones we carry wrapped in foil to cook on or beside the coals. People who stay at sporting camps often are given sandwiches for lunch. Most of these taste better when toasted on one of the roasting sticks illustrated here. A roasting stick is a green stick three or four feet long, selected because it has two or three branches extending from the same crotch. These are cut off and pointed four or five inches from the crotch, so that a sandwich can be laid on them for toasting, or so that a game bird or fish can be impaled on them for roasting—as we did with the grouse breasts.

Fish are excellent when roasted this way, especially if a bacon strip or two, or some salt pork, can be added to baste and flavor the food. The sticks can be stuck in the ground at an angle (like the dingle stick) and can be moved or turned occasionally to roast the food uniformly in the heat of the fire. Slow cooking makes such meat and fish turn a golden brown by the time it is cooked through. We can't hurry the process too much, or the outside will be burned while the inside still is raw. Don't add salt until the food is removed from the fire, because salt tends to draw out the juices and make the food tough.

A GOOD CUP OF COFFEE!

Here's the way woodsmen in the Northeast brew their coffee. If a beverage pot is lacking, any metal container will do, such as a large, clean tin can. Puncture the can on opposite sides close to the top, so wire can be inserted to make a bail. Put in a handful or two of coffee (at least a heaping tablespoonful per cup) and fill the container with water to within an inch or two from the top. When the coffee begins to

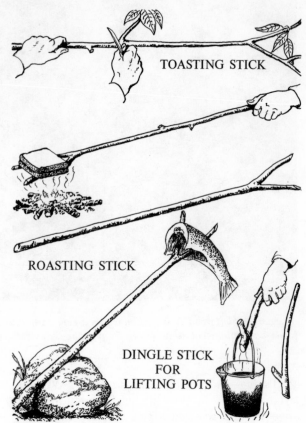

TOASTING STICK

ROASTING STICK

DINGLE STICK FOR LIFTING POTS

boil briskly, remove it from the heat and let it cool for four or five minutes. Then put it back over the fire and let it come to a boil again. Clear coffee, free from grounds, should result when the coffee is decanted into cups.

There are other ways of "settling the grounds" when making coffee out of doors. In the above method, we have to watch the coffee closely and take it off the fire as soon as it comes to a boil, to prevent it from boiling over. To avoid this tendency to boil over, some woodsmen do not add the coffee until the water has come to a boil. They then stir it and set it aside for several minutes to settle the grounds, and then heat it up again. Others add a little cold water after the coffee has come to a boil. In these various similar methods we see that the idea is to bring the coffee to a boil; to cool it a bit by one means or another, and then to bring it to a boil again. Most people prefer not to boil it very long, because excess boiling releases acids that tend to make it bitter.

All of us have heard of the old formula of adding eggshells, a whole broken egg, or a pinch of dehydrated egg powder to the boiled coffee

With the beverage can heating on the dingle stick and food sputtering in the skillet, these Boy Scouts will enjoy a good meal.

to settle the grounds. If one of the above methods is used, adding egg is not necessary—and many woodsmen think that the addition of egg is harmful to the coffee's body and flavor.

INSTANT BEVERAGES

In this day and age, many modern outdoorsmen prefer instant coffees because they are less bulky and are easier to prepare. Be traditional, if you wish, but try a good brand of instant coffee. So many improvements have been made that few can tell the instant types from the bulkier varieties.

To remove the pot from the dingle stick (if we have used one), merely pull the stick to one side. If the bail is hot, use a pothook (cut from a green branch, as shown). Decant the coffee into cups, and remember that woodsmen like it very strong!

As a pleasant change from the perhaps too often used coffee, why not try tea or cocoa? To me, the most delicious and most easily prepared cocoa is "Nestlé's EverReady," because it has

whole milk and sugar already in it. All that's necessary is to put two or three heaping teaspoonfuls in a cup and add very hot water.

Old-timers may not take to the idea of using instant beverages, such as tea, coffee, cocoa, and bouillons, but this is because they don't realize how delicious and easy these instant drinks are today. You may like them better, or not as well, but it is common sense to try them. Instant soups, such as "Maggi" and "Lipton's," also are delicious and easy to carry. They come in a score of varieties and are prepared merely by heating with boiling water for a few minutes.

Last in the "Let's Boil the Kettle" department is a tasty and invigorating drink called "mocha." This is merely hot black coffee to which cocoa has been added—about a heaping teaspoonful per cup.

When using a dingle-stick fire, we don't have any support for cooking, except for the dingle stick itself. To use other pots and pans, we need a simple fireplace, such as one of those described below.

THE "U" FIREPLACE

When rocks are available, the "U" fireplace will do everything from making coffee to baking pies and cakes, although for people "on the go" the simpler foods usually will suffice.

This fireplace can be built in minutes, merely by scraping a depression in the ground and fitting rocks around it in the form of three sides of a rectangle or square. The opening of the rectangle should be toward the direction from which the prevailing wind is blowing, so that smoke (if any) will blow away from the cook. The rocks should be fitted and chinked rather tightly and should be set level and fairly flat at the top. The top surface of the fireplace need not be over eight inches (or a foot, at the most) from the bottom of the small pit in which the fire is to be built.

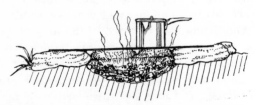

We'll set a grating, or iron bars, over the top to hold cooking utensils. If a grating or iron bars are unavailable, the stones should be laid in a very narrow rectangle, so cooking utensils can be set directly on them, over the fire.

The size of this fireplace depends on the size of the available grid (or metal supports). An ideal type of grid is a wire tray such as the ones that come in the refrigerator or cooking range we have at home. One of these usually can be spared for the purpose, and can be carried between folded newspapers to keep other equipment clean.

On hiking trips, pack trips, etc., such a grid may be too cumbersome to bother with. In this case, two or three flat steel strips about one eighth of an inch in thickness, between one and two inches wide, and fifteen or so inches long, form a compact (and usually not too heavy) bundle. These can be laid on the rocks over the fire pit, to serve the same purpose as the grid. Almost any junk yard or ironworking plant can supply them, properly cut to size.

A third alternative is to get one or two lengths of small-diameter iron or copper pipe about thirty inches long, and to bend each section of pipe into the form of a "U." The legs of the "U" should be about fifteen inches long and four or five inches apart. These, when laid on the rocks over the fire pit, also make good supports on which to rest utensils for cooking.

Both the bars and the bent pipe are fairly compact and light. When conditions permit, the metal tray is superior, because it provides a more secure cooking surface on which heavy-duty aluminum foil can be laid for the frying of foods.

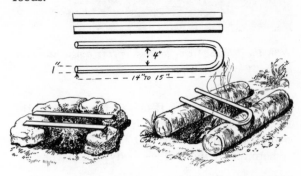

For a single meal or two, this type of fireplace can be made very quickly and roughly. If we're camping for any length of time in one place, we may want to make it a bit more elaborate. The basic layer of rocks should not extend higher above the fire bed than recommended, because the higher they are, the more heat will be lost, thus calling for too big a fire and the use of too much wood. If we want to raise the metal tray higher, temporarily, a top rim of flat rocks can be laid on top of the basic layer to accomplish this.

Since these metal trays are fairly wide, we can enjoy almost any degree of cooking heat by poking the bed of coals to one side of the fireplace or the other. This gives us a very hot area to cook over; also an area of lesser heat where foods can simmer or be kept warm.

In the chapter on aluminum foil cooking, we'll see that a doubled sheet of heavy-duty aluminum foil can be laid over the metal tray and used as a frying surface on which to cook griddle cakes, bacon and eggs, hamburg patties, frankfurters, and many other things. These foods are turned with a spatula, of course being careful not to puncture or disarrange the metal foil. When taking the family on a cookout, this may offer the solution for preparing such foods for the whole group. Rolls and bread can be toasted by laying them on the foil. If they soak up a little of the juices and the fat with which the foil has been greased, this may make them taste even better!

While steaks, chops, broilers, fish, etc., can be cooked directly on the wire tray (usually without the foil), a folding wire broiler is handy to contain such foods because, with it, they all can be turned over together without the use of a fork. A fork punctures the foods and wastes the juices. If such foods are turned without the use of a folding wire broiler (which may not be convenient to carry) it is more advisable to use a pair of tongs.

To indicate the variety of uses of such a simple fireplace, we can bake breads, pies, and cakes in or on it in either of two ways: we can put these foods in a pan or skillet right on the grayed coals (being sure they are not too hot). By laying a strip of aluminum foil over the wire tray, the heat also will be reflected downward to bake and to brown the top of the food.

If the coals are fairly hot, we may burn the food by baking it this way. In this case, lay the bread, pie, or cake on the wire tray over medium heat and put a "tent" of foil over the food to reflect heat downward.

This fireplace can also be used to bake vegetables and other foods wrapped in aluminum foil; put the foil-wrapped vegetables very near the heat of the fire, or even in the coals, if they are nearly reduced to ashes.

But let's not get off the point of how to build the various types of fireplaces. We'll learn more about outdoor cooking methods later.

THE "V" FIREPLACE

This one is not a favorite of mine except when rocks are unavailable—and in some localities suitable rocks are hard to find. The "V" fireplace is made by cutting two green hardwood logs about six inches in diameter into lengths about three feet long. These two logs are set close together at one end and about a foot apart at the other end. The open end (preferably) is toward the direction from which the prevailing wind blows. If a somewhat larger log is split into two equal pieces, these can be set, flat side up, to provide a handy flat surface on which to rest cooking utensils, thus minimizing the danger of slipping.

With the two logs thus set, use a stick, flat rock, or some other tool to scrape a depression between the logs. This can be about six inches deep, if possible, but the depth is unimportant. The hardwood fire is built in this depression between the logs, and it can be fed by long pieces of hardwood branches which are poked farther into the fire as they burn.

Utensils are placed over the fire, resting on the logs, and can be moved to one place or another along the length of the logs, depending on the size of the utensils and the amount of heat desired. One or more dingle sticks on which to hang pots over the fire can be used.

A wire tray, or the irons previously described, can be placed over the logs to support utensils but, with this type of fireplace, such rarely seem to be used. This "V" fireplace seems much less useful than the "U" fireplace or the parallel log fireplace that comes next on the list. If rocks are available, we might as well forget it, although in many localities it is a popular cooking arrangement for a very few people and for simple meals.

THE PARALLEL LOG FIREPLACE

For a long camping period in one place, or for a quick meal on the go, the parallel log fireplace can be as small or as large as needed. It

The parallel log fireplace can be as small or as large as needed; it is ideal for a quick meal on the go.

provides a better draft than the "V" fireplace, and (in my opinion) offers a better arrangement for using a cooking fire.

Here again, we cut two green hardwood logs six inches or larger in diameter and at least three feet long. We dig a trench about eight inches deep and eight inches wide, as long as the logs are. We set the two logs (held firmly by dirt or rocks) one on each side of the trench at whatever distance apart we wish them to be to support utensils, the wire grid, or the fire irons over the fire. We build a hardwood fire in the trench, feeding it from one end only. Thus we have a hot end and a cooler end, and we can rake coals from the hot end toward the cooler end to provide whatever heat is desired for the kind of cooking being done.

Since the fire is well down in the trench, and is fed gradually, rather than too much at once, the flames should not burn the logs to any great extent. If this fireplace is used for a prolonged time, these logs may need replacement every few days. Here again, if we split a large log (instead of using two), the two sections of split log can be set with the flat sides uppermost, thus providing a flat surface on which to rest cooking utensils. In all of the enclosed fireplaces, the logs or rocks have the dual purpose of retaining heat inside the enclosed area and of providing supports on which to set equipment.

They also help to keep sparks and embers from getting out of control—an important point when a sudden wind comes up.

If the trench is wide enough, or if the logs are set at a slight angle, we can do simple baking in the cinder end of the trench by setting the covered baking pans on hot ashes far enough away from the hotter part of the fire to provide correct baking heat. This sort of arrangement should be adequate for biscuits or muffins, but we'll probably need something a bit more elaborate for pies and cakes, as we shall see. The covered biscuit or muffin pan should be rotated occasionally to equalize the cooking heat. A section of aluminum foil, propped or bent over the pan so as to reflect heat down onto it, helps in providing even heat.

The dingle-stick pole is supported by two crotched green sticks, as this illustration shows. (Abercrombie)

THE REFLECTOR FIREPLACE

This is a solution for a good cooking and warming fire when staying in the woods overnight. Cut two green hardwood logs or branches that are three or four inches in diameter, about four feet long, and fairly straight. Since these are used as stakes, one end of each should be pointed. Set these in the ground about two feet apart where the back of the fire is to be, and tilt them slightly backward. If the ground is fairly soft, perhaps we can pound these in securely with an ax. If not, we may need to dig holes for each stake, then set them in place and firm dirt or rocks around them. In any event, the stakes should be set very securely. If we are staying in a tent or lean-to, the fire should be as close to its opening as is convenient and safe, because part of the idea of this reflector fire is to reflect heat toward the spot where we sleep.

With the two green stakes thus set, we cut a dozen or more fairly straight green hardwood logs or branches four or five inches in diameter and three or four feet long. We pile some of these, one on top of another, against the two stakes. Since the stakes are leaning backward slightly, the wall of logs should not roll off this support.

The fire is built close to the logs. For cooking, it should be a fairly small fire, as usual. We can set large rocks or logs conveniently, as previously described, on which to place pots and pans for cooking and/or we can make a dingle-stick pole. The dingle-stick pole often is used with this type of fireplace.

To make the dingle-stick pole support, we cut two saplings that are two or three inches thick and about four feet long, each of which has a crotch or small branch at one end cut so as to extend four or five inches from the main branch. The illustration should make this clear—and it is much quicker and easier than it sounds. We drive these stakes perpendicularly into the ground, one on each side of the fireplace, and far enough away from the fire so they won't burn —about five feet apart. When driven solidly into the ground, the crotch on each stake is at the same height—about three feet from the ground. A straight, stiff, green sapling about two inches in diameter is cut about six feet long, so that it will rest solidly on the two crotches to make a level pole on which to hang the dingle sticks.

There are many ways to make dingle sticks, as the illustration shows. Basically, these usually

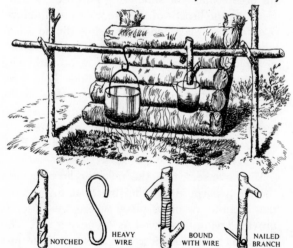

NOTCHED   HEAVY WIRE   BOUND WITH WIRE   NAILED BRANCH

are green sticks of various lengths cut so that each has a crotch that can be hung downward on the dingle-stick pole. To hang pots and other utensils on these dingle sticks, we'll have to fix up something for them to hang on. A way to do it is to cut one or more notches downward into the dingle stick, as shown. Another way is to drive a nail or two into the dingle stick to hold the bail of the utensil. These dingle sticks should be in various lengths, so that one or more of them will be of the right length to hold the utensil at the proper height over the fire. To move utensils from one dingle stick to another (higher or lower from the fire, or nearer or farther from it) we cut another crotched branch to use as a hook. By hooking the bail of the utensil with this crotched green branch, we can move the utensil from one place to another, even if the fire or the utensil is hot.

We can also grasp the upper part of a dingle stick on which a pot is suspended and move the whole thing from one place to another on the pole, thus transferring it from a hot place over the fire to a cooler place, or removing it altogether.

Dingle sticks need not be made of wood. Many campers make them of heavy wire, or of metal rods, and carry them as part of their equipment. As shown in Chapter Seven, dingle sticks can be made by cutting and bending coat-hanger wire, although these may not be strong enough for some purposes.

The dingle-stick pole and dingle sticks are used for boiling water or hot beverages, for boiling vegetables, for making stews and soups, and for other boiling or simmering purposes. We fry foods on the hearth of the fire, as we did before. We broil or roast foods by using dingle sticks stuck in the ground (as we did with the grouse) or by wrapping large pieces of meat with wire and hanging them on dingle sticks held over the fire by the dingle-stick support thus made. We bake foods in front of the fire by using a reflector baker (or a makeshift one made of aluminum foil), as described in Chapters Four and Five.

We have seen that the reflector fireplace has the main purpose of reflecting heat toward the tent, lean-to, or other place where we sleep. It provides warmth as well as a cooking fire. The fire is not built against the backlogs, but just

in front of them. However, the lower logs will burn through from time to time. When this happens, they are kicked from the backlog support into the fire, and other logs are allowed to slide down to take their place, more being added at the top to replace those used. In the preceding chapter we learned what varieties of green woods are best for this purpose.

Campers who are gadget-minded will be interested in camp grids, as illustrated. Obtainable in hardware stores and housewares departments anywhere, these strong, folding grids can be stuck in the ground at any desired height over the coals to support pots, pans, broilers, and

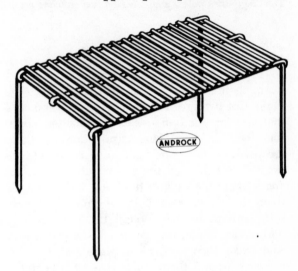

other utensils used in cooking. Because these have leg supports, they may be preferable for many purposes to the wire tray previously mentioned.

When dinner is over and the stars are beginning to come out, we can remove the dingle-stick pole and toss some logs on the fire, so we can bask in its warmth before turning in. The backlogs will feed the fire and reflect it toward us for hours—although we may need to get up to add logs once or twice. When morning comes, enough embers should remain to help us get the breakfast fire going quickly.

THE STOVEPIPE STOVE

Earlier in this book we stated that many practical outdoor cooking devices can be obtained for little or nothing. One of them is a very useful stove made from a section of stovepipe (or a similar cylindrical piece of metal).

The stovepipe stove was developed by Walt Whittum, a neighbor and bow-hunting companion of mine, and we have used it most successfully on cold and wet hunting trips in the Vermont woods on many occasions. Walt also prefers it for back yard cooking, and prepares an amazing variety of foods with it—even to pies and biscuits!

To make a stovepipe stove, we merely explore a junk yard and locate a section of stovepipe about fifteen inches in diameter and about fifteen inches long, but preferably of a diameter that can be covered comfortably by an ash-can cover. We set the piece of stovepipe upright on three or four flat rocks, and we push dirt all around the bottom to exclude air. Then we use a stick to poke a hole in the dirt under the stovepipe on the side from which the wind is blowing, thus making an air vent.

The stovepipe stove will burn almost anything and is excellent for warmth as well as for cooking. So—just throw in twigs, branches, chips, cut wood, or whatever is handy, and make a brisk fire in the stovepipe. Add some hardwood (if cooking is to be done) and let this burn down to coals.

Since we'll need a surface on top of the stovepipe for cooking, we find a square of heavy wire mesh to fit the top of the stovepipe, and we bend down the four corners to fit the top securely. This surface can be used for cooking.

A good point about this arrangement is that we can poke open the vent hole in the dirt to provide more draft, or we can scuff dirt into the hole to shut off the air. If we have an ash-can cover for the top, this will seal off the top completely so that, when the dirt vent is closed, almost no air can enter the stovepipe. The advantage of this is that, when we want to bank the fire at night, or in the morning before going hunting, we can leave a good fire burning; seal off the lower vent; put on the cover, and let the fire smolder until we want to use it again. Thus, many hours later, when we remove the cover and poke open the vent, we will find that the wood has reduced to charcoal, which the renewed air supply will quickly transform to glowing coals. When used properly, there's no need to kindle a new fire in the stovepipe. All we need to do is adjust the vent and add some more hardwood occasionally.

Another advantage of the stovepipe stove is that the fire is completely enclosed. It is safe from the wind and the rain. It certainly is comforting for a group of tired and cold hunters to return to camp and find the stovepipe stove smoldering contentedly, instantly ready to warm cold hands and quickly prepared to burst into a roaring fire when it is opened up and when fresh hardwood is added.

This stove throws so much heat that foil-wrapped vegetables can be placed around the outside of the pipe on the ground for baking. We can lay a doubled layer of aluminum foil over part of the wire mesh and use this surface for frying many kinds of foods, if no skillet is handy. We can boil or broil foods on the wire mesh. We can make delicious pies, cakes, and biscuits by putting them in pans on the wire mesh and tenting them with aluminum foil to reflect the heat downward onto the top of the foods. If the fire's heat is incorrect, it can quickly be adjusted by opening or closing the dirt vent. This sensible stove is ideal for cooking for up to six people, although, if a good deal of cooking is to be done, we may need two of these stoves, or one of the other types of fireplaces.

The disadvantages of the stovepipe stove are few. The main one is that it is rather bulky, and (if not cleaned) may be rather dirty to carry. We have a section of stovepipe that fits comfortably into a lightweight ash can, complete with cover. We fill the inside space with billets of hardwood, or with a bag of charcoal or briquettes. We include a fire starter, and we keep things from rattling by including a few newspapers with which we can clean out the stovepipe before starting home. The ash can is used as a refuse container while camping, and burnable refuse can be burned up in the stovepipe when cooking is done.

TIN-CAN STOVES

These, essentially, are little brothers of the stovepipe stove; they are handy for cooking very simple meals, for preparing hot beverages, for warming cold hands in a duck blind, in an ice-fishing shack, or on a deer stand. We can use them either with wood fuel or with "Canned Heat."

To make a wood-burning tin-can stove, find a fairly large and clean tin can or pail (such as a lard pail, obtainable from a restaurant) and, using tin snips, cut a rectangular hole two or three inches square on the curved part of the top; cut a similar hole on the opposite side at the bottom of the inverted can. Using a beer-can opener, cut about six triangular holes in the bottom of the can so that, when it is inverted, this will serve as a burner. Fill the can lightly with kindling; invert it on the ground and light the contents. Now, all we need to do to keep the fire going is to stoke it with small sticks which can be added either from the top or from the bottom.

If we are using a fairly large tin can, this little device is practical for providing warmth and for heating beverages or simple foods. If the can should be a small one, the stove would be little more than a toy.

If "Canned Heat" fuel is available, the tin-can stove is easier and more practical to operate. Since this fuel can be purchased at low prices almost anywhere, it is convenient to have on hand, especially for use as a fire starter. Being solid, it won't leak while being carried. Since it is smokeless, nearly odorless, and quite inexpensive, it is ideal for this purpose. To use it in the tin-can stove, find a tin can, as before, and use a beer-can opener to cut about six triangles equally spaced around the edge of the bottom of the can. Now, cut about six more triangles around the sides of the bottom of the can in between those that were cut before. Cut three or four more triangular holes in one part of the top of the can. All this takes only a few minutes when using a beer-can opener, and is done as shown in the sketch.

To start the stove, light a large (7-ounce size) can of "Sterno" and set it on a convenient surface. Invert the tin can over the fuel and the tin-can stove is in operation! To extinguish the fuel, remove the tin can (by knocking it over) and slide the fuel-can cover over the flame. When the can cools, replace the cover tightly so that the remaining fuel will be conserved for use later.

This type of tin-can stove makes an ideal warmer for cold hands and for heating a small space, such as an ice-fishing enclosure. The fuel burns about two hours, and extra cans are light and compact to carry. It will boil a beverage pot quickly, and it does a good job of warming canned goods or of preparing foods that can be cooked in a small skillet. The stove, however, is a small one, so don't expect too much of it. Remember that it costs nothing, and that a can of the fuel can be purchased almost anywhere for about the cost of a package of cigarettes.

The stoves and fireplaces discussed in this chapter are mostly ones that use wood fuel and cost little or nothing. Other stoves and grills, suitable for station wagon camping and for picnics, are described in Chapter Six.

PLAN WHAT YOU'LL TAKE ALONG

When cooking outdoors away from home, it is usual to forget a few necessities or conveniences, unless we have developed a check list to assure that all is included. Remarks like "Oh, I forgot it!" or "I thought you'd bring that," don't add to the fun of camping or cookouts. One man's check list may be entirely inappropriate for another, and various kinds and lengths of trips require different varieties of equipment. So —beyond the list of equipment recommended in the Emergency Kit in Chapter Five, we shall leave it to the reader to prepare his own check list, with the suggestion that it be prepared well in advance; revised as necessary; and kept in a

Thanksgiving dinner can be enjoyed in the "grand manner" even in the lower Mojave Desert. The folding table is set with a matching paper food service of disposable plates, cups, place mats, and napkins. The sixteen-pound turkey was roasted for four hours over charcoal briquettes arranged around an aluminum foil drip-pan in an aluminum-foil-lined fire pit about 2 feet by 2½ feet by 8 inches deep. Note the ingenious portable spit which can lower or raise the roasting food by means of a chain winch. An aluminum-foil shield was placed over the turkey to conserve heat and to act as a reflector. This dinner included all the "fixin's," cooked in foil or in skillets—plus a tasty tossed salad and wine carried to the spot in portable refrigerators in the Volkswagen Camper. (Photos: Farley Manning Associates)

convenient place, such as pasted in the back of this book. Then the wrong answer to questions like "What did you do with the icepick?" won't start a Civil War in the family!

Many of us simplify such problems by having on hand an "outdoor box" of essentials, such as knives, forks, spoons, carving knife, tongs, serving spoons, spatula, can opener, icepick, fire starter, aluminum foil, plates and cups, condiments, nested cooking kit, etc. This "outdoor box" is for outdoor use only and never is raided for use in the home. (That is, it never should be!) With this as a starter, it's fairly easy to pack the food and get moving. It's also easier to put things away when we return home again!

The Campers Kitchen requires little room in a station wagon—can contain food for a family for a week, plus stove, fuel, and other utensils. (Campers Kitchen)

Ed Hodgson's Rangeland Cafeteria now serves visitors to famed Jackson Hole, Wyoming, just as it did when it rolled across plains and mountains following mighty herds of cattle being driven to market. Ed follows a check list to keep his chuck wagon well stocked in order to feed hungry cowpokes on long trips. His Dutch ovens work overtime turning out real cowboy chow—such as beef, beans, spuds, and sourdough biscuits, washed down with strong black coffee. (Ed Hodgson, Jackson, Wyoming)

Chapter Three

QUICK TRICKS
WITH THE SKILLET

A big part of the fun of being outdoors is to hunt or fish all morning and then to meet for lunch when an early arrival has the fire going and food sputtering in the skillet. The blending of odors of spruce trees, hardwood smoke, bubbling coffee, and cooking food combine to make a backwoods perfume eagerly anticipated by the hungry sportsman as he rounds a bend in the trail to find his companions chatting before the fire while lunch is being prepared.

This midday siesta is always a happy occasion, but to me it seems especially so in the backwoods of Maine in the crisp, bright-leafed autumn before the fishing season has ended and when the bird-hunting season has begun.

There are many favorite spots in Maine for this brief period of combined hunting and fishing. One of them is the relatively unspoiled back country in the vicinity of Jackman—a cozy rural town near the Canadian border where the wilderness is lavishly sprinkled with big lakes, rocky streams, spruce and hardwood forests, and old logging roads where partridges sun themselves during the day. What more can a man ask of life than to mosey along a trail beside a stream in a spruce forest with a fly rod in his hand, plus one or two fat trout in his jacket, and perhaps a spruce partridge shot with a hand gun on the way to the luncheon spot?

Sportsmen can drive or fly to Jackman. If they fly they can land small airplanes on the grassy air strip in front of Sky Lodge—an amazing log cabin, boasting no less than sixty rooms, and with two tremendous fireplaces that provide a rustic setting undreamed of, even in the movies! Ed Landgraf, who runs the lodge, provides such an abundance of good food that his guests must hunt or fish all day to avoid getting fat.

When Ben Pike and I arrived, Bud Dilihunt (who presides over the Jackman Chamber of Commerce) was there to meet us. We were up before daybreak and, well fortified with Ed's abundant country sausage and flapjacks, we set out in the battered Jeep over otherwise impassable old logging roads to a log bridge across a rocky stream. Here we parked the Jeep, with the arrangement that we would go fly-fishing until noon and then meet for lunch.

After six hours of climbing over rocks along the fast stream, breakfast seemed only an ancient memory. Thus, when I rounded the bend in the trail, with the trout and the bird in my pocket, the smells of bubbling black coffee and sizzling brook trout made it seem as if I hadn't eaten in days.

Now there are many ways of cooking a trout, and many ways of preparing a partridge, as this book soon will tell—but one of the most toothsome methods is the way the old-timers do it in the backwoods of Maine.

The breast is removed from the partridge, since, for a hasty lunch, the rest is not worth the bother. The trout are cleaned and, if small, are fried whole. Both are dusted liberally with flour (which usually is carried in a small plastic bag); are salted and peppered and then fried slowly in bubbling bacon fat until they are crisp, golden brown. The birds and the fish are fried separately, of course, and nothing else is added to interfere with the delicate flavors of the foods. When cooked, they are drained on paper towels while corn bread is toasted on a forked stick.

This, with a mug of black, scalding coffee, provides a lunch beyond compare.

Cooking in a skillet is very simple—yet there are an abundance of foods that can be prepared this way. Since a frying pan is one of the most often used pieces of equipment in the woodsman's kit, it should be selected with care. The aluminum pans commonly provided with cooking kits often are so thin that they overheat and scorch the food. The ideal choice (if we have room to carry it) is the old-fashioned cast-iron skillet. Since this obviously is too heavy for a packsack, woodsmen usually settle for one made of steel—preferably with a folding handle. Outfitters and camping supply stores sell these with folding handles of heavy wire, so made that a stick can be inserted to extend the length of the handle. Two such skillets, one slightly smaller than the other to allow them to nest together, make an ideal combination. Two skillets often are handy in cooking a meal. One can be used as a cover for the other, and both provide an oven.

There's almost no end to the variety of tasty foods that can be cooked in a skillet over an open fire. Many favorite recipes will be found in following chapters. But since so many of us want a few quick and easy combinations for a simple lunch or dinner on a day's outing, it may be helpful to give a few of them here.

MEASURING

Before starting, however, let's lay down a few ground rules concerning measurements, so we won't put in too much of one thing and too little of another.

Beginners waste a lot of time by measuring ingredients too carefully. A little too much or too little sugar, flour, or milk, for example, usually makes little or no difference. Adding such things as salt, pepper, condiments, and spices takes a little more care. The best rule is to stay on the safe side and to add a little more of one thing or another later on, if the "taste test" indicates this is necessary. Most such ingredients vary widely anyway, depending on who made them and how long they have been kept. Some people like foods more or less highly flavored, or thicker or thinner, than others. Thus, no matter what the cookbook says, the cook must use judgment (and perhaps a little ingenuity and experimentation) in how he interprets the recipes. Recipes usually are not hard and fast rules. They merely tell how certain people do it.

We rarely need to cook by the clock, either. We cook foods until they are done, and we try to take them off before they become overdone. We try to cook at the right temperatures, but even this isn't too important, if we don't go to extremes.

Experienced cooks usually just toss in the ingredients and rarely bother to measure anything. They know instinctively how much or how little to put in, and when to do it. (And my sister said that I should take care not to write this book that way!) The answer to the whole thing is to just go ahead and cook. We'll be surprised at how easy it is—and we'll learn as we go along.

With all this in mind, though, let's still mention the ground rules of measurement, because they are what the cook had in mind when he wrote the recipe. A measurement, such as a cupful or a teaspoonful, means a level one, unless it is specified as "heaping" or "rounded." We could go astray on this if we don't remember it, because a rounded teaspoonful equals two level ones, and a heaping teaspoonful equals three. Three teaspoonfuls equal a tablespoonful. A cupful is half a pint, and an ordinary drinking cup is about a cook's "cupful" if it is filled only about three fourths full.

With this in mind, let's get on with a few "quick tricks with the skillet":

Bannock (Skillet Bread)

 1 cup flour
 1 teaspoon baking powder
 1 cup water
 Dash of salt (about ¼ teaspoon)

The dry ingredients can be sifted together at home, using several times this recipe if the trip is to be of long duration. It is handy to carry them in a plastic bag. Before starting to make the bannock, grease the skillet and keep it moderately warm over the fire.

Put the dry ingredients into a receptacle and quickly mix them with enough water to form a stiff dough. Before handling the dough, dust hands with some of the flour. Now mold the dough into a round, flat cake, using as few motions as possible. Dust the cake with flour and set it in the warm skillet. Many outdoor cooks poke a hole in the middle of the bannock, with the idea that this cooks it a little faster and provides more crust. The cake can be of any size, but should not be over an inch thick.

There are several ways to bake bannock over an open fire. The skillet can be left over moderate heat until the bottom of the bannock is crusted and lightly browned. Then it can be flipped over to brown the other side.

Another way is to use a reflector baker, such as will be discussed in Chapter Five. A makeshift one (which works very well) is made by propping a section of heavy-duty aluminum foil at an angle toward the skillet so that the heat of the fire will be reflected toward the top of the cake. The skillet is propped in front of the fire, as shown in the sketch.

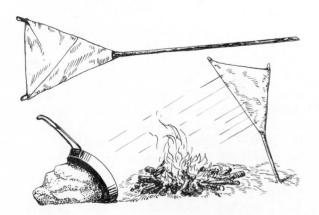

A simpler way (if we don't plan to do very much baking) is to leave the skillet over moderate heat and to prop a piece of aluminum foil over it, like a tent. This accomplishes the same purpose of reflecting heat onto the cake. We use this method with the stovepipe stove while deer hunting, and find that it works nicely.

After making a few bannocks, it will be unnecessary to bother to test them to be sure they are done. To be sure, however, stick a splinter or small twig into the cake. If no dough adheres to it, the bannock should be done. Slow heat is necessary in order to cook it through while the outside remains a golden brown. Break it apart while it is hot, and serve it with butter and jam.

This same simple baking method works equally well with corn bread, muffins, prepared mixes, and even with cakes and pies. Many of these don't need to be baked in a skillet. Try doing them in a pan fashioned from aluminum foil, as described in the next chapter.

Sweet Beans and Bacon

 8 slices bacon (cut in 1-inch pieces)
 1 can brown beans
 2 small cans tomato sauce
 ¼ cup brown sugar

Fry the bacon, but not crisp. Pour off most of the fat. Add the beans and tomato sauce. Bring this to a boil and let it simmer. Sprinkle in the brown sugar and continue simmering for 10 or 15 minutes.

Small pieces of ham can be used instead of the bacon, or canned pork and beans can be used in place of either. Another idea is to slice frankfurters into small sections and add these to the beans.

Spanish Burgers

 2 tablespoons bacon fat or 1 cube butter
 2 pounds hamburg
 1 onion, chopped fine

1 can chicken gumbo soup
3 tablespoons catsup
3 tablespoons prepared mustard or ½ teaspoon dry mustard
½ teaspoon salt
¼ teaspoon pepper

Brown the hamburg and onion in the bacon fat or butter until the red color is out of the meat. Add the remaining ingredients and simmer for about 15 minutes. Add a little water, if the mixture cooks dry.

This is very good on toasted rolls or on biscuits.

Camp Chowder

3 tablespoons butter
1 onion, chopped
1 can whole-kernel corn
1 can tomatoes
1 can string beans
1 teaspoon salt
1 pint milk or 1 can evaporated milk

Sauté the onion in butter until it is transparent. Add the other vegetables and the salt. Simmer about 15 minutes, then add the milk. Heat until very hot, without allowing the chowder to boil.

If fresh fish is available, add some small chunks that are free from skin and bones. This makes a very good fish chowder. A can of cream of celery soup can be used instead of the milk. In this case, thin the chowder with water to the desired consistency. A teaspoonful of dried herbs, such as basil, thyme, or tarragon, contributes excellent flavor to this dish. Fresh vegetables may be used instead of the canned ones, if they are available.

Fish Chowder

4 strips bacon or equivalent salt pork, diced
1 medium-sized onion, chopped coarsely
2 or 3 potatoes, diced
3 cups water
1 pound or 2 cups fish, free of skin and bones, and cut in small chunks
1 pint milk or 1 can evaporated milk
1 can cream of celery soup
1 teaspoon dried herbs (tarragon, thyme, savory, or herb blend)
½ teaspoon salt
½ teaspoon pepper

Fry the bacon or pork until crisp. Remove from grease and dry on paper towel. Sauté the onion in the grease until it is transparent. Add

potatoes and water, and boil slowly until nearly done. Add remaining ingredients and simmer (do not boil) for about 15 minutes, or until the fish is done. Sprinkle the bacon or pork on top of the chowder before serving.

The cream of celery soup and the herbs are not essential, but they add greatly to the flavor. Other vegetable cream soups can be used instead of the cream of celery soup, but most people seem to prefer the celery flavor.

This recipe makes an excellent clam chowder, if chopped or coarsely ground hard-shell clams are used in place of the fish. In this case, leave out the cream of celery soup, and go a bit light on the herbs to retain all possible of the clam flavor. Shuck the clams into a pail or bowl to save the liquor, which should be added to the chowder. If the clams are freshly dug, it may be well to let them clean themselves in cold water for an hour or two to be sure they are free from sand.

Squaw Corn

½ pound sliced bacon, cut in 1-inch pieces
1 can whole-kernel corn
8 eggs
Dash of pepper

Fry the bacon until crisp, and pour off the fat. Add the drained corn. When this begins to bubble, break in the eggs, one at a time. Add pepper. Stir gently until the eggs are scrambled and well set. Add a little salt, if necessary, but the amount in the bacon should be enough.

For an added touch, place 3 or 4 slices of American cheese on top; cover, and set the skillet in the "warming oven" part of the fireplace until the cheese has melted. Another idea is to fry a small chopped onion when frying the bacon. If you like chili powder, stir in a teaspoonful of it. Mexican-type corn can be used instead of the regular corn, and is especially good if you have added the chili powder.

Skillet Dinner

3 tablespoons bacon fat, oil, or shortening
1 medium-sized onion, sliced
1 pound lean ground beef
1 bell pepper
1 can red kidney beans
1 can whole-kernel golden corn
1 teaspoon garlic salt
¼ teaspoon black pepper

Sauté peeled sliced onion in skillet in hot fat until tender. Remove onion from skillet, leaving the hot fat. Break ground beef into small pieces and brown slowly in hot fat in skillet. When meat is light brown, pour off the fat and add the sautéed onion, seeded and sliced bell pepper, kidney beans with gravy, corn drained of liquor, salt and pepper. Simmer in skillet until bell pepper is tender (about 10 minutes).

This is one of the most widely used of all outdoor recipes; prepared with a variety of ingredients, which depend on what is available and who is doing the cooking. If the pepper or the corn isn't available, either or both can be left out. If a can of tomato sauce, a can of tomatoes, or some catsup is at hand, one of these can be added. Stir in 1 tablespoon or more of chili powder, if you wish, and if you have added tomatoes. This makes a dish very much like chili con carne. In this version, the corn can be left out. Add 1 level teaspoonful dried sage for a flavor preferred by many campers. A little grated cheese sprinkled over the top of each serving is popular. If you plan to simmer this dish longer than usual, add the kidney beans last, to avoid their getting mushy. If ground beef (hamburg) isn't handy, break up the contents of a can of corned beef, and use this instead.

Corned Beef Pancakes

1 can corned beef
Pancake mix

Remove the corned beef from the can in one chunk and slice it as thin as possible. Dip each slice in thin pancake batter, and fry in the skillet until golden brown.

Gingerbread Pancakes

1 package gingerbread mix
⅔ cup semi-sweet chocolate morsels

Prepare the gingerbread mix according to directions on the package and add the chocolate morsels. Let this stand about half an hour, then spoon 2 tablespoons of the mixture onto a moderately hot greased skillet. Brown the cakes on both sides, turning only once. Eat them while they are warm.

If you want to be a bit fancy with this recipe, roll up each pancake and sprinkle it with sugar.

Potato Pancakes (and Other Kinds)

1 cup pancake mix
1 potato, peeled and coarsely grated
1 onion, chopped fine
¼ teaspoon salt
Dash of pepper

Prepare the pancake mix by making a moderately thin batter according to directions on the package. Stir in the potato, onion, salt and pepper. Spoon the batter onto a moderately hot griddle to make cakes of the desired size; turn them only once when they are a golden brown. Eat them while they're hot—without syrup, of course.

Since pancakes are a staple outdoor diet, let's take a minute to describe the uses of prepared mixes in this skillet section, despite the fact that breads and biscuits are discussed in Chapter Nineteen. Pancakes made from prepared mixes are excellent when the rules on the box are followed, but they are even better when an egg and 1 tablespoon of hot bacon fat are stirred or beaten into the mix. The usual recipe also can be varied by peeling, coring, and slicing or dicing an apple into tiny pieces and adding this to the batter. Also try a finely sliced or diced banana. We can make a very tasty "dessert pancake" by adding a handful of semi-sweet chocolate morsels to the mix. This tastes something like the famous Toll House cookies the girls make at home.

Mountain Potatoes

4 large potatoes, peeled and sliced thin
2 medium-sized onions, peeled and sliced thin
4 slices bacon, cut in small squares
1 cup water
Salt
Pepper

Fry the bacon until crisp. Remove from grease and dry on a paper towel. Fry the potatoes and onions in the grease until they are lightly browned (for color). Add salt, pepper, and the bacon. Add enough water barely to cover. Simmer slowly over a moderate fire for 15 minutes or so—until tender.

The water will cook away. When it does, the potatoes can be turned over with a spatula, and can be browned and crisped a bit, if you like them that way.

(This dish goes nicely with fried or broiled trout, and a green vegetable such as peas.)

Skillet Pudding

1 can (1⅔ cups) evaporated milk
¾ cup "Nestlé's EverReady" cocoa
½ cup sugar
¾ cup water
Graham crackers, cookies, etc.

Put the first four ingredients in a skillet and bring them to a boil, stirring constantly. Add 10 or so coarsely broken graham crackers; cover, and cook over low heat for about half an hour, stirring occasionally. Then spoon the pudding into dishes.

If graham crackers are not handy, other kinds of cookies can be used, or breakfast foods such as corn flakes—even if they are a bit soggy! This is an easy, tasty dessert, and is a good way to use up items that might otherwise be thrown away.

Frying-Pan Rice

½ cup bacon fat
½ cup uncooked rice
1 onion, chopped fine
1 teaspoon salt
Dash of pepper
1 can tomato soup
3 cups hot water

Heat the fat in the skillet and stir in the rice. When the rice is lightly browned, add the onion, salt, and pepper. Cook this for about 5 minutes (until the onion becomes transparent), then add the tomato soup and the water. Put the skillet over a slow fire and let the food simmer for about 20 minutes.

The rice will absorb the water as it cooks. If it becomes dry before it is done, add a little more water. Rice cooked this way is excellent, as is, but the recipe can be varied by adding cooked bacon, chipped (dried) beef, hamburg steak, or sausage. We also can use another kind of soup instead of tomato—such as mushroom, cream of chicken, cream of celery, etc.

Mulligan Stew

1 or 2 onions, cut in small chunks
2 cups water
1 can corned beef, cut in small chunks
1 can green peas
Dash of salt
Dash of pepper

Boil the onion in water for about 5 minutes. Add remaining ingredients and boil slowly until the onions are done. Avoid overcooking, so the onions will not get mushy. Other vegetables, such as green beans and carrots, can be added, if handy. A dash of herb blend adds to the flavor.

French Toast I

4 eggs
¼ cup milk
6 slices bread

Mix (or beat) eggs and milk until thoroughly blended. Dip bread slices in the mixture and allow them to soak for a few minutes. Fry them in a lightly greased skillet over moderately high heat until they are brown on both sides.

Another version is to add 1 tablespoon prepared pancake flour to the above mixture, plus enough more milk to make a thin batter. This is also good for dipping fish fillets, sections of small game, or pieces of chicken or game birds preparatory to frying them in enough fat to cover the bottom of the skillet liberally. In the cases of meat and birds, turn the pieces until they are golden brown; then cover them and put the skillet over low heat for about half an hour, or slightly longer, until the meat is tender. When cooking fish or browning other foods, the fat should be bubbling but not smoking.

French toast, of course, tastes good with syrup, jelly, jam, or creamed foods such as creamed dried beef. To make camp syrup, boil together 1 cup sugar, ½ cup water, and ¼ teaspoon of concentrated maple flavoring. Add the flavoring after the sugar has dissolved.

These few "quick tricks with the skillet" are intended merely to illustrate that it is very easy to prepare a wide variety of good foods this way, rather than remain in the all too common rut of frying bacon and eggs, hamburgs and "hot dogs." But skillet cooking is far more versatile than these brief typical recipes might indicate. By browsing through the chapters on outdoor recipes that appear later in this book, you'll find that skillet cooking can be so varied that you could go on scores of outdoor trips without ever having to repeat the menu!

In skillet cooking, there is always a tendency to use too much fat—or to use the skillet when it is at an incorrect heat. A good rule is to use as little fat as possible—usually only enough to prevent the foods from sticking to the pan. Another rule is to put in foods (that are to be fried) only when the skillet is at the correct heat. After a little experience, we know the correct heat instinctively. The fat is actively simmering in the skillet, but it is not hot enough to cause it to smoke. When butter is used, it bubbles merrily but does not lose its golden color. The man who presides over the skillet observes how its contents are being affected by the heat of the fire—and he moves the skillet to a hotter or a cooler place until the cooking heat seems to be suitable. When we cook in fat that is insufficiently hot, the fat soaks into the food, with a rather unsavory result. When we cook in fat that is too hot, we burn the food before it is cooked through.

CLEANING METHODS AND OTHER TRICKS

Woodsmen take as good care of their skillets as they do of their axes and other favorite equipment. They try to avoid scratching the inside of the skillet excessively, because a badly scratched skillet causes foods to stick.

One of the ways to clean a skillet is to scoop into it some of the fine gray ashes from the fire, fill the skillet with water, and bring this to a boil. Fire ashes contain mineral salts that help to dissolve fats somewhat in the way soap does. Scouring with fine sand (or even leaves or grass) is another method; after this the cook boils water in the skillet and then wipes it dry.

Soaped steel wool pads do a good job, although one pad will last for only a few applications, since the steel wool tends to rust. Copper scouring pads don't rust, and the finely meshed types provide longer service. If the outside of the skillet is rubbed with a bar of soap before each use, accumulated soot rinses off more easily.

Chapter Four

HOW TO COOK WITH ALUMINUM FOIL

The trout fishing is almost always good in Jackson Hole, Wyoming, but it is especially so between first light and sunrise. Before the last stars had disappeared, we parked the station wagon by the main road, climbed down the bank to a beaver meadow, and were fishing in less than half an hour after leaving the lodge.

In this place, the beavers' expert engineering forms a complex of dams and waterways ideal for big fish. A cast to the far bank with a Lady Doctor fly brought a splashing strike from a big cutthroat trout that tested the tiny Orvis tackle to the utmost. In the cool gray dawn of the brightening June day, nearly every cast brought a smashing strike. I pinched the barb off the hook, because one brightly colored three-pounder was enough for lunch.

While roaming the beaver meadow, I lost my way on a watery peat bog of an island whose every border seemed to present channels too deep to wade and too wide to jump. The solution came in following an elk trail, on the theory that elk dislike swimming as much as booted anglers do. This trail led through a cottonwood forest, which proved to be a rookery for great blue herons. The great ungainly birds rose by scores in squawking flight from their immense treetop nests, but finally returned from their circling when I stood still to watch them.

The humus of the forest floor in places was scattered with morel mushrooms, rising to spongy inverted cones on thick stalks. Since these are an unmistakable variety and considered a rare delicacy, I filled a raincoat with them, topping the pile with a heap of succulent dandelion greens, selected from young plants that had not yet come into flower.

Beside the rocky river my companions waited, the faint blue smoke from their fire rising toward the blue sky against the awesome background of the snow-capped Grand Teton Mountains. All we had brought from home for food were a few strips of bacon; some corn bread mix in a plastic bag; an envelope of condiments; a small can of prepared cocoa; and some folded aluminum foil.

We filleted the trout and sealed it in foil, along with two bacon strips and a dash of condiments —salt and pepper mixed with a powdered herb blend. We washed some of the mushrooms and prepared these in the same way. We did the same with the dandelion greens, except that we added a little water to the foil package. Cups for the hot beverage were made by crimping a doubled thickness of foil around a fist, then folding down the edges to provide a secure rim and twisting part of the excess foil into a handle. All that was necessary to prepare the corn bread was to knead it with water into dough in the bag; then to squeeze out the dough into aluminum foil, shaped somewhat like a pie plate.

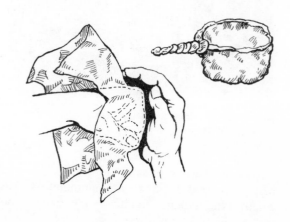

By this time the hardwood fire was a mass of graying coals. Since these varieties of foods would require similar cooking times, we laid them all on the coals together, turning the tightly sealed packages occasionally during the fifteen minutes or so necessary for them to cook. Then we poked the packages from the coals and opened them on a hummock of grass that served for a table.

These sealed packages act as small pressure cookers. Foods cook rapidly in them, and little if any moisture is able to escape. A generous amount of the cocoa, stirred into the cups of boiling water, made a delicious beverage. When the packets of fish were opened, there was enough bacon gravy with which to flavor the greens, which we chopped up with a pocket knife. The mushrooms also were abundant in gravy, so we added some of this to the greens too. The opened heavy-duty aluminum foil packets served as plates; the grass hummock as our table; the gorgeous scenery as our dining room; the songs of birds and the splashing of the stream provided background music—all fitting accompaniments to a delicious meal almost entirely provided by the bounties of nature! When the last crumb had been consumed, all we needed to do to clean up was to crumple the foil and bury it, while someone stirred water into the few coals that remained of the fire.

Aluminum foil eliminates the necessity of carrying and cleaning heavy and bulky utensils. (Boy Scouts of America)

Now there still are many old-time guides who will affirm that cooking with aluminum foil is strictly a fad indulged in only by city people and sissies. The fathers of these narrow-minded pundits probably would have assured anyone who would listen that the automobile was a fad, too, and certainly was not here to stay! Innocent readers of certain magazine articles and commercial booklets might be inclined to agree with these old-timers, if they know anything at all about outdoor cooking.

But the fact remains that in this day and age the use of aluminum foil in outdoor (and indoor) cooking is a major factor in the culinary arts. Aluminum foil can cook many kinds of foods in many ways in a manner far superior to any other method. For the outdoorsman, it also eliminates the necessity of carrying and cleaning heavy and bulky utensils. It saves time, adds to convenience, and often makes the foods taste better. So it will be well worth while to go into aluminum foil cooking in some detail. Some of the suggestions herein may seem rather elementary to veteran outdoorsmen—but they are very practical at times, and we can adopt them or ignore them, as we choose.

FACTS ABOUT FOIL

First, a few words about selecting foil. It is usually purchased in rolls, available in a range of lengths, widths, and thicknesses. While these should be selected with an eye toward the uses to which they will put, the heavy-duty thicknesses are preferable for most purposes in the outdoor cooking of foods. If only a roll of the lightweight material is available, of course it can be used in double thickness, but the light (or thin) weights are inclined to puncture easily.

Outdoorsmen often find that the bulkiness of foil in rolls makes it awkward to carry. A solution to this problem is to reroll the round roll onto a flat rectangle of cardboard, so that the resulting package will be flat. Another way (less advisable unless it seems necessary) is to tear squares of foil from the roll and fold several such squares together, handkerchief-fashion, for carrying in a pocket. Rolls of aluminum foil also can be flattened for greater compactness.

Usually aluminum foil has a very shiny side and a less shiny side. It helps slightly in heat absorption to fashion packages or containers so that the duller side is on the outside. This point has been developed in a type of foil which is jet black on one side. When this foil is used, the black surface is always on the outside. The

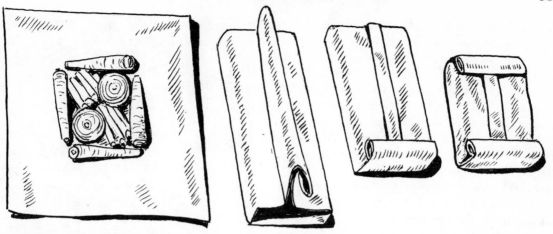

Drugstore fold—sealed at top

principle of this is that the black outside surface allows the penetration of infrared (heat) rays that a bright surface would tend to reflect. The use of this black-on-one-side foil results in cooking foods up to twice as fast as when regular foil is used. Since this foil is considerably more expensive, the user must decide whether or not the shorter period of cooking time is worth the added cost. According to the manufacturer, another advantage of it is that foods brown faster in it, because of the increased penetration of infrared rays.

SEALING FOOD PACKAGES

One of the very important points in cooking foods in foil packages is to seal the packages tightly in order to retain steam and juices and, at the same time, to keep out ashes and dirt. This is easily done by using what is called the "drugstore" fold (among various names for it). The fold consists merely of bringing two opposite sides of the foil together, around the foods to be cooked, and folding the edges over together at least twice, as shown in the sketch. A way to do it is to bring two opposite edges of foil together over the top of the food, and to fold these over together two or three times so that the final fold lies flat over the top of the food package. Then the two ends are sealed in the same way. Another method is to fold the foil over the food by bringing the top side over the food to meet the bottom edge, and to fold these two edges two or three times over together so that the seal is on the side of the package, rather than on the top. Then the other two sides are folded similarly, each fold being about a half inch wide. If the foil is thin, it should be doubled before doing this. An advantage of the side-fold method is that foods cook more evenly on both top and bottom if the fold is on the side, rather than on the top.

When foil packages are to be cooked in or on

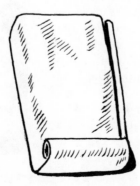

Drugstore fold—sealed on side

the coals, it is well to add a second foil covering over the first one. By so doing, we accomplish two results. The package is tighter and less inclined to puncture and allow steam and juices to escape. Also, when the outer covering is removed, the inside package will be clean, and the opened foil can be used as a plate.

When the food is cooked the package can be opened by unfolding it or by tearing off one of the crimped edges. When in the woods, we use a stick to turn over the package on the coals, so that both sides will cook evenly, and we use the stick to poke the package out of the fire, when done. In back yard cooking, a pair of tongs is more convenient. When removed from the fire, the hot foil cools to the heat of the food within, so that a man with tough fingers can open the package without using gloves. When this job is done for several people, the use of cloth gloves may prevent a blister or two.

Whether these foil packets are cooked on, in, or beside the coals is a matter of judgment that depends on the heat of the fire and on how fast or slowly the foods are to be cooked. Various persons have various ways of doing this. Some cooks like to pat the coals flat with a stick and then cover them with ashes before putting the package on the fire. Others poke hot ashes or coals over the top of the package, instead of turning it over when they think it is half cooked. A little experimentation usually solves such minor problems.

While cooking time is a matter of judgment, a foil package about an inch or two thick should require about twenty minutes' cooking time—ten minutes to a side. Larger packages, such as a roast or a fairly large game bird, may require an hour or more.

How tightly should these foil packages be sealed—that is, how much air space should be left in them? When cooking meats and fish, the packages can be sealed with very little or no air space. In this case, close contact between food and foil and fire helps to brown the food evenly. In cooking vegetables or other foods, when steam will help to blend the flavors, more air space inside the package is advisable. In this case, the extra air space allows the package to act as a pressure cooker, blending the juices because of the steam inside.

Finally, if the foods being cooked (vegetables, for instance) do not contain natural fats of their

This Hot Dinner Package is being prepared with hamburg, bacon, carrots, and potatoes.

Season the food and wrap it securely in a doubled sheet of heavy-duty aluminum foil.

When cooked on the coals, the food should be done in about 15 minutes. Use the foil as a plate. (Boy Scouts of America)

For spit cooking over charcoal, a drip pan made of a single or doubled sheet of aluminum foil will save juices for gravy—at the same time preventing flare-ups from spattering grease. The pan need be no larger than necessary to catch the juices. Use a straight edge (such as a short board) to bend up the edges evenly, and crimp the corners to make them secure. Pans for baking breads and biscuits are made similarly. (Alcoa Wrap)

own, it helps flavor to add a little fat, such as butter, margarine, or bacon grease, along with the usual condiments.

THE HOT DINNER PACKAGE

Those of us who are tired of cold sandwiches on outdoor trips will find the "hot dinner package" an excellent way of providing a hot meal quickly and easily. Lay a bacon strip or two on a piece of foil. On this place a large hamburg patty. Top with some finely sliced potatoes, onions, carrots, or other vegetables. Add salt and pepper (and a pat of butter, if you wish). Fold this into a double packet. This can be done the night before, and left in the refrigerator until time to leave. Then just put the package in your pocket and cook it over hot coals when meal-

time comes. You may wish to take along a fork, but nothing else is necessary because the foil can be used as a plate. For hungry outdoorsmen, an apple or a banana adds to this meal—and perhaps a chocolate bar, for dessert.

Quite obviously there are many variations to this hot dinner package: a big slice of ham topped with sweet potato and apple slices; a chicken leg or breast with bacon, potato slices, and carrot slivers; liver, onions, and bacon—and so on. If we expect to catch a fish or shoot a partridge, we could risk leaving the meat out. Just take along some heavy-duty foil folded handkerchiefwise, with a strip or two of bacon, the vegetables, and some salt and pepper. With these, the meat or fish course can be a hot dinner package made up on the spot!

FOIL CUPS, PLATES, AND PANS

We agree that most utensils fashioned from foil are less desirable than the real thing, but if the real thing isn't handy it is helpful to know how to rig a makeshift to take its place.

Previously we mentioned making a cup by molding foil over a fist and crimping down the edges to make a rim. There are better ways. One

is to press a doubled sheet of foil around a metal can of the right size. With the base of the cup thus fashioned, remove the foil and crimp down the edges to make a secure rim. The longest part of the excess foil can also be twisted to provide a handle. Plates and larger cups and pans can be fashioned similarly by molding the doubled sheet of foil over a small, flat stump, over the end of a log, or something else.

If a rectangular pan is desired, rather than a round one, lay a doubled rectangular sheet of foil on a flat surface and bend up the sides with the use of a straight edge, as indicated by the sketch. The corners are bent against the pan edge and are crimped in place to make them secure. This makes a good pan for baking breads and biscuits, and also a drip pan to catch juices when it is placed under foods that are being broiled on a spit.

If we have an old wire coat hanger and a pair of metal-cutting pliers, here's a way to make a rim and handle for cups such as mentioned above. Cut the hook off the coat hanger and straighten the wire. Bend the mid-section of the wire around a can of suitable size, or something similar. Twist the wire with at least one or two turns to make the loop secure. Then use the pliers to bend the remaining two equally lengthed ends into a handle, as the illustration shows.

The cup to fit inside this rim is made by molding a doubled square of foil over the same form we used to make the wire loop. When the cup is so fashioned, remove it from the form and slide it into the wire loop (which will be about of the same size). Then crimp the jagged edges of the top of the cup down around the wire rim to make the cup and rim handle secure.

This reminds me of a way we poach eggs when usual utensils are not available. To make an egg poacher, merely lay a doubled sheet of foil over the wire rim discussed above. Depress the center of the foil about half an inch or so, and crimp the foil edges securely underneath the rim. Put a small amount of water in this little pan and, when it is boiling, drop an egg into it.

The egg will poach nicely over the fire and will come out as round and even as if it had been poached in the kind of an egg poacher we use at home. When the egg is cooked, pour off the remaining water; add butter, salt, and pepper, and slide the egg onto a piece of toast!

THE COAT-HANGER FRYING PAN

There are many uses for wire coat hangers in making makeshift items useful around camp. One of them is the coat-hanger frying pan—very handy when the real thing isn't available.

To make this, merely pull the bottom of a coat hanger into a square of wire, as shown. Bend the hook around so it points downward to make a handle. Fold a length of heavy-duty foil into a doubled square and slip the wire between. Fold and crimp the three foil edges under the rim, and the pan is made! When cooking in it, note that foods will depress the center slightly, thus preventing liquids from running off. Bacon and eggs, toast, pancakes, meats, and many other foods can be cooked with this simple implement. Washing is easy, too. Just remove the foil and wad and bury it! If a frying pan is made for each person, each can use it as a plate.

Fashioning cooking utensils from aluminum foil and sturdy wire is easy, as these pictures and the text describe. (Boy Scouts of America)

COOKING VEGETABLES AND FRUITS IN FOIL

Vegetables and fruits cooked in foil are a real taste treat, very easy to prepare, and considered by many outdoor cooks to be superior in flavor to those cooked in other ways. Those requiring long cooking time, such as potatoes and onions, should be placed beside the fire, rather than in it, so they will bake slowly and be cooked through before being burned. Potatoes and onions, for example, need nearly an hour to cook through in this slow heat. Leave them in a hot

place at the edge of the fire and turn them occasionally, perhaps moving them nearer to the fire as it burns down. We don't need to wait until the fire has burned down to do this. It may take nearly an hour for the fire to burn to cooking coals—and about as long to cook the vegetables. So put them near the fire as soon as it is lighted, or shortly afterward.

We have two ways of wrapping vegetables in heavy-duty foil. Roundish ones, like onions and apples, are placed on a square of foil whose sides are drawn up tightly around the vegetable and twisted together on top. Longish ones, such as potatoes and squash, are rolled in a small sheet of foil, and then the ends are twisted tightly. (In cooking whole vegetables, the drugstore fold is unnecessary.) These twisted ends of foil serve as handles, making it easy to turn them and to adjust their position (with gloves, tongs, a stick, or even with bare hands).

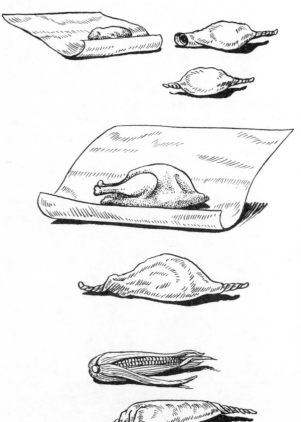

SOME EASY FRUIT AND VEGETABLE RECIPES

Baked Apples

These are favorites with outdoor cooks. Core each apple, trying to leave ½ inch or so of the bottom intact. Peel each apple about a third of the way down. Fill the cavity with sugar, butter, and a dash of cinnamon (if you have it). Also add a few seedless raisins, if handy. Place each apple on a doubled square of foil; bring the foil up around the sides and twist it on top. Bake slowly in the heat of the coals for nearly an hour.

Bananas

Peel the banana and slice it in half lengthwise. Add a little brown sugar, honey, or white sugar (preference in that order). Roll up in foil, twisting the ends. These need only about 10 minutes to cook when the fire is fairly hot. An excellent variation: sprinkle between the banana halves a small handful of semi-sweet chocolate morsels. A package of these small pieces of semi-sweet chocolate is usually in sportsmen's kits, because they are tasty and nourishing to munch on along the trail.

Vegetables wrapped in foil should bake in moderate heat beside the fire or in the coals. Turn them frequently to insure even cooking. When unwrapped, they are as clean as if cooked in the kitchen range at home—and usually more delicious. Use a double wrapping if vegetables (such as potatoes) are to be served in foil. Remove the outer foil covering and the inner one will be clean and, when opened, can be used as a plate. The corn, potatoes, and onions shown above are about to be baked for a cookout on the beach. (Alcoa Wrap)

Cabbage

Cut out the stem part of a small or medium-sized cabbage and fill the cavity with butter, plus some salt and pepper. Place this on a large, doubled square of foil; gather the foil loosely up around the cabbage and twist the gathered foil together on top. Cook slowly beside the coals.

Carrots

Scrape clean, cutting off ends. Then either slice or sliver the carrots. Lay the pile together on a doubled rectangle of foil, and add butter, salt, and pepper. Wrap and seal with a drugstore fold and cook the packet in the coals. (This is a vegetable many outdoor cooks like to "caramelize" a bit. If you like the sweetness of the caramel flavor, put the packet on the coals for a few minutes, just before it is done.)

Corn on the Cob

It is not at all necessary to prepare corn in any way or to use foil in cooking it. Without opening the ears, just line them up on the grid over the flaming fire and let them cook until the outside husks are so charred and blackened that people will think the corn is being badly over-cooked. Turn and alternate the ears, using tongs, so all will be blackened evenly, and most of the outside silk will be burned off. Then put 4 or 5 ears on several thicknesses of opened newspaper and roll them up into a tight bundle, tying this with string or putting it in a paper bag. Make as many such packages as necessary.

The corn will continue to steam in the insulation of the newspapers, and will keep hot for half an hour or more. When serving time comes, the husks and remaining silk will strip off very easily. If the corn is browned by the fire in a few places, remember that many people prefer it that way.

Now, if you prefer to use foil, strip off some of the outside husk and, by opening the inside husk, remove the silk. Spread butter on the corn and replace the inside husk. Then roll each ear in foil and twist the ends. Roast the corn over the coals for about 20 minutes, turning it frequently. Add more butter and some salt when the corn is removed from the wrappers.

Eggplant

Peel, cut off ends, and slice about 1 inch thick. Add a little butter, salt, and pepper. Seal with the drugstore fold and cook beside the coals until soft. For a variation, include slices of Bermuda onion, tomato, and Italian cheese between the slices of eggplant. If you have any Italian-style herbs, such as powdered rosemary, savory, or orégano, sprinkle on a very small amount and cook as above.

Onions

Cut off tops and bottoms (and peel them, if you wish). Place each on a square of foil, adding butter, salt, and pepper. Gather the foil around the onion and twist it tightly on top. Another way is to slice the peeled onions thickly, season them, and reassemble. Then wrap them in foil, as before. In cooking onions (which take about as long as potatoes), many people like to set the wrapped packages on the coals for a few minutes toward the end of the cooking time. This burns, or caramelizes, them slightly. This sugary caramel flavor is delicious.

For a variation, use the large Bermuda variety. Just put them on the grill over a hot fire (without wrapping them in foil) and let them cook until the outside crust is black—usually about 45 minutes. When the black crust is peeled off, the inside should be soft and delicious.

Potatoes

Scrub them and (preferably) rub them with bacon grease. Roll each in foil, twisting the ends, to make handles. Or peel each potato and cut it in thick slices. Put a little butter and some salt and pepper between the slices. Reassemble and bake them in foil.

Summer Squash

Wash, cut off ends, slice in half (the long way). Put some finely sliced onion, a small bacon strip, and salt and pepper between the halves. Reassemble each squash and roll it in foil, twisting the ends, and bake.

Sweet Potatoes

Wash (and peel, if you wish) medium-sized sweet potatoes. Cut them in half, lengthwise. Scoop 1 teaspoonful of the raw potato from the center of each half. Fill this with butter, brown, white, or maple sugar, and a little nutmeg, cinnamon, or other spices. Put the halves together again; roll them in foil; twist the ends, and bake beside the heat of the fire for about an hour. Turn frequently while cooking.

BAKING AND REFLECTOR COOKING

Reflector cooking, used primarily in outdoor cooking for the baking of breads, pies, cakes, and biscuits, requires nothing more or less than a means of reflecting heat onto the top of the foods (to brown and to help cook them) while these foods also are being cooked by heat coming up from the bottom. Reflector bakers can be purchased from camping supply houses and are discussed in Chapter Five. Recipes will be found in Chapter Nineteen.

Since aluminum foil is a very shiny and adjustable material, it makes an ideal reflector for this kind of cooking. Let's start by reducing the matter to elementals, as we did in Vermont when we made corn bread and biscuits on the stovepipe stove described in Chapter Two.

Outdoor cooking in the wilderness often becomes a matter of experimentation and improvisation. Since we had left our reflector baker at home, we decided to see what we could do with aluminum foil. We made a pan of foil, as previously described, and poured into it some corn-bread mix, prepared per instructions on the package. (These prepared mixes are very handy, if there is room to carry them.) We put the pan of corn bread on the grid over a low fire in the stovepipe stove. To make the reflector, we merely laid a large piece of heavy-duty foil over the pan, sort of tent fashion, so the rising heat could reflect off the roof of foil and down onto the top of the bread. Gradually the bread took on a beautiful golden color and, when this color seemed about right, we tested the bread for doneness with a small sliver of wood. The sliver came out with no dough adhering to it, thus indicating that the bread was done.

This simple method could have been used on a grid or rack over almost any kind of a slow fire that had reduced to coals. Thus we see that there is nothing at all difficult or mysterious about baking over an open fire.

The next step toward the popular and economical commercial folding reflector baker is to make one from aluminum foil. To do this, we take a wide roll of heavy-duty foil and cut off a sheet about four feet long. We cut two straight green sticks about a foot longer than the foil is wide, and we point them, to make stakes. We lay a stick at each end of the foil strip and roll the two sticks toward each other until three or four tight turns of foil have been made around each stick, to hold the foil securely. Then we drive these two stakes into the ground in front of the fire so that each stake is inclined at an angle of about 45° toward the fire, and so that the sheet of foil is taut between them.

The grill can be used as a reflector baker by doubling a large sheet of heavy-duty aluminum foil and molding it over the rear of the grill to make a hood, as shown above. This reflects heat downward onto the top of the food while it also cooks from below. Biscuits, breads, pies, and cakes can be baked in this manner, as well as vegetables and other foods. The foil hood, crimped to the steel or wire grid, also acts as a windscreen. If a wind is blowing, flatten the hood along the bottom edge and use stones to hold it in place. (Reynolds Wrap)

For reflected heat and light from an open fire, crimp a sheet of aluminum foil around a steel or wire grid and prop the grid behind the fire, as this hunter is doing while preparing his dinner after dark. (George X. Sand)

To cook with this reflector baker, we set the pan of whatever is to be cooked between the fire and the reflector, so that the fire's heat will reflect down onto the food. By building up the fire a bit, or by letting it burn down somewhat, we can adjust it to provide correct heat. Don't let the reflector become discolored by soot, because it is the shiny surface that does the reflecting.

If we want to get a bit more complicated, we can build the sort of reflector baker that is modeled after the commercial type, similar to the sketch. I shall not go into much detail on this, because the previous two methods do the job well enough; because this one wastes too much foil; because it is rather flimsy; and because it is so much trouble that we'll wish we had brought along a regular reflector baker, instead of bothering with it. Anyway, here's the idea, for whatever it is worth:

Drive four stakes into the ground in front of the fire. Each two should be about a foot and a half apart, with one pair about fourteen inches behind the other, to form a rectangle. The four stakes will extend about two feet above ground. Now lash crosspieces to the forward and rear pairs of stakes, so that each is horizontally about eight inches above the ground. Lash another horizontal crosspiece on the front pair of stakes about eight inches above the lower one. Using a double or treble sheet of the heaviest available aluminum foil (or a piece of sheet metal), cover the two lower horizontal bars to make a shelf. Fasten another long sheet of foil to the top horizontal bar, bringing it down around the back lower one, and then forward to the front stakes, where it can be held in place by flat stones or by small pegs. This results in a flat bed on which the food is placed, plus a top reflector and a bottom reflector, each extending from the back at an angle of about 45° upward and downward from the shelf.

To bake food on this reflector, we'll need a hot, flaming fire, because the heat must extend upward to a considerable degree to bake the food properly. The fire should be directly in front of the baker, and not over a foot or two away from it, this distance depending on how large and how hot the fire is.

Now, to get back to something a little more logical, we can take an extra wire tray (or grid) and cover it with foil. By propping this up at the correct angle, we have a fairly sensible reflector with which to bake foods that also are being cooked from the bottom because they are resting on warm ashes beside the fire.

FRYING ON FOIL

In the absence of a skillet or other receptacle suitable for frying, we can lay a doubled sheet of heavy-duty aluminum foil over the wire tray over the fire and use this to fry foods placed on it. We can do the same with a foil-covered wire tray placed over a folding charcoal grill—or even lay the foil directly over the burners of camp stoves. In the latter case, the fire may be too hot in one place and not hot enough in others, but this will depend on the type of stove being used.

Whether or not a skillet is available, the idea of cooking on foil placed over a wire tray over an open fire has merit because it affords a wide surface on which to cook. It is a good suggestion when we are cooking simple foods such as hamburg patties or hot dogs for a large number of people. If the coals are raked to one side of the fire bed, we have a hot side on which to cook, as well as a side of less heat where foods can be kept simmering. The foil should be well greased, so foods will not stick to it. In using spatulas, forks, and other tools, care must be taken not to puncture the foil.

OTHER USES FOR FOIL IN COOKING

When the bottom of an aluminum foil cup (described earlier) is punctured with small holes (as with a nail) it makes a handy strainer.

Make a bread board by laying a strip of foil on any flat surface. Rolling pin? Use a round bottle.

Small items, such as knives, forks, and spoons, can be kept clean and together without rattling by packaging them in foil.

Prevent dampness by wrapping items such as sugar, flour, and salt in foil.

Make a dishpan by scooping a hole in the ground and lining it with foil. If the foil is too narrow, combine two lengths by fastening with the drugstore fold along one edge. (Use a straight edge, such as a yardstick or a board, to do it neatly.) When the two combined strips are opened up, they will be nearly of double width. Fill the hole with hot water for washing your dishes.

When roasting food on a spit, the food can be wrapped in foil to keep in juices. This automatically bastes the food. It may be necessary to remove the foil when the food is nearly done, to allow it to brown properly.

COOKING MEATS, FISH, AND BIRDS IN FOIL

Finally, here are a few additional easy recipes that should suggest a good outdoor dinner or two, especially when served with some of the foil-baked vegetables suggested earlier. Many of these foil packets can be made up at home, to make cooking simple when lunchtime comes. To avoid repetition, all these should be wrapped securely in foil, as previously described. A double wrapping of foil is even better.

Fish

Clean, and scale if necessary. Remove the head if you wish. Large fish should be cut into fillets. Lay a slice of bacon on a piece of foil; put a serving of fish on top; add a slice of lemon and one or two of onion (if available), and salt and pepper to taste. (If the fish lacks flavor, a little Worcestershire sauce, or something similar, may help.) Package in foil; turn frequently while cooking.

Fish Dinner

Lay a slice of bacon on a piece of foil, and on this put a cleaned fish weighing about a pound. Put slices of a potato and an onion on the fish. Top this with another slice of bacon and some seasoning. Seal in foil, and cook in the coals for about 20 minutes. Here again, the cooking time depends on the size of the package and the heat of the fire.

Stuffed Fish

For this, we'll need a fairly large fish, of 4 or 5 pounds or so. After cleaning (and scaling, if necessary), stuff the fish with mixed, coarsely chopped apples, onions, and celery—or one of the other stuffings suggested in Chapter Fourteen. Season to taste—perhaps including a little garlic salt. Package in foil and bake in the coals. With a large fish such as this, sprinkling a few coals over the top would help. Fish should not be overcooked. This should not need much more than half an hour in the coals, depending on the size of the fish and the heat of the fire.

Hamburg with Cheese

Divide the hamburg in half, to make two flat patties. Place one on foil, and in the center of it place minced onion and sharp Cheddar cheese. Lay the second patty on this, and crimp the two patties together, to make one cake. Season. Seal in foil and cook on the coals, turning the package once or twice.

Hamburg with Potato

Mix a pound or so of hamburg with 1 or 2 grated potatoes (depending on size) and a small chopped onion. Add salt and pepper, and 1 tablespoon chopped parsley, if you have it. Seal in foil and cook on the coals, turning the package once or twice. Spread some mustard on the patty, if desired.

Hashed Brown Potatoes

Grate 4 large pared potatoes onto a section of foil. Grate or chop a large onion, and add this, along with seasoning. Add two tablespoons of butter, and pour a small amount of cream (or substitute) over this. Seal the package in foil and cook on the coals for from 30 to 45 minutes, turning the package occasionally.

Foods can be wrapped in foil at home and carried in the pocket. When lunchtime comes, cook them on or beside the coals, turning each package occasionally. Use a stick if the fire is hot! (Boy Scouts of America)

Pot Roast

Using a 3- to 3½-pound chuck pot roast, cut about 2 inches thick, sear both sides of the roast on the grate over hot coals. Put this on a large piece of heavy-duty foil and add sliced potatoes, onions, carrots, or other vegetables in whatever quantity is desirable. Season to taste. Seal in foil (double-package this one!), and cook on hot coals for about an hour, turning the package occasionally. Open the package carefully, because it should contain some delicious gravy.

Roast Partridge

(Other kinds of game birds or chicken are cooked the same way.) Clean and pluck the bird, and put an onion in the body cavity. If the bird is a wild one, tie legs and wings and tuck in 2 or 3 strips of bacon. If it is a chicken, dot it with butter. Season; sprinkle lightly with flour, if available, and package tightly in foil. Roast the package on the coals, turning frequently, for about an hour. (The purpose of the onion in the wild bird is to draw out some of the gamy taste. You may wish to discard it later.)

Sausage Potato

Clean a baking-size potato and drill a hole through it with an apple corer. Push a large pork sausage into the hole and wrap the potato in foil. Cook this for nearly an hour in the coals. (With this, try the baked apple recipe mentioned earlier.)

Chapter Five

NOTES ON EQUIPMENT AND CONVENIENCES

Having started with the basic elements of outdoor cooking, we know how to prepare a wide variety of well-balanced meals with little or no equipment. But such primitive methods, even though necessary at times, are usually makeshift. To do the job comfortably and efficiently, we should have proper equipment—and the array available is almost limitless. From this, we will select whatever we wish, but perhaps the information in the next few pages will help decide which items are basic; which ones further contribute to efficiency; and which ones fall in the gadget category and may be eliminated.

In this book there is occasional mention of brand names because certain products are readily available favorites of the author and of other outdoorsmen. The illustrations of equipment, however, are intended to be typical or of special interest, and not necessarily preferable to something similar. Hundreds of manufacturers offer excellent products. It is unfortunate that the limitations of this book prevent showing them all.

KNIVES, AND HOW TO SELECT THEM

Professional cooks know that few, if any, items contribute more to the pleasure and efficiency of cooking than a set of good knives, and the ability to keep them razor sharp. Unfortunately the tendency is to buy cheap ones—gleaming stainless-steel delusions with flexible blades that never keep an edge. We buy them innocently and we put up with them because they are there. It would be better immediately to bury them in a deep hole, to throw them in the ocean,

French cook's knife
Steak knife
Narrow boning knife
Spear-point paring knife
Slicer
Two-tined fork
Heavy-duty cake turner
Spreader
Hunting knife
Steel

QUALITY CUTLERY IS AN ESSENTIAL AID TO ANY COOK. (Dexter)

or to send them to some well-known character in the Kremlin or in Cuba with an appropriate suggestion for their final use—and then to go out and buy a truly efficient set that will be lifetime companions and heirlooms for future generations.

Fine knives cost little, if any, more than cheap varieties, but they are made by a relatively few firms, and one must seek them out in the stores. Perhaps the most widely used by both amateurs and professionals is the "Dexter" brand, made by the Russell-Harrington Cutlery Company in Southbridge, Massachusetts—a firm of dedicated New England craftsmen which has been in the fine cutlery business for more than a hundred and fifty years.

From Russell-Harrington's catalog of hundreds of varieties, I have selected five to recommend to the outdoor cook for both outdoor and indoor uses. These, as illustrated, are the French cook's knife, the steak knife, the narrow boning knife, the spear-point paring knife, and the slicer. In addition, the well-heeled cook will need a long-handled and a short-handled two-tined fork, a heavy-duty cake turner, and perhaps a spreader. A fine hunting knife in a sheath should be the lifetime companion of every sportsman. This has to double for all the others on occasion. It should have a fairly short (four to five inches) boning type blade, preferably with a serrated upper edge that can be used for the scaling of fish. On long trips, a carborundum stone can keep these knives in top condition. At home, the connoisseur will use a steel to maintain the edge, although many will prefer an electric knife sharpener. Of course we could go on and on to mention spatulas, cleavers, oyster and clam knives, and other types. Start with the essentials and go on from there—but be sure that whatever is selected is the finest obtainable.

How do we select the "finest obtainable?" Here are six points to consider:

1. Purchase the cutlery from a reliable manufacturer known for providing high-quality blades with long-lasting edges.

2. Heft the knife to be sure it is well balanced.

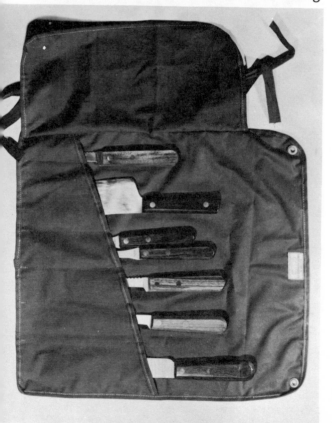

Cutlery roll (Abercrombie)

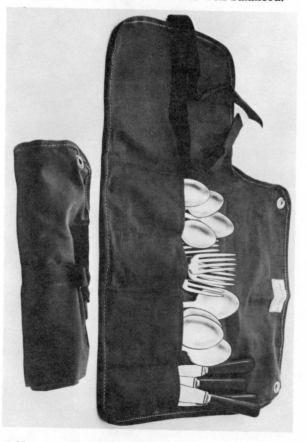

Tableware roll (Abercrombie)

3. Examine the handle for quality of hardwood (or durable plastic), and be sure the finish is stain- and moisture-resistant.

4. The blade should be secured to the handle by rivets, and should run either half the length or the full length of the handle.

5. Examine the edge—hollow ground for a keen cutting edge; rolled edge and canneled edge for heavy-duty cutting; and scalloped or serrated edge for slicing bread, vegetables, and fruit.

6. A matter of major importance is the type of steel. High-carbon steel or high-carbon stainless steel is used in the manufacture of quality cutlery. High-carbon steel will stain, but it provides a much better edge, holding qualities, and toughness than does stainless steel. High-carbon stainless steel has less carbon content than carbon

steel. It will not rust or stain, and will retain a fairly good cutting edge. (My own cooking knives are all of high-carbon steel because I consider its ability to hold an edge much more important than its tendency to stain.)

Perhaps this author could be accused of being something of a "nut about knives," but my set has provided exceptional efficiency for more than twenty-five years. Therefore, perhaps I may be excused for stressing the importance of the subject.

Illustrated on page 49 are a cutlery and a tableware roll that keep such objects clean, compact, and ready for use when needed. If such rolls are not handy, the utensils can be wrapped in a dish towel. Long-handled tools, which will be mentioned next, can be stored in the same way. Knife blades can be protected in folded cardboard.

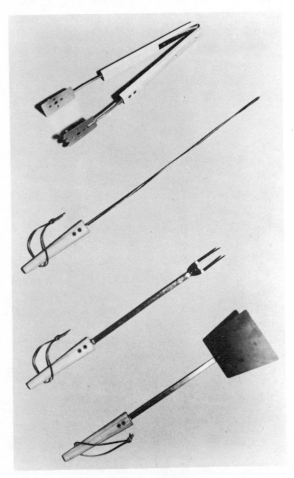

Barbecue tongs Skewer Barbecue fork Turner

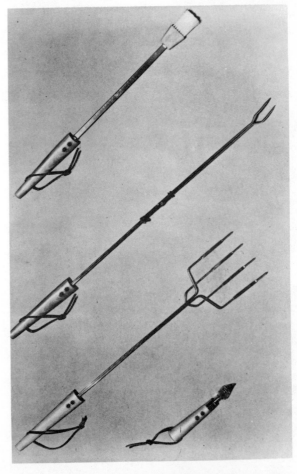

Basting brush Extension fork Hot dog roaster Bottle opener Barbecue tools (Androck)

ESSENTIAL TOOLS, AND OTHERS

Barbecue chefs are fond of long-handled tools, several of which are shown here. Some are important; others much less so. Long-handled tongs are almost indispensable for turning meats and vegetables over an open fire. A brush (preferably long-handled) is necessary for basting meats and fish with gravy or barbecue sauces. Regular light-bristled paintbrushes are obtainable at low cost from hardware stores and can be spliced to extend the handle, if long-handled barbecue brushes are temporarily unavailable. When long-handled barbecue brushes are purchased, be sure the brush ends are removable, and buy several at the same time. The brush ends last only for a few cookouts, and need to be replaced often. Many of these brush ends are made of bristles of synthetic plastic material, and will crinkle and disintegrate if washed in very hot water. If you have no basting brush, an acceptable substitute can be made by winding and tying a strip of clean white cloth about three inches wide around the end of a green stick so that about two inches of the cloth protrude from the end of the stick.

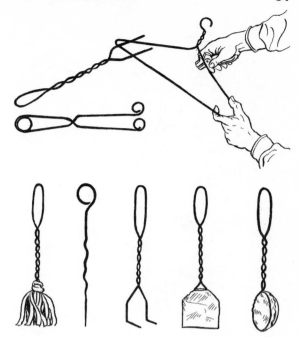

Wire coat hangers can be bent and shaped into many helpful implements with wire-cutting pliers, as the sketch shows. Here illustrated are a fork, tongs, basting brush, skewer, rake, spatula, and ladle. The last two are lined with heavy-duty aluminum foil.

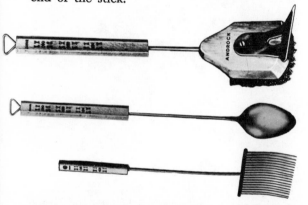

Barbecue brush and scraper Barbecue spoon Flexible turner (for reaching down between wires of a grill to lift sticky foods, such as hamburgs or fish) Barbecue tools (Androck)

If we may retrogress to the elementals with which this book was begun, let's bear in mind that many of these tools can be fashioned from strong wire (such as coat-hanger wire) if commercial products are not handy. If the wire has been painted, the paint on the parts of the tools that are to touch food should be burned and scraped off.

In cooking with wire grids and broilers, a combination wire brush and scraper, as illustrated, is very useful to keep the wire clean. Wire brushes such as are used by painters are obtainable from hardware stores and serve essentially the same purpose. These wire grids and broilers can be transported wrapped in newspapers or in aluminum foil, thus keeping everything clean.

In selecting cooking tools such as these, what may seem most desirable to one cook may appear entirely useless to another. Each of us develops his favorite types of cooking fires and cooking methods—and each of us therefore will prefer a different assortment of tools.

WIRE BROILERS

An appliance that is essential to almost everybody, however, is a wire broiler—or a small collection of them, because in such a broiler one can cook all sorts of fish, meats, and game, adjusting the foods at will to suitable cooking heat and turning the broiler frequently to assure correct cooking on both sides.

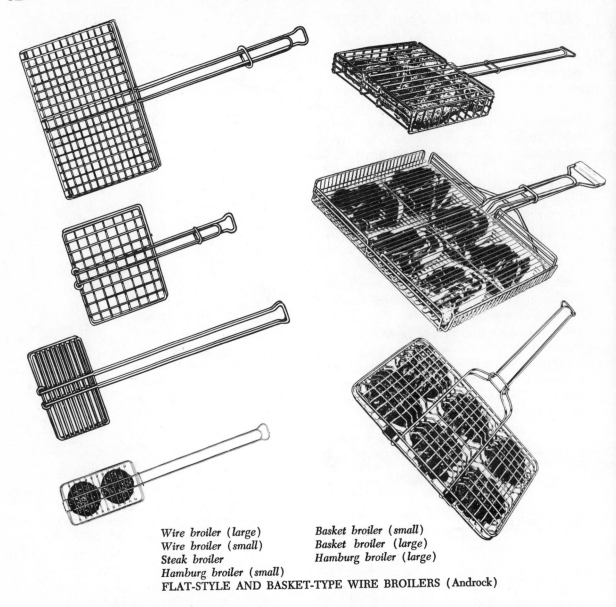

Wire broiler (large)
Wire broiler (small)
Steak broiler
Hamburg broiler (small)

Basket broiler (small)
Basket broiler (large)
Hamburg broiler (large)

FLAT-STYLE AND BASKET-TYPE WIRE BROILERS (Androck)

Here again, quality is important, because a well-made broiler will last for years, while a cheap one soon will become warped, rusted, and bent. Even top manufacturers, such as The Washburn Company of Worcester, Massachusetts (which produces the "Androck" brand of outdoor cooking equipment), make broilers priced for limited budgets as well as highest-quality products providing years of efficient service. A respected trade name assures that the buyer will get best value in whatever degree of quality he selects. In buying wire broilers for long service, look for those with strong bars on heavy frames to prevent warping; quality plat-

ing to prevent rusting and sticking; and firmly welded joints to prevent wires from becoming detached from each other.

While the size of broiler one selects is a matter of choice, several types are worthy of mention. Most commonly used is the steak broiler, which also will handle other foods of uniform thickness. Foods not uniformly thick may need a basket broiler to prevent pieces from dropping out. Basket broilers have sides as well as tops and bottoms. The tops are usually adjustable to hold foods firmly, whether they be thick or thin. Since hamburgs are popular fare in outdoor cooking, special wire broilers are made to keep the patties separated and uncompressed, as the illustration shows. There are also special ones for frankfurters and other foods; broilers designed for uses on rotating spits; and giant sizes for quantity cooking, as shown in Chapter Six.

This reflector baker can do a professional job of baking foods before an open fire. This one is the folding type. (Abercrombie)

To prevent foods from sticking when being cooked, raise the wings of the broiler from the food occasionally to lubricate the wires with the fats oozing from the food. Clean the broiler as soon as possible after use to keep the wires free from carbon. Selecting broilers with mirror chrome-plated finishes also helps.

THE REFLECTOR BAKER

In this book we have recommended two outdoor cooking utensils more valuable to the seasoned camper than to the back yard cook. These are the folding reflector baker and the Dutch oven. The reflector baker can do a really professional job of baking pies, cakes, and biscuits, as well as preparing casseroles and other foods that need to be baked. To use this properly, we need a high open fire that will throw heat into the baker so that its slanting top and bottom will re-

flect heat evenly toward both the top and bottom of the pan of food being baked. With a good fire going, we can move the baker toward the heat or farther away from it, as desirable.

THE DUTCH OVEN

The Dutch oven is a metal cooking pot, usually of cast iron, which has a recessed or flanged cover to allow hot coals to be placed on it. When this oven is placed on a bed of coals and when other coals are heaped on the lid, it provides a serviceable "oven," as the name implies. Heat can be adjusted by the hotness and quantity of the coals being used. Those on top need only to be partially poked off to inspect the contents—which can be a pie, a cake, a batch of biscuits, a stew, a roast, or whatever else can be cooked in the family oven or range back home.

NESTED COOKING KITS

Nested cooking kits are handy items for campers because numerous utensils, such as frying pans (with detachable handles), pots, plates, cups, and cutlery, all can be nested together compactly for easy transportation. Here again, quality counts. Get a sturdy, well-made set, and avoid the thin utensils that do not hold heat well and therefore are more inclined to scorch the food.

After buying such a set, and before using it for cooking, it is well to wash it thoroughly with strong soap and hot water. If this has not been done at the factory, some of the oils used in fabrication may still coat the metal and would impart an unpleasant taste to the food.

DISPOSABLE PANS

For casual cooking on picnics or as a camp or back yard cooking accessory, a set or two of "Disposa-Pans" is an investment worth far more than the small cost. This is a set of several pie-plate-like aluminum pans and a handle holder to fit them. Use the holder and a pan to cook with, and then remove the pan from the holder and use it as a plate. The pans can be discarded after use, since replacements are available in stores. A set of "Disposa-Pans" and a reflector baker quite obviously provide a most useful combination, because this set then can be used to bake breads, pies, cakes, and casseroles, as well as for its more frequent uses of frying foods over an open fire.

DUTCH OVENS

Note the flanged lid, which allows coals to be piled on the lid to provide heat from the top while the oven (resting on or in the coals of an open fire) also heats from the bottom. In the lower picture, these Boy Scouts have used Dutch ovens to prepare a meal of vegetables, chicken, biscuits, and baked apples. (Boy Scouts of America)

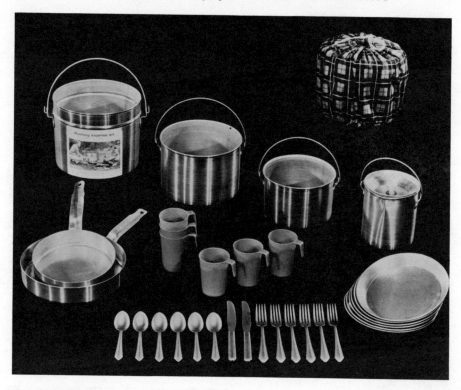

(Mustang)

NESTED COOKING KITS

All utensils shown nest compactly in the large kettle. Skillet handles are detachable, so skillets also can be used as kettle covers. There is room for cutlery, condiments, and other small items too.

(Abercrombie)

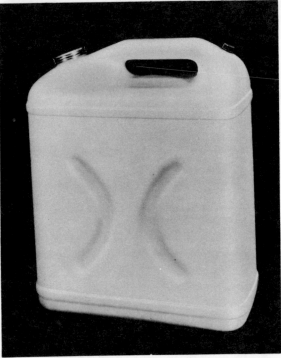

Disposa-Pan sets include a frying-pan frame and eight disposable aluminum plates. Set a plate in the frame; cook the food in this skillet and serve it on the plate. (Disposa-Pan)

A camp lantern is important when darkness falls. This one uses any automobile gasoline, so carrying special fuel is unnecessary. (Thermos)

This giant aluminum griddle is 16 inches in diameter; has a folding handle—ideal for frying almost anything and for carrying the food to the table for serving. (Bethany)

Porta-Perk makes coffee anywhere, using pressurized gas in disposable cylinders. Turn it on, light up, and coffee will be perking in minutes! (Blu-Burn-R)

This light and sturdy plastic Tote-Can holds 3 gallons— ideal for transportation and providing a water supply around camp. (Carry-Lite)

CHECK LIST OF EQUIPMENT

"What to take along?" usually poses a problem because the inexperienced camper often carries unnecessary items, while leaving a few essentials at home. The answer to this is to prepare a check list, and to adjust it from time to time as seems necessary. When the list has simmered down to a sensible one, why not type it and fasten it into this book? Many chronic campers keep their non-perishable items in a kit, or portable pantry, and avoid borrowing from it for household needs. Then all they need to do is put it in the car and be on their way. Such kits may be as simple as essential items packed in a carton or they may extend to very elaborate portable pantries, custom-designed and handmade from plywood and other materials, complete with partitions, drawers, and doors.

AN EMERGENCY FOOD KIT

Since nearly everyone drives a car these days, readers may be interested in a compact "emergency kit" the author put together for preparing impromptu meals beside the road, in motels, or at home during power failures. This kit, once stocked, need not be revised for months, except for replacements. It provides between sixteen and twenty meals, including choices of hot beverages, main courses, and desserts. Obviously, contents can be varied according to individual taste, but let's use the contents of the author's kit as a basis, and see how much can be fitted into a small space.

A portable refrigerator makes an ideal container because it secures foods from rodents, insects, dust, and moisture, while keeping the contents at a fairly even temperature. My choice was a foam plastic box, because these are very light and have few parts that can corrode or rust. The inside capacity is 9×10×18 inches, or 1620 cubic inches—only about a cubic foot. This size accommodates all the items listed, with a little room to spare.

The compact portable stove problem is solved by the sturdy "Sterno" double-burner folding cook stove, which folds flat to only 13×7×½ inches. For heat, we take along four 7-ounce cans of "Sterno" solidified alcohol fuel. Since each can burns for nearly two hours, this provides almost eight hours of burning time at a cost of only twenty cents per hour. This little stove, costing less than two dollars, can be picked up at almost any hardware or sporting goods store. It is perfectly safe, and there's nothing to get out of order. Keep the stove in its original box. It won't get smudgy, because "Sterno" fuel doesn't smoke. The fuel can be extinguished easily, and can be reused until the cans are empty.

With these two problems solved, all we need is to stock the kit with foods and equipment. Everything listed will fit into the container described—with room to spare:

1 *Portable refrigerator (or similar box, as described)*
1 *"Sterno" two-burner folding cook stove*
1 *aluminum beverage pot (2-quart size, with bail or detachable handle, and cover)*
2 *aluminum boilers (with folding handles and covers; about 1 pint capacity)*
4 *cans of "Sterno Canned Heat" fuel (7-ounce size)*
4 *nested aluminum cups (or about 16 nested paper hot-beverage cups)*
4 *nested small aluminum plates (or about 16 paper plates)*
4 *sets of knives, forks, spoons (all cutlery, etc., in plastic bag, secured with rubber bands)*
1 *short-blade carving or hunting knife*
1 *wheel-type can opener*
1 *serving spoon*
1 *small spatula*
2 *dozen paper napkins*
2 *dish cloths (or dish towels)*
1 *bar of soap (or small container of detergent)*
25 *feet or so of heavy-duty aluminum foil (wound flat on cardboard about 2 inches wide)*
1 *package "Barrier" insect repellent*
1 *small container of wooden matches*
1 *small container of vegetable oil*
1 *small container of salt*
1 *small container of pepper*
1 *small container of sugar*
1 *small container of pancake flour*
1 *can of cocoa (1-pound can)*
1 *jar of instant coffee (2-ounce jar)*
1 *small jar of chicken or beef bouillon (granulated or cubes)*
8 *envelopes of dehydrated soups (assorted varieties)*
2 *cans of corned beef hash*
2 *cans of pork and beans*
2 *cans of beef ravioli in sauce*
1 *can of macaroni and cheese*
1 *can of Maine sardines*

Photographs at left and at top are of the author's Emergency Kit, as described here. Photograph at bottom suggests equipment (less food) that might be needed by a party of not more than four people on a short camping trip. Incidentally, the rifle used to bag this eight-point buck in the Jackman region of Maine was the famous Ruger .44 Magnum Carbine. When the deer is in the car, it's time to open the Emergency Kit and enjoy a hot beverage such as is being made on the little Sterno stove on the car's tailgate. (Photo at bottom right by Ford Times Magazine. Other photos by the Maine Development Commission)

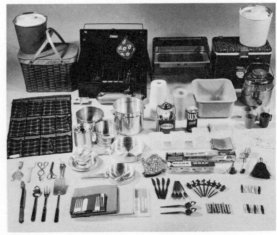

Properly prepared food and comfortable accommodations are essentials in station wagon camping. These photographs show three sensible station wagon camping lay-outs. In the top picture, a Para-Wing shelters the dining table and cooking area, flanked by a large Pop-Tent which comfortably accommodates another couple. In the bottom picture, a family enjoys a view of Wyoming's Grand Tetons while serving dinner on the car's tailgate near their wall tent. (Photos: top Ford Times, middle Pop-Tent, lower Coleman)

1 small tin of crackers
1 small jar of powdered cream
6 bars of chocolate (large size)
1 bag of semi-sweet chocolate morsels

Condiments and other small items can be stored in the cooking pots. Set the folding stove on its side, for easy removal. Include other small items, such as gum or rolls of hard candy if you wish—but avoid cramming the kit too tightly.

The use of paper plates, cups, and aluminum foil makes cleaning dishes unnecessary. Lay a doubled sheet of foil over the stove burners to fry fish and other foods. Use the vegetable oil to grease the foil or pans, if necessary. Use the flour for dusting the fish you catch. If there's a chance that pure water may not be available, carry some in a water jug—or boil questionable water before using. The "small containers" mentioned above can be screw-top glass or plastic jars such as condiments come in. Just clean the jars and label their new contents. Most of these jars have both shaker tops and screw covers. The size of the jars should be varied, depending on the volume of contents that will be used.

With the Emergency Food Kit assembled, store it at home in case of need, and take it along when going on trips. Replace the foods used promptly, and keep the kit fully equipped for enjoying a few tasty and easy meals wherever you may be. It's then ready to go—whenever you are. Just put it in the car and be on your way!

CAMP SANITATION

Insect repellent is an item many outdoor cooks forget to take along—and fervently wish they had! Everyone has his favorite, and mine is a type that repels all sorts of flying insects for hours and does not come in a bottle or jar that would take up unnecessary room and might break or leak. This is a product called "Barrier," and is in the form of small paper napkins impregnated with the repellent, each contained in a protective envelope no larger than an envelope of sugar. We tuck several of these in fishing jackets, camping kits, and in the glove compartment of the car. When needed, merely open an envelope and wipe exposed body parts with the damp napkins. That ends the bug problem!

Another problem in outdoor cooking is the disposal of garbage, which draws flies and tempts animals if not taken care of. Merely throwing it on a fire is not the solution, because it must be at least partially dry for it to burn. One solution is to dig a deep trench and build a fire in it. Lay green sticks side by side across the trench and dump the garbage on them. By the time the green sticks have burned through, the garbage has dried and will burn easily. Squash cans flat, and crumple up used foil. Bury them and other such refuse in the garbage pit, because such things never add to the beauty of the landscape.

While touching upon camp sanitation, it may be appropriate to include a few remarks that may prevent digestive ailments and other troubles. All cooking utensils should be sterilized

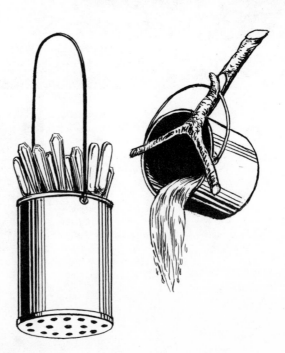

with boiling water and a detergent. A handy way to sterilize cutlery is to punch some holes in the bottom of a can and rig a bail at the top. Put the washed cutlery in this can, and dip it in boiling water. (Don't do this to wooden handles, because it will gradually ruin them.) Keep opened foods cool or cold, and use them as soon as possible. Never warm up leftovers more than once, and be sure they are untainted. Boil dish cloths and towels, and dry them in the sun. Taking along plenty of paper towels is a big help. Use them to drain fried foods, because solid fats can ruin the taste of food, as well as our digestions. Don't let the cook taste foods and then use the same fork or spoon for cooking before washing it again. He may be coming down with a cold or sore throat before he knows it! Don't trust water unless you're sure it is pure. If there's any doubt, boil it, or treat it with water purification tablets.

If you run out of soap, remember that wood ashes provide a good substitute. When combined with water, the potash and soda in the ashes help to dissolve grease. Then rub the utensils with dry grass, if no towels are handy. To avoid blackening pots and pans with soot over an open fire, rub bottoms and sides with soap that has soaked in a little water to make a paste. After use, this coating and the soot both wash off easily.

MAKING A FIRELESS COOKER

And finally in this chapter on equipment and conveniences, here's an interesting idea sent to me by my old friend, Bill Bragg, from Jackson Hole, Wyoming. It's a fireless cooker made with a box and some hay, and here's how Bill says it works:

"Take a double armful of alfalfa hay. Take a pail of water. Take a straight-sided kettle, and a wooden box like an ammunition box. Wet the hay, handfuls at a time, and tamp a layer firm and flat in the bottom of the box. Place the kettle on the hay, and pack wet hay all around between the kettle and the box. Then set the whole affair aside for about a week, until the tightly packed hay dries out. Then the kettle will slip in and out of its hay nest perfectly.

"Now, if you are in a hunters' camp, fix up a stew in the kettle. Bring it to a boil over the fire, and then put it in its hay nest. Leave it all day, and it will simmer and cook for hours. Cowboys and sheepherders used to do this when they wanted a good warm meal waiting for them after a day in the saddle. They called this contraption the 'Wooden Wife from Wyoming,' and when they returned they would find it had cooked their evening meal for them!"

Chapter Six

FIREPLACES, STOVES, AND GRILLS

"What to cook on" should not be a problem because an almost inexhaustible array of portable camp stoves and grills is available everywhere in every price range and size and for every outdoor cooking purpose. Camp stoves double as an indoor convenience for use in camps and during emergencies such as power failures. We can take them along on trips and enjoy hot outdoor meals anywhere, regardless of fire restrictions. The small charcoal stoves or grills also double as an indoor convenience because we can use them on the patio or in the fireplace to broil foods and to bake vegetables regardless of weather.

But there's something about an outdoor fireplace that seems to put it in a spot of its own in the hearts of outdoor cooks. Perhaps it's because we especially enjoy cooking on something we have created ourselves. Perhaps it's because it may be more picturesque, or because it may provide a larger cooking surface. Or it may be because, when the meal is over, we can remove the grid and pile on some wood and enjoy after-dinner beverages before an open fire while the shadows fall.

FIREPLACES: HOMEMADE, AND MORE ELABORATE

The open fireplace need not be elaborate. Fancy ones of iron and masonry later may turn out to be inefficient eyesores, very difficult to move or to remodel. Let's discuss a basic outdoor fireplace that will serve its purpose well and can be moved or remodeled quickly when desirable. If readers want the more elaborate masonry designs, outdoor magazines usually are happy to answer letters requesting plans for them.

This basic fireplace can be made from flat rocks, but it usually is preferable to build it with cinder blocks or large fire bricks obtainable at low cost from building supply establishments. The cooking surface is a wire rack or tray such as comes in refrigerators or kitchen ranges. This wire rack should be as large and as sturdy as possible. If it cannot be found at home, junk yards or hardware stores can supply one. Modern plating on such racks usually is non-toxic, and never should peel off. In the very rare cases when it does peel off, it can be kept smooth with a wire brush, but it would be preferable to discard such a rack in favor of one of higher quality.

The size of the rack dictates the size of the fireplace. Lay a bed of a dozen or so cinder blocks tightly together on level ground with the smooth sides of the blocks uppermost. Lay the wire tray on this, and fit a row of cinder blocks

on back and sides of the fireplace, as the sketch shows. A third row on top of the lower two will aid the draft.

Now, to hold the rack at the desired height above the fire bed, merely set rows of bricks on each side. These can be adjusted to any height desired. Build the fire as explained in Chapter One, and we are ready to cook! Masonry is unnecessary, but we could use mortar to apply a facing of bricks or rocks to the outside if better appearance is desired. We could also raise the height of the fireplace by adding another layer or two of cinder blocks to the base. Such a fireplace should be adequate for family and guests, but we could make it double in size, if need be. The direction in which the fireplace faces with respect to prevailing breezes is unimportant, as there is enough natural draft to maintain good fires.

Remember previous comments about building the fire on one side of the fire bed, or raking coals to one side or the other. This gives us a hot side and a cooler side, which often is desirable because it provides a side for hot cooking and a side for slow cooking or simmering. Remember what was said in Chapter One about building fires, and the relative burning time of charcoal and of briquettes.

A little ingenuity can adapt this fireplace to rotary spit cooking. A spit and a battery-operated or plug-in electric motor can be obtained from hardware stores. The supports may need to be

improvised from metal, but they can be kept in place by fitting them between the cinder blocks. For smoke cooking, a cover can be made to order at a metalworking shop, but a common ash-can cover will suffice for usual purposes.

The author's fireplace is in a woodsy cookout area and has been in use without repair for ten years. Cinder blocks were laid as described and were faced with Indiana limestone left over from building a house. This fireplace required only an hour or two to build. No mortar was used in its construction.

The little Taykit pocket stove uses almost any kind of fuel—it is light and compact for carrying in a pocket. The famous Primus is available in several models; it is enclosed in a metal box and burns ordinary gasoline. The foolproof Sterno is available in double- or single-burner models; burns approximately two hours on a can of Sterno Canned Heat; folds to ½-inch thickness and is very light and economical.

The Sportster, by Coleman, is a miniature 5×5-inch model that uses unleaded gasoline and fits in an aluminum container also usable as a fry pan and a saucepan. A heat drum (right) converts this stove into a heater.

SMALL CAMP STOVES

One of a wide selection of Coleman camp stoves, this double-burner model accommodates two 9-inch pans; folds compactly into a steel carrying case. The stove burns special Coleman fuel or unleaded gasoline.

This Insta-Lite stove is available in single- and double-burner models; burns L.P. gas fuel from disposable cylinders. This double-burner model folds into a carrying case holding a spare pair of cylinders—enough fuel for three meals a day for six days for a family of four.

STOVES OF VARIOUS KINDS

The selection of a stove or grill quite obviously is a matter of choosing a type suitable to the uses to which it will be put—at a price we are willing to pay. From the many excellent ones available, let's discuss a few as typical examples.

Among the little ones, suitable for pack carrying and for cooking simple meals, the several "Primus" stoves are well known as having been used by famous explorers on mountain-climbing expeditions. The "Primus" is a collapsible stove, weighing little more than a pound, that operates on ordinary gasoline or white gas. It will boil a pint of water in a matter of minutes and operates for between one and two hours on a filling.

Somewhat similar in usefulness is the "Taykit" pocket stove, which uses almost any type of fuel, including gasolines, outboard motor fuel, or lighter fluid. This folding stove requires no pump to keep pressure up, and it regulates itself. Weight, fuel consumption, and burning time are similar to the "Primus."

Thermos makes several two- and three-burner camp stoves equipped with windshields folding into a suitcase-type carrying case. Tanks hold approximately one quart of fuel, providing from four to five hours' burning time.

A feature of Thermos cook stoves is that they burn ordinary gasoline which, if the regular supply runs out, can be siphoned into the fuel tank directly from an automobile gasoline tank.

Among the lowest cost and lightest in the small portable stove line are the "Sterno" one- or two-burner folding stoves; also ideal for pack carrying because they fold compactly to only half an inch in thickness, and weigh almost nothing. These stoves burn "Sterno Canned Heat." For stove use, the 7-ounce can is more economical than the smaller one, since it provides greater heat at a burning time of about two hours. The "Sterno" fuel, which has been mentioned previously, is notable because it is solidified alcohol, which is smokeless and won't spill or leak.

Another practical item in the one-burner portable stove class is the "Coleman Sportster," which can be obtained in an aluminum case whose bottom doubles as a two-quart saucepan and whose top provides a six-inch frying pan. Both have detachable handles. This stove burns unleaded gasoline and has an accessory that converts it into a practical heater. Coleman also offers larger two-burner camp stoves in carrying cases provided with windscreens. An accessory also adaptable to charcoal grills is a folding oven about twelve inches square that breaks down into a package less than three inches thick. This oven has an adjustable steel rack, front-opening door, and heat indicator.

Among the many other two-burner gasoline stoves available in carrying cases fitted with windscreens, the "Holiday" stove made by "Thermos" is notable because it burns regular automobile gasoline. As the illustration shows, the stove's fuel tank can be removed and filled by siphoning gas from an automobile's gasoline tank.

Other folding camp stoves burn propane or butane pressurized gas (or a mixture of the two) obtainable in cans or cylinders that are discarded after use. Some of these stoves are practically foolproof; others perhaps less so. A very popular model burning butane fuel (L.P. gas) in light and economical disposable cylinders is the "Insta-Lite," obtainable in both one- and two-burner models. The two-burner stove folds into a carrying case measuring $13 \times 9\frac{1}{4} \times 7\frac{5}{8}$ inches and weighs less than ten pounds with four fuel refills. Two of these are carried as spares. This should be adequate for preparing about eighteen meals for a family of four.

While most portable stoves burn gas, gasoline, or similar fuels, there are a few that burn wood,

PORTABLE OVENS FOR CAMP STOVES
(*Ford Times*)

Folding ovens, such as the Coleman model above, convert camp stoves into ovens capable of baking, roasting, and warming foods. Another type is shown in use on a camp stove in the illustration below.

2

4

1

3

5

A WOOD OR COAL COOK STOVE

Since the Raemco folding stove burns wood or coal, as well as charcoal or briquettes, it is ideal for use in both tents and camps and for outdoor cooking. Stovepipe sections are available, if needed for indoor use. This stove can be set up in a choice of seven positions including (1) carrying position, (2) frying, (3) open rotisserie, (4) broiling, (5) baking. The stove weighs about 28 pounds and measures 10¼✕19✕9½ inches in carrying position. Oven and other basic accessories can be packed inside.

coal, charcoal, or briquettes. One of the most versatile of these is the "Raemco 7 in 1" portable stove, which as the name implies can be set up in a choice of any of seven ways to permit broiling, baking, barbecuing, frying, smoke cooking, spit roasting, or heating. For indoor or tent use this stove can be obtained with lengths of stove-pipe, which are unnecessary otherwise. All parts except the optional extension legs can be carried in the stove box, which measures 10¼✕19✕9½ inches. The complete unit weighs just less than twenty-eight pounds. As shown in the illustrations, the legs fold upward to provide a carrying handle.

GRILLS, AND HOW TO SELECT THEM

The third principal type of unit used to provide heat for outdoor cooking usually depends upon wood, charcoal, or briquettes for fuel. Grills essentially are fireplaces that are more or less transportable.

In Chapter One we learned easy ways to build efficient fires, using wood kindling or a commercial fire starter to get cooking fires going quickly. These methods are better than using paper as kindling, because paper burns to sooty flakes that waft upward and often settle in undesirable places, including the food. We also observed that the simplest forms of grills consist of wire racks or metal rods supported by rocks or logs over a small open fire. Let's go on from there.

If we want to take our grill with us in one of its simplest forms, we can use a wire rack fitted with folding wire legs that can be pushed into the ground to the desired cooking height over a wood fire built on the ground. We can surround this simple cooking unit with a windscreen of rocks, logs, or something else, if need be.

Proceeding from these basic appliances to more elaborate grills, we find types fitted with a firebox, such as the two "Androck" examples shown here. These provide low-cost, lightweight folding portable units in which fires for broiling can be built with little danger of damage caused by dropping coals.

These simple grills and the portable stoves we have been discussing are intended primarily for transportation, as when going on picnics and camping trips. For back yard cooking, it is more practical and more enjoyable to use grills of a more versatile nature, such as the examples to be discussed from now on.

The famous "Curtis Cooker" is a grill small enough to transport or to use in the fireplace, yet ideal for many forms of back yard cooking. Let's look at it in some detail, because it possesses many advantages that a practical portable grill should have. Important among these are provisions for adjusting the draft to hasten or to slow down a fire, plus a quickly adjustable firebox that can be lowered to twelve inches below the food or raised to four inches under the grilling

Simple wire rack grills (Androck)

In these Eclipse grills, a crank raises the grid as the fire-box lowers, thus providing adjustable cooking heat. The unit can be obtained with a rotary spit and is suitable for cooking in a fireplace. Eclipse makes grills in a wide variety and price range.

MORE ELABORATE PORTABLE GRILLS

Above left is the Curtis Cooker, described in the text. The extension legs can be folded back or removed for fireplace use. Above right is the 18-inch-diameter cast-iron Charcoal King, which also can be used as a large hibachi, as described in Chapter Nine.

surface. The grilling surface measures a very adequate 17×15 inches. For fireplace use, the legs can be folded to reduce the height to eighteen inches; or they can be extended to thirty inches for outdoor cooking. The complete unit weighs sixteen pounds.

The base of the "Curtis Cooker" firebox is in the form of a truncated inverted pyramid, which causes coals to settle in the middle of the box. This, and the sealed sides of the box, force heat upward and make it possible to use much less charcoal than in grills built differently. The base of the firebox terminates in a small removable or adjustable drawer that seals off draft when closed and allows the desirable amount of draft when opened. The manufacturer recommends starting the grill by lighting a "Sterno" charcoal lighter cube placed in the drawer. One cube, and the excellent draft provided, gets a brisk fire going and ready for cooking in about five minutes. This fire is regulated by opening or closing the drawer and by raising or lowering the firebox by means of handles on its sides. Optionally, the cooker is obtainable with shelves that fit on the sides, and with a battery-operated or a plug-in spit.

Another excellent grill constructed along somewhat similar lines is the "Eclipse 365." This one is a little larger (16×18 inches) and heavier (twenty-five pounds) than the "Curtis Cooker." It has the very desirable feature of an adjustable cooking surface, which is controlled by means of a crank that raises the grid while at the same time lowering the firebox. An electric spit is available. The Eclipse Manufacturing Corporation also manufactures a very wide range of more and less elaborate grills, about which information can be obtained on request. One of these is illustrated.

The "Charcoal King" is a cast-iron grill that is actually a large-sized hibachi, obtainable in two sizes of 13¼-inch or 18-inch diameters and weighing twenty-three pounds and thirty-one pounds respectively. Both of these units are 9 inches high and have heat controls operated by sliding doors in the front of the base. One of the advantages of this excellent grill is that the base is sealed to prevent ashes and coals from dropping onto the table. Foil-wrapped vegetables can be baked in the oven in the base of the larger model while other foods are being broiled on top. The illustration shows this grill being used to pre-

pare a meal on a boat—a purpose for which the two grills mentioned previously also are adapted.

And—if readers are yachtsmen who want something similar that is really fancy, there is illustrated a grill mounted in gimbals so that the grill won't tilt when the boat rocks!

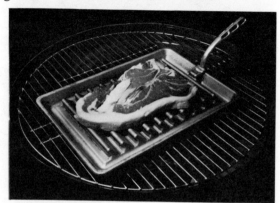

The J-T Flameless Grill is made of heavy aluminum, with a detachable handle. It weighs 5 pounds and measures 10½×15 inches.

An item that will appeal to chefs who dislike foods flavored with smoke caused by the occasional flare-up of dripping fat is the "J-T Flameless Grill." This unit allows the food to be charcoal-broiled on the grill but it catches dripping fat in the wells or channels between the slits in the grill. These fats then can be used for basting, if desired. The unit can be used on the range at home, as well as for outdoor cooking.

Finally, for outdoor cooking in the grand manner, let's look at the types of grills so large that they need to be wheeled from place to place. These are available in infinite variety and price range, many equipped with hoods and with electric spits. To show them all would transform this book into an immense catalog, so we'll have to be content with the typical examples illustrated here. Two of these have hoods that completely enclose the firebox, thus making it possible to impart to the food the smoky charcoal flavor some outdoor cooks consider essential, though to others it is undesirable. However, the hood provides an excellent windscreen and is a very efficient aid in baking vegetables and other foods. Whether we cook with it opened or closed is entirely optional. An important point to look for is the provision for raising or lowering the cooking surface to aid in adjusting cooking heat. The illustrations show that on one of these grills this

OUTDOOR COOKING AFLOAT

Cooking on deck, at anchor or on a calm sea, makes it of little importance whether or not the boat boasts a galley. Small cook stoves make it possible to brew a beverage or to prepare a hot snack on the seat or on the floor boards of a small boat, even while trolling. If the boat is larger, we can be a bit more elaborate, even to preparing a lobster dinner on a Charcoal King broiler, as shown in the top picture, where the potatoes and corn are being cooked in aluminum foil on the grill. The cook stove in the picture at bottom is mounted in gimbals, so that it won't tilt as the boat rocks.

(middle photo by Province of Ontario; others by Evinrude)

is accomplished by levers; on another by a crank; and on the third by handles that can be raised or lowered to bring the cooking surface to the desired distance from the coals.

When the type and size of grill has been decided upon, what else should we look for in selecting one of these more expensive grills? As in other products, we'll find grills with flashy and perhaps unnecessary gadgets and with fire pits made of metal so thin that they may wear through in a single season. It would be better to ignore these fancy accessories in favor of a less ornate product so substantially made that it will last and look well for many seasons. Quality should be a primary consideration. As we have said, the grill should have an efficient means of raising and lowering the cooking surface, because adjustable heat is to be preferred to having to add fuel to too slow a fire, or having to squirt water on one that is too hot. This also suggests the advisability of an adjustable draft—a means of forcing air through the coals to increase heat, or shutting off air to decrease it.

Do we need a hood or cover of some sort? Decidedly yes, even though we may not always use it. The hood protects food from wind and dust while aiding even cooking by retaining heat and reflecting it toward what is being cooked. (Remember that an ash-can cover will do the job, if the grill selected has no hood and if no revolving spit is to be used.)

SPITS AND SPIT ROASTING

Do we need a revolving spit? Only if we plan to cook items such as whole chickens and roasts. There's something very enticing about watching a roast or chicken turning on a spit and basting itself in its own juices and the sauces that may be added from time to time. So, if the budget permits, by all means include a spit—but get an electric one, even though it must be battery-operated. Turning the spit by hand for an hour or so seems to be too much of a chore, when three or four flashlight batteries will do the job for several hours. If the grill is to be used where there is an electrical outlet, the plug-in type spit is ideal, because batteries and how long they will last no longer are a problem.

If the grill is purchased with a spit, the spit will be equipped with prongs as shown in the picture of a duck being roasted. Ducks, chickens,

BACK YARD AND PATIO GRILLS

Top left: A simple open grill whose grid is raised and lowered by a lever. (Accessories by Androck)

Top right: An elaborate stove-type grill whose fire bed is raised and lowered by handles (Char-Broil)

Middle: Another covered grill whose grid can be raised, lowered, or tilted by knob handles (Hi-Lo)

Lower left: a hooded grill whose grid can be raised or lowered by means of a crank (Eclipse)

Lower right: A grill with smoke-control lid that can be removed from its cart for table use (Nesco)

These typical back yard and patio grills, varying widely in price, illustrate the wide choice of features available for broiling, roasting or spit cooking, baking, boiling, frying, smoke cooking, or any other kind of food preparation that can be done in the home kitchen. The outdoor cook has several advantages over most indoor cooks. He can prepare food with that delicious charcoal-broiled or smoky flavor—and he knows that foods always taste best when cooked outdoors!

1   (Reynolds Wrap)   2   (Androck)   3   (Androck)

4   (Androck)   5   (Androck)

ROTARY SPITS AND ACCESSORIES

Outdoor cooks have all the equipment available that any man could wish for. In the realm of rotary spit cooking, here are a few of many conveniences: (1) the usual type of pronged spit, on which a duck is being roasted. (Note the aluminum-foil drip pan to catch juices, and the position of the briquettes behind the pan.) (2) A rotary roast rack, used instead of a spit bar. (3) A chicken basket, for broiling disjointed chickens. (4) A balanced spit basket for chops, chicken, spareribs, and other foods. (5) A shish kebaber with demountable skewers. These are typical of a wide range of similar products that are helpful (although not necessary) for back yard cooking.

turkeys, and other birds first are trussed with skewers and/or string to hold wings and legs in place. The spit rod then is run through the bird as shown in the photograph in such a manner that the meat is balanced on the spit so that it will turn evenly without forcing the motor. When properly balanced, the prongs are slid down the spit rod, pressed into the meat, and tightened in place. Roasts are balanced on the spit similarly; first being tied compactly with string, if necessary. Haunch meats, like a leg of lamb or a ham, sometimes present a bit of a balancing problem, and the spit may need to be

driven through the meat with a hammer. In balancing a ham, it may need to be cut in halves diagonally so that the spit can be run through each half with the bone offset to provide correct balance and so that the bone will not interfere with the insertion of the spit rod.

All this is made easier by the roasting rack illustrated, which is obtainable as a complete unit that will fit the aperture in the motor. The rack is adjustable to roasts of normal size, and can be balanced by screw clamps that center the weight. This eliminates the necessity of puncturing the meat and the difficulty of experimenting until it is properly balanced on a spit rod.

When cooking for a crowd, larger than usual grills can be made easily from grease cans or oil drums, as the text describes. This method of above-ground pit cooking makes it possible to broil over 1000 (count them!) chicken halves at a time at the famous Belfast Broiler Festival in Belfast, Maine. The racks used are made similarly to those described in the text. (Maine Development Commission)

Other aids to spit cooking are illustrated here —a spit basket, for chops, chicken parts, frankfurters, and other foods, that is adjustable to food thicknesses ranging from a strip of bacon to chops or steaks 2½ inches thick; an attachment for spit-roasting shish kebabs; a chicken-broiling basket; and other similar appliances for the rotisserie cooking of vegetables or what have you.

While the time needed to roast these meats can be estimated, the safest way is to use a meat thermometer. The point should be driven into the exact center of the meat and, to get a true reading, care should be taken that it does not come in contact with the spit rod or with bone. Just before the meat is done (as indicated by the thermometer), reduce heat by removing or poking away some of the coals, and remove the meat from the fire as soon as the desired temperature is reached. The heat of the fire will not harm a well-made meat thermometer.

GRILLS FOR A CROWD

Now, if you're going to invite the Kiwanis Club or the local chapter of the Izaak Walton League, or your Boy or Girl Scout troop or some other hungry crowd over for a cookout, it's quite obvious that none of the grills discussed in this chapter will be adequate to do the job. But don't despair, because you can make your own. Just take a look at the picture of over a thousand chicken broiler halves all being cooked at one time at the Belfast (Maine) Broiler Festival, and you'll see how easy it is. Only two or three of the boys seem to be doing any work at all!

The idea for a very sensible large grill made from an oil drum was provided through the kindness of Mr. P. H. Gooding, of the Clemson Agricultural College in Clemson, South Carolina. By observing the pictures, the following explanation should make the construction and operation of the grill fairly easy.

Make your own barbecue stand from 10-, 15-, or 35-gallon grease cans, or from 55-gallon oil drums. Stands made from 10-gallon cans will broil eight chicken halves at a time. Stands from 15-gallon cans will do ten halves at a time; from 35-gallon cans fourteen at a time; and those made from 55-gallon drums will broil twenty halves at a time. Of course these stands will also broil steaks, chops, or any other foods other grills will broil.

The stands are made by cutting the cans or drums in halves lengthwise. Then ½-inch pipes cut 6 inches long are welded on each corner. Legs 30 inches long made from ½-inch steel reinforcing rods are inserted into the short pipes. This method enables the legs to be removed so that the stand can be transported in the trunk of a car.

Grills to go on top of the stands consist of a frame of ½-inch steel rods welded at each of the four corners with the lengthwise rods extending out 6 inches or more on each end for handles. One-inch × 2-inch welded wire, 14 gauge, is cut about ⅜ inch smaller than the frame. The welded wire is attached inside the frame with No. 3 hog rings.

For crowds of two hundred or more (as in the picture of the Belfast Broiler Festival), barbecue pits can be made from cinder blocks. A rectangular wall composed of two tiers of blocks should suffice and, since these blocks are not cemented, the whole thing can be moved with little difficulty. Grills such as those used on the 55-gallon drums may be used on the pits. Two grills may be used by placing the second one on top of the chicken halves, similar to a sandwich, and by having two people turn this double grill, as shown in the illustration.

The fire is made with charcoal briquettes, allowing about one pound per chicken. These are piled in one end of the barbecue pit and are ignited by pouring kerosene on them and dropping a lighted match into the pit. When the briquettes are burning well, spread them evenly over the bottom of the stand with an iron rake or shovel. The fire is started about half an hour before the food is put on.

HOW TO BROIL LOTS OF CHICKENS!

Broilers weighing about 2 or 2½ pounds are used. To split them properly into halves, remove the backbone by cutting down each side of it with a sharp knife. Then press open the bird to expose the breastbone and pull it out with the white piece of cartilage that is attached to it. It then is easy to cut the broiler into equal halves. Chickens may be quartered by splitting them

*Here's how they broil chickens for a crowd at Severance Lodge, Lake Kezar, Maine. The giant **Androck basket broilers** are ingeniously propped on logs over a charcoal fire that also is brewing coffee and baking vegetables for 100 hungry guests.*

again just back of the ribs, between breast and thigh. You may wish to remove the neck also. The backbone and neck supply little meat, and the broilers cook faster without them. Turkey broilers and other large birds, such as pheasants, can be handled similarly.

Put the chickens on the grill, skin side up, and as close together as possible without overlapping. This keeps heat from escaping through the open spaces, avoids uneven cooking, and saves fuel. Turn the halves as soon as they look as if they might blister or burn. If they should start burning, turn them (all at once) continuously, raise the grill, or sprinkle water on the fire. Basting (with one of the barbecue sauces described in this book) helps prevent burning. Turn the halves every 5 or 10 minutes, basting them with sauce before each turning. Cooking time should be about an hour, or perhaps a little more, depending on the heat. A way to tell when the broilers are done is to hold a broiler down with one hand and turn the bone of the drumstick. If it turns loose from the meat, it is done.

Chickens should be removed from the heat as soon as they are done, because they will dry out if cooked too long. To store them for a short time, wrap the broilers together in aluminum foil, or pack them in a covered box lined with foil. This should keep them hot for an hour or more.

While chickens have been used as an example in these methods of quantity cooking, anything that can be prepared on a small grill can be done similarly on a larger one. The only difference is that there's more of it. One rack can hold steaks, chops, or fish fillets. Another can hold potatoes and onions wrapped in foil. Corn, just as it comes from the field, can be roasted on another. Decide on the menu depending on what's available, and plan the cooking to take care of the crowd.

ROASTING A SIDE OF LAMB

Once, for example, we did a whole side of lamb on such a cinder block grill as we have described. The meat was wired to ½-inch pipes fastened together in the form of a double cross—like two plus signs joined together. This pipe rack made it easy to turn and to baste the meat with barbecue sauce, adjusting its position from time to time to be sure that the thicker parts were done properly. Carving was equally simple. We did it on a table cleanly covered with strips of heavy-duty aluminum foil.

PIT-COOKING, RANGE STYLE

This method of roasting a side of lamb is about as near to the true barbecue method as most outdoor cooks will want to get. The word "barbecue" has been badly abused lately. When the term came into being generations ago it referred to outdoor cooking in the grand manner—nothing smaller than a side or a quarter of a large animal; lots of people to eat the food; and cooking in a sealed pit rather than above ground.

You would dig a pit several feet deep and several feet wide—the length being decided by the number of animals to be cooked. For a really big crowd, the pit might be a hundred feet long, or more. In this pit you would build a fire to get coals nearly a foot deep. The sides of beef (or other animal) might be wrapped in burlap soaked in barbecue sauce, but they always were bound with heavy wire so they could be removed from the pit more easily, and all in one piece.

When the fire was right, the cook would set the meat directly on the coals. (The juices caked the coals under the meat and kept it rea-

sonably clean.) The pit then was covered tightly by sheets of steel that were covered with earth from the pit. This sealed everything in so almost no steam could escape. Thus, during cooking, the steam and barbecue juices would penetrate the meat, making even the toughest animals reasonably tender. The method evidently was developed as being the only way tough range cattle could be cooked satisfactorily for a large number of ranch hands.

This slow cooking in the subterranean fireless cooker went on for half a day or more—usually all night. Then the pits were carefully uncovered, the meat removed, and everybody enjoyed a true barbecue. Vegetables frequently were cooked in the same way—something like the New England Clambake described in Chapter Twelve. Barbecue experts considered that the underground pit held heat better than contrivances like the cinder block pit built above ground. Anyway, they didn't have any cinder blocks.

Barbecue sauce was an important ingredient in this kind of cooking. Meats were basted liberally with it, and it was served as a gravy. Each cook had his own formula, but evidently all were based on using an abundance of tomatoes, sugar, vinegar, and condiments, all cooked together very slowly for several hours. Recipes for several of these historic barbecue sauces are given in Chapter Fifteen.

OTHER IMPROVISED GRILLS

Commercial cook stoves and grills are attractive and efficient—and every outdoor cook should own one or more types in the highest quality that seems sensible. But it may be impractical to take an expensive and bulky grill to our hunting or fishing camp, or to our vacation spot in the summer. In this case, remember the simple fireplaces and the very efficient stovepipe stove described in Chapter Two.

Usually we can find a steel wheelbarrow around somewhere, and it's simple to transform it into an efficient outdoor grill that can be wheeled easily from place to place.

To keep the heat from harming the wheelbarrow, shovel a heavy layer of sand or gravel into it to a depth of three or four inches. Then, as shown in the sketch, use bricks or flat rocks to hold a wire rack from six to eight inches above the sand or gravel. Build the charcoal fire on this base under the rack, and you're ready to cook anywhere where the wheelbarrow can be taken!

If it's windy, a windscreen can be fashioned from rocks or aluminum foil. To keep heat in, use an ash-can cover. To fry simple foods like hamburgs or frankfurters, crimp a doubled layer of heavy-duty aluminum foil over the wire rack, and use this foil for the cooking surface. Bread and rolls can be toasted on it too. When you're cooking for a small crowd it's an idea worth remembering!

Chapter Seven

BACK YARD COOKING IS FUN!

Nowadays most of us with back yards enjoy outdoor cooking in one form or another whenever weather and time permit. After having read about methods and equipment, let's put things together and see how easy it is to enjoy a cookout almost anywhere. In so doing, let's get away from those too familiar hot dogs and hamburgs, at least for a while. Let's roll out the carpet for the Jones family and show them we really know how to cook!

HOW TO PLAN A BACK YARD MEAL

What'll we have? The menus, as we are beginning to see, are infinite and easy. Let's settle on some hot hors d'oeuvres, such as broiled baby sausages and chicken livers wrapped in bacon. These are cooked on an hibachi, as described in Chapter Nine. Put Mrs. Jones in charge of this, and let Mr. Jones supervise the cold beverages. This helps to keep people occupied while the chef is busy.

For the main course, how about chicken broilers with barbecue sauce, baked potatoes with sour cream dressing, squash and onions baked in foil, and roast corn, fresh from the fields? This, with iced or hot coffee or tea, can be followed by flaming bananas, with or without ice cream, for dessert.

PRIOR PREPARATION MAKES IT EASY

To make things easy, a little prior preparation is necessary, so when the Joneses arrive all we have to do is cook, eat, and have fun.

First prepare the barbecue sauce. While any of the tomato-based sauces recommended in this book is excellent for basting chicken, here is a different one used with disjointed chicken that many people like:

½ cup salad oil
¾ tablespoon soy sauce
½ teaspoon powdered ginger
1 teaspoon garlic salt

Mix above ingredients and marinate the chicken pieces in the mixture for an hour or two or overnight. Then broil the chicken on the grill, basting it occasionally with the remaining sauce.

The halved broilers are in a pan in the icebox. We'll take them out to the cooking area with a jar of barbecue sauce, a pair of tongs, and a basting brush. We have selected potatoes of equal size, scrubbed them, rubbed them with butter or bacon fat, and sealed them in aluminum foil.

The sour cream can be used just as it comes from the dairy. To be a little fancier, beat it with an equal part of cottage cheese, 1 tablespoon minced or grated onion, and a dash of salt. If chives are in the garden, cut some up fine for use as an added garnish.

The squash should be the small yellow summer variety, but other kinds will do as well. Remove ends and cut each squash in half lengthwise. Make a "sandwich" with each pair of halves by putting some onion slices, butter, salt, and pepper in between. Seal these in foil. Getting the normal table equipment ready about completes the prior preparation.

When foil-wrapped foods have been grilled and the fire has died down, they can be kept warm on the grill until ready to serve. If the packages have been double-wrapped, the outer foil wrapping can be discarded and the clean inner wrapping turned back so it can be used as a plate or serving dish. In this case, the inner wrapping usually should be heavy-duty foil, but the outer wrapping could be thinner. (Alcoa Wrap)

COOKING A TYPICAL BACK YARD DINNER

About half an hour before the guests arrive, start a charcoal or briquette fire in the hibachi, so it will be ready for use. The fireplace fire will need about half an hour to reduce itself to cooking coals, and the chickens and vegetables will need another hour to cook, so start the fire an hour and a half before mealtime.

When the fire is burning briskly, with lots of flames, put on the corn. (Yes—an hour or more before you plan to eat it!) Lay the ears in a row on the wire grate and let them char until the outside is black—and I mean *black*. This will take 10 or 15 minutes. Turn them and shift them around with tongs. Put them on just as they come from the field—no need to fuss with the husks or tassels, and no need to wrap them in foil. So what could be easier?

When the corn is well blackened, wrap each 6 ears or so in several sheets of opened newspaper. Wrap them tightly, so they will keep hot and continue to steam in the heavy newspaper insulation. This way, they should keep hot for an hour or more.

Set the potatoes and squash against the coals where the heat is so intense that you have to handle them with tongs. Do this when you put the corn on, if the vegetables are large. If they are smaller, they can be cooked with the chickens.

Now, when the fire has burned down to coals, lay the chicken halves or sections on the grill, skin side up. They must be cooked slowly, so don't let them burn. If they start to burn, move them away from the heat temporarily. The idea is to cook them through and still to have them remain a golden brown.

While this is going on and everyone else is waiting on you and trying to boss the job, check on the vegetables. Be sure they are cooking—but not too fast. Lay them on the coals for a while, if advisable. Shift them and turn them with the tongs.

When the broilers have begun to brown on the bottom, turn them over, keeping them close together without overlapping. Baste them liberally with barbecue sauce during the last part of their cooking period. (Basting them too early will burn the tomato in the sauce and make the chickens a bit too dark in color.) Baste with butter or vegetable oil, if you prefer.

During this cooking period the chef has little to do except to be sure the fire is at the right temperature and to turn the food to insure even cooking. The hostess has little to do except to set the table and see that the senior Joneses are happy with their jobs of presiding over the hibachi and the beverage department. The Jones kids can be deterred from running through the flower gardens by giving them a hibachi of their own over which to broil frankfurters cut into 1-inch sections, stuffed olives wrapped in bacon, or some other sort of toothsome tidbits suitable for hungry youngsters.

When the cooking and gossip hour is about over the chef again tests the foods with his long-handled fork and announces that dinner is ready. Vegetables have been removed from the fire to allow them to cool slightly. Potatoes are removed from foil, the skins sliced crosswise, fluffed open, given a dash of dressing, a garnish of chives, and are served on paper plates. The squash with onions is removed from the foil and served with its savory juices. Broiled chicken is added to each plate, and a dish of barbecue sauce is on the table in case anyone wants a little more. The hostess has poured the beverages, and everyone except the chef sits down to enjoy this delicious outdoor meal.

The chef has one more little job to do. He removes the corn from the newspapers and removes husks and silk from each ear. Since the corn has been steaming in the newspapers, husks and silk strip off quickly and easily. We hope the kernels have been browned in a few spots, because this slight caramelizing adds to the flavor—or at least most people think it does.

Optionally, the chef could have put the cooked chickens back in their pan and have kept them warm while he roasted the corn after the other foods were cooked. This, however, requires building up the fire again, and allowing the corn to steam for at least 15 minutes in its insulation of newspapers makes it easier to handle and seems to add to its flavor.

When the main course is about over, the chef gets busy with the dessert. Flaming bananas should be prepared in a chafing dish, but they can be prepared in a skillet. Merely peel them and cut them in halves lengthwise, and then into quarters crosswise. Sauté them lightly in butter for a few minutes, and sprinkle them with sugar and nutmeg. When they have turned a golden brown, pour over them a few ounces of brandy, rum, or Southern Comfort and light them. After exhibiting this simple and rather spectacular dish to the guests, spoon the bananas and sauce into dishes, or serve it with vanilla ice cream. Other suitable canned or brandied fruits, such as clingstone peaches, pears, cherries, or dates, can be served similarly.

MORE ABOUT COOKING VEGETABLES

A large variety of vegetables can be cooked in foil, as described in Chapter Four. Frozen vegetables can be removed from the package and the frozen cake wrapped in foil, using the drugstore fold. Before sealing, add a tablespoon or two of water, plus butter and seasoning, if desired. Cook these on or beside the coals, or on top of the grid, turning the package occasionally. Cooking time can be estimated from the directions on the package. Remember, however, that frozen foods must thaw before they begin to cook, so allow enough time for this.

In season, fresh asparagus is delicious when cooked this way. Wash the stalks and cut off the tough ends. Wrap them as above in a double thickness of heavy-duty foil, adding a little water, salt, pepper, and butter. The cooking time for a wrapped bunch of asparagus should be about half an hour.

Those who have taken time to investigate the various chapters of this book will see that the variety of outdoor menus suitable for back yard grill cooking is almost endless. Plan a menu suitable to the season; make the prior preparations and, when the guests arrive, the rest is easy.

To make this chapter on back yard cooking complete, however, let's discuss the outdoor cooking of meats and fish—not the kinds Daddy brings home from hunting and fishing trips, but the kinds we buy at the store.

TRICKS IN COOKING MEATS

Chops, such as lamb and pork, are easy to broil on the outdoor grill. Order them fairly thick, and trim off all but ¼ inch of the fat. Too much fat dripping into the fire causes too much flame, which may burn the meat.

The secret of broiling meats is to do it quite slowly. When cooked too fast, too much of the juice is drawn from the meat, thus tending to make it tough. Slow cooking imparts a true charcoal flavor. Fast cooking causes too much undesirable carbon to collect on the surface of the meat, as well as making it tough.

Try basting pork chops with barbecue sauce, as we did when cooking the chickens. This seems to add to the flavor of pork, but it does not add to the flavor of meats such as lamb and beef steaks.

There probably are as many theories on how to broil a beef steak—and what kind to get—as there are on how to mix a martini. Without attempting to influence fixed opinions, here are a few suggestions that seem to make sense.

The steak should be cut fairly thick—between an inch and a half and two inches. Enclose it in a wire steak broiler, placed on the grill, or, as second choice, turn it with tongs. Using a fork punctures the meat, thus allowing sealed-in juices to drip out. Adding salt before cooking also tends to draw out desirable juices, so do the seasonings after the steak has been broiled. If cooked in a wire broiler, the meat can be prevented from sticking by raising the wings of the broiler occasionally to free the meat from contact with the wire enough to lubricate the wire with the steak juices.

How do we tell when a steak is done without having to cut into it? If cooked fairly slowly, the steak should be done when the fat has become dark and crusted and has stopped dripping. Experienced cooks can tell the proper time by the appearance of the meat, and they allow a little longer if the steak is a very thick one. Slow cooking will make the meat a beautiful pink all the way through. If broiled too fast, the meat will be blackened on the outside when it is almost raw on the inside—but some people like it that way.

There's a trick in carving, too. Use a sturdy knife, and have it very sharp. Carve the steak (after buttering it and adding salt and pepper) on a board that will catch the juices. First cut out the bone, if any. Then carve the meat thinly at an angle of 45° or more. This makes the slices wider and cuts the meat across the grain, thus adding to tenderness.

Serving the thin slices as steak sandwiches makes a steak go farther. One way is to put the slices and juices in a pan and add a little A-1 or Worcestershire sauce, if desired. Serve the slices on toasted bread or hamburg rolls, with some of the juices.

A very economical and excellent steak is the London broil often ordered in restaurants. Buy a flank steak and sprinkle it with meat tenderizer an hour or so before cooking. Broil it the same way as any other beef steak, preferably brushing it with salad oil before broiling and using garlic salt instead of regular salt after the steak is done. London broil should be served bright pink, and must be carved thinly on a slant with a sharp knife if it is to be tender.

Here's a way to do a toothsome job of broiling a leg of lamb on a grill without using a spit. Purchase a young leg of lamb and have the market bone it and flatten it. If fresh mint is available, puncture the meat here and there and insert rolled or folded bits of mint leaves. Put the flattened meat in a wire steak broiler and broil it slowly over the coals for 30 to 45 minutes (depending on the intensity of the fire). While the meat is broiling, baste it with the following sauce:

- *1 stick butter*
- *½ clove garlic*
- *1 tablespoon minced onion*
- *¼ teaspoon salt*
- *⅛ teaspoon pepper*
- *½ cup finely chopped fresh mint*

Melt the butter and add the garlic clove, onion, and seasoning. Sauté the onion until transparent, then discard the garlic, so only a suggestion of the flavor remains. Stir in the mint. Baste the lamb frequently with this sauce. The lamb should not be overcooked; it tastes better when it is light pink inside.

Another very popular meat for back yard cooking is barbecued spareribs. Cut them three ribs to a section and boil them in about 3 cups water for 5 to 10 minutes, or simmer them slowly for about 30 minutes. This helps to tenderize the ribs and makes their cooking quicker on the outdoor grill. The tenderizing can be done a day or two in advance.

Barbecuing spareribs is very simple. Merely broil them over the coals until they are nicely browned and crisp on both sides. When they

After grilling the spareribs, this chef is keeping them warm in a dish of heavy-duty foil. Frozen peas have been cooked on the grill in foil while potatoes were baking in the coals. The outer wrapping of foil on the vegetables has been removed and the inner wrapping turned back to act as a plate or serving dish. (Reynolds Wrap)

begin to brown, brush them liberally with barbecue sauce. The usual allowance is a pound of ribs per person, but it is well to order more if people are very hungry.

Broiling meats on an electrically operated spit is much simpler than it might seem, and is an ideal way to feed a large number of people.

Truss the meat if necessary and balance it on the spit as explained in Chapter Six. The balancing is very important because an unbalanced roast or bird will not revolve evenly on the spit, and may stall the motor. If a spit rod is used, rather than the spit baskets described in Chapter Six, insert the rod through the center of the meat and check it for balance by holding the ends of the rod lightly in the fingers. If the meat revolves in the hands it is unbalanced, and the spit rod must be partially withdrawn and inserted again toward the heavier side of the roast. This may need to be attempted two or three times, until the above test indicates that the rod is balanced to make it revolve evenly. The prongs then are pushed into the meat securely and tightly clamped in place.

Since roasting will take an hour or more, the use of briquettes is superior to charcoal because briquettes burn longer. To start the fire, pile about two dozen briquettes in the middle of the grill and light them, using a fire starter. Let them burn in a pile until each is burning well, and then use tongs to place them equally spaced in the back of the grill. Make an aluminum foil drip pan (Chapter Four) and place it under the position the roast will occupy to catch the drippings. The pan should be no larger than necessary to do this. The briquettes are spaced behind or around the pan. When gray ash begins to show on the briquettes, the spitted meat is put in position on the grill and the motor is turned on. As the meat revolves, juices will run out of the meat and baste it as it turns. Some of these will drop into the pan, which is intended to catch the juices rather than allow them to drop and flame and sputter on the coals. If juices drop excessively or cause any flare-up, the fire is too hot, and some of the briquettes should be removed with tongs. These can be dropped into a pail of water and later can be dried out and used again.

Once started, the spit should not be stopped until the meat is done, because stopping the motor may cause excessive juices to drop from the meat and to flare up.

The number and spacing of briquettes in this illustration are correct for usual grill requirements. (Chefs often use too many briquettes—which is wasteful and results in too hot a fire). Lining the bed of the grill with foil is not necessary, but it serves to keep the grill clean and to reflect more heat upward. (Alcoa Wrap)

Since cooking time will vary somewhat, depending on the heat of the fire, the usual rule of roasting meats a half hour to the pound (for medium) cannot be followed exactly. The chef, however, can make a pretty good guess at it by considering the heat of the fire and the amount of dripping from the roast and its general appearance while being cooked. The best plan is to use a meat thermometer. As was said in Chapter Six, this must not come in contact with the spit rod or with bone, and the tip must be in the exact center of the meat in order to get a true reading. This will be 125° for very rare and 130° for rare meat. Remember that meat will continue to cook slowly for ten or fifteen minutes after being removed from the fire. When the desired temperature is nearly reached, push the briquettes to the back of the grill, or remove some of them, so the meat will reach the proper temperature more slowly.

When the meat begins to cook, many chefs like to sprinkle a tablespoonful or two of sugar over the roast to help seal in juices and make the meat tenderer. When the meat is nearly done it can be basted with barbecue sauce. If the fire seems to need more fuel, remember that tapping the briquettes to remove some of the gray ash will help to increase the heat. Additional briquettes can be added to the outside of the fire and can be moved inward when they are burning properly.

The juices in the drip pan can be used to make gravy, as described in Chapter Fifteen.

Roast pork should always be well done, and it is especially good when basted with barbecue sauce. Meats with little or no fat, such as veal, should be wrapped with fat, or skewered with bacon, or basted with bacon fat or something similar.

ROASTING FISH

Little need be said here on the preparation of fish because the subject is covered fairly thoroughly in Chapter Eleven. However, it seems suitable to remind back yard cooks that the fish they catch taste especially good when done on the outdoor grill. Large ones can be stuffed and roasted on the spit. Since the prongs may not hold them securely, they may need to be wired in place. Large fillets can be broiled in the wire steak broiler. Put strips of bacon between the fish and the wire so the skin won't stick. Bacon, as we shall see in Chapter Eleven, is very important in cooking lean fish, but not important in broiling fat fishes such as bluefish and mackerel.

Those who are near enough to the sea to obtain swordfish steaks in season should by all means enjoy their deliciousness when broiled over an outdoor grill. If possible, have them cut specially to a thickness of about an inch and a half. Cook them just as you would a beef steak, in the wire steak broiler, so the delicate meat won't fall apart in turning. Broil the swordfish very slowly so that it will be golden brown on the outside when it is done in the middle. Very slow broiling is one of the secrets. Another is to spread

This chef, who is broiling spareribs on a spit, evidently has an abundance of aluminum foil, but his uses of it are of interest. The bed of the grill has been lined with foil to keep it clean and to reflect more heat upward. The hood of the grill also has been lined with foil to reflect more heat outward. The foil drip pan is unnecessarily large. (Alcoa Wrap)

plenty of melted butter over it before carving. Serve it with lemon wedges and, if possible, garnish it with parsley or chopped chives.

AND IF IT RAINS . . .

More often than not, when we invite some people for a back yard cookout, the weather is perfect. But as soon as things get going, gray clouds appear, and before the meal is over it starts to rain. So this author rigged up a tarpaulin that makes dining outdoors enjoyable in everything but a downpour.

The ideal tarpaulin to protect a picnic table is a "Para-Wing," made by the American Thermos Products Company of Norwich, Connecticut, and invented by my old friend Bill Moss, a genius who has invented many other conveniences for outdoor living.

The "Para-Wing" is a very large tarpaulin, gaily and widely striped in red and white or in other colors. It is intended as a rain guard and sun shade for use in station wagon camping, but it is equally valuable for back yard use. It comes with 8-foot sturdy aluminum sectional poles for the ends and with guy ropes for the other two corners, so nothing else is needed to erect it.

Mine is slung over the picnic table by small pulleys and ropes between two trees, so the aluminum poles are used to hold up the other two corners. This provides a colorful canopy at least eight feet above the ground which very effectively protects the picnic table and everyone sitting there. This canopy provides protection from showers as well as from being bombed by acorns from our oak trees and from the occasional discourtesy of birds. A "Para-Wing," or something similar, is recommended highly for outdoor cooking.

But of course if the rain comes down really seriously, probably there's nothing left to do except high-tail for the house!

Chapter Eight

FOODS ON THE FLAMING SWORD

Back in prehistoric times our bearded ancestors broiled meats and roots over wood fires by impaling the foods on straight sticks of green wood. They pulled off the food and ate it with their fingers—or gnawed it from the stick, as we eat corn on the cob. These, of course, were the days before forks, and table manners had not been invented. (Neither had tables.)

Later on, when men had learned how to make swords and sabers of metal, they used these for the same purpose, mainly because they were handy. In those days you didn't even have to finish eating to be ready to defend yourself!

Nowadays, in our retrogression to outdoor cooking, we've become rather fancy. We go to expensive restaurants for foods broiled similarly but much more flavorsomely. The restaurants try to justify their high prices by calling these dishes *"shish kebab,"* which merely means meat broiled on skewers, as the ancient Greeks, Turks, and Armenians prepared it—or *en brochette,* which is the French for about the same thing.

But no matter what you call it, meats and vegetables properly broiled on skewers are so delicious and so easy to prepare that every back yard cook and camper should include them in his bag of tricks. To cook foods properly this way, there are only a few things to remember.

NOTES ON EQUIPMENT

Skewers, made of stainless steel or heavy wire, are so inexpensive that there's little sense in trying to make your own. In an emergency, they can be fashioned from coat-hanger wire, although the paint should be burned or scraped off. To hold meats and vegetables firmly, the

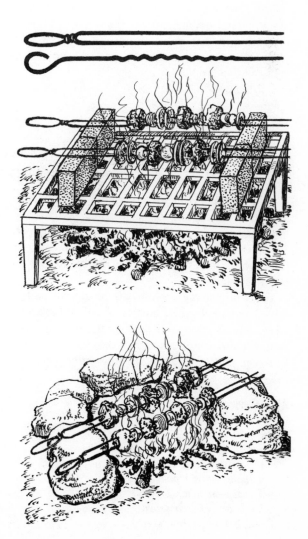

double-tined or fork-type homemade skewer works best. If the single skewer is used, the wire should be bent with pliers into a wavy or saw-toothed shape so the foods won't rotate around it when being turned. The loaded skewers can be rested between bricks laid on the wire grid over the fire, or between flat stones over a small bed of coals.

Skewers purchased in stores are from a few inches to two feet long, the choice depending on the uses to which they will be put. For most purposes they should be at least a foot long, because the food should occupy only the middle section, allowing the skewer ends to be rested on supports. All skewers for use in broiling should have a means of preventing the foods from turning on the skewer, such as is found on the two-tined type or the twisted-ribbon type.

Most skewers are obtainable in sets of six or so; many of the sets include a square or rectangular metal frame that holds the skewers parallel to each other over the wire grid of the fireplace or grill.

MARINADES

Raw meats, such as lamb, pork and beef, should be tenderized or marinated before broiling. The marinating of vegetables is optional, but many cooks think it improves their flavor. Thorough marination requires at least two or three hours', and preferably overnight, storage in the refrigerator.

There are many recipes for meat marinades, which essentially are blends of oil, vinegar or wine, lemon juice, and seasonings. As we have said, their purpose is to tenderize the meat and to flavor the foods. Here are four from which to select:

Meat Marinade I
4 tablespoons olive oil
5 tablespoons soy sauce
1 tablespoon Worcestershire sauce
1 medium-sized onion, finely chopped
3 tablespoons lemon juice
½ teaspoon black or white pepper
Dash of Tabasco sauce
Combine ingredients.

Meat Marinade II
½ cup tomato catsup
2 tablespoons A-1 sauce
2 tablespoons sugar
2 tablespoons cider or wine vinegar
2 tablespoons Worcestershire sauce
2 tablespoons salad oil
¼ cup water
1 teaspoon salt
Combine ingredients and heat. Allow to simmer slowly, covered, for a few minutes. Heat again after marinating, if the sauce is used for basting.

Meat Marinade III
½ cup red wine
1 teaspoon Worcestershire sauce
1 garlic clove, minced
½ cup salad oil
1 tablespoon vinegar
½ teaspoon monosodium glutamate
¼ cup tomato catsup
1 tablespoon sugar
1 teaspoon dried herbs
½ teaspoon salt
Combine ingredients and bring to a boil. Allow to cool, and marinate meat in the mixture. Use it also for basting.

Meat Marinade IV
2 tablespoons salad oil
¼ cup soy sauce
2 tablespoons lemon juice
Combine ingredients and pour over the meat. Allow the combination to stand for at least 2 hours. Also use the sauce for basting.

TRICKS IN SKEWER COOKING

Lamb is the historic meat for skewer broiling —preferably young spring lamb rather than that from an older animal. The lean meat is cut in cubes approximately 2 inches in size. Tomatoes, onions, and some other vegetables are easiest to use when cut in large wedges, rather than in slices, because they stay on the skewers better that way. Vegetables such as potatoes, eggplant, and squash usually are cut in chunks and are parboiled slightly in salted water so they will cook more quickly when placed on the skewers over the open fire.

With the foods thus prepared, the various chunks or pieces are alternated on the skewers —for instance, meat, onion, pepper (slices),

Shish kebabs provide a complete meal without having to do the dishes. Peeled green sticks provide the skewers for these Boy Scouts, who are preparing a combination of meat, squash, onions, and peppers. A comment about these pictures might be that the skewers are unnecessarily long, which would make it difficult to put on the food securely. (Boy Scouts of America)

(Russell-Harrington)

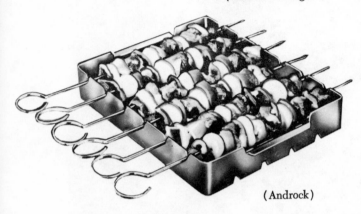

(Androck)

Typical skewer sets, and racks to hold them. The foil-type skewers in the upper picture have juice guards and wooden handles. The rack clamps to the wires of the grill grid. The lower picture shows metal skewers on a rack that sets on the grill. It is turned over when four or less skewers are used.

mushroom caps—until the desired amounts of food have been added. Avoid filling the skewers too full, and leave a little space between the foods so they will cook thoroughly. Baste with the marinade or with a barbecue sauce while cooking. The broiling should be done slowly over a bed of coals, rather than over a flaming fire.

MEAT AND SEAFOOD KEBABS

Here are a few suggestions, from which readers can improvise others of their own:

Chicken Liver Kebab

> Chicken livers, cut to desired size
> Bacon strips, cut in squares
> Mushroom caps
> Bread crumbs
> Olive oil

Dry the livers on absorbent paper, and put a liver, a bacon square, and a mushroom cap on the skewer, repeating as desired. Baste with oil and roll in crumbs. Broil until bacon is crisp. Push from skewer onto a plate and season with salt and pepper.

Frankfurter Kebab

> Frankfurters, sliced in thirds
> Dill pickles (large slices)
> Onions (small ones, sliced)
> Prepared mustard
> Frankfurter rolls

Alternate the foods on skewers; brush on the desired amount of mustard, and broil until the frankfurters are well browned. Push from skewer onto an opened and toasted long roll. Baste with barbecue sauce while cooking, if desired.

Ham Kebab

> Ham steak, precooked and sliced in squares
> Pineapple rings, quartered
> ½ cup pineapple juice
> ½ cup brown sugar or honey

Melt the pineapple juice and the sugar or honey until blended. Alternate the ham and pineapple on skewers. Baste with the sauce, and broil until nicely browned. Parboiled sweet potato chunks go well with this.

Lamb Kebab

> 2 pounds spring lamb, cubed
> 2 medium-sized onions, sliced in half and quartered into wedges
> 1 dozen mushroom caps
> 2 tomatoes, cut in wedges
> 2 green peppers, cut in squares
> Marinade

Put lamb cubes in marinade for from 2 hours to overnight (in refrigerator). String lamb and vegetables alternately on skewers. Baste with the marinade, and broil until done, basting again occasionally.

Beef Steak Kebab

Use a good grade of thick beef steak, cut in cubes. Prepare the same as Lamb Kebab, above.

Veal Kebab

Cut veal in cubes, marinate, and string loosely on skewers. Baste with Meat Marinade IV. Serve with Vegetable Kebab.

Scallop Kebab

> 1 pound (or more) sea scallops
> 1 dozen mushroom caps
> 4 pineapple rings, quartered
> 8 slices bacon, squared

Shish kebabs are turned and basted with sauce frequently while being broiled. If the chef in this picture should place the rack so that the skewer handles were not above the heat, she would not have to take the chance of scorching her fingers. (Androck)

Put all but the bacon in a bowl, and add the following marinade, allowing the mixture to stand in a cool place for at least an hour. Alternate scallops, mushrooms, pineapple, and bacon on skewers, with the bacon squares on each side of the scallops. Broil until bacon is crisp. Do not overcook.

Sea Food Marinade

¼ cup salad oil
¼ cup soy sauce
¼ cup lemon juice
½ teaspoon salt
2 tablespoons minced parsley
Dash of pepper

Combine ingredients. Use the sauce both for marinating and for basting.

Sea Food Kebab

Almost any kind, or several kinds, of fish and shellfish can be used, such as bass, dolphin, swordfish, halibut, shrimps, scallops, lobster, etc.

Sea food, cut to desired size
Green pepper, cut in squares
Mushroom caps
Tomato wedges
Onion wedges (small)
Bacon squares (unless the fish is a fatty kind)
Melted butter
Lemon juice
Chopped parsley

Alternate fish, bacon, and vegetables on skewers; season with salt and pepper, and broil for about 10 minutes, until done. Push from skewer onto plate, and add a sauce of melted butter, lemon juice, and chopped parsley to the fish.

VEGETABLE KEBAB

Because some vegetables cook faster than large meat cubes, or because a vegetable kebab may be desired to serve with meat or fish prepared in another way, many cooks prefer to kebab their vegetables separately. To do this, parboil small whole onions, cubes of sweet or white potatoes, eggplant, squash, zucchini, etc., together until they are about half cooked. Then string them on skewers with raw (unpeeled) tomato wedges, green pepper squares, or whatever else is desired. Brush with oil; season with salt and pepper, and continue cooking over the coals until done.

FLAMING FOODS ON SKEWERS

Finally, we get to the "flaming sword" part.

This, of course, is strictly "window dressing," and most outdoor cooks won't want to bother with it—but it may cause a murmur of approval if you're entertaining someone from the city or a few of your daughter's friends from college! It can be done in two ways:

One way is merely to pour a little brandy over the kebab after it has been removed from the fire. Touch the kebab to the coals, and the food will burst into a brief blue flame. Let your guests see what is going on, because the flame only lasts for a minute. (Use low-cost domestic brandy for this.)

Another way is to push a small wad of cotton onto the tip of the skewer. Pour a little brandy on this and light it. The flame will be only at the tip, but it will last longer. The cotton, if any remains, can be pushed off the skewer before serving.

Chapter Nine

BROILING ON HIBACHIS

Since we buried the hatchet with the Japanese, the sons of Nippon have been shipping over here almost everything imaginable in the popular international quest for the good old Yankee dollar. Included in this is their favorite way of cooking—on miniature cast-iron or enamel stoves, known as hibachis.

HIBACHIS, LARGE AND SMALL

In Japan and in other places in the Pacific, people cook almost everything on hibachis, or on very similar contraptions. Since these stoves are heavy, the ones being imported are quite small, with square or round cooking surfaces usually not more than ten inches in diameter. As such, the imported versions seem, so far as we are concerned, to be strictly in the "hot hors d'oeuvre department." But here, the little cast-iron hibachi can work wonders of gastronomic delight. Everyone gathers around the hibachi (you should have two or more for a crowd) to broil his own tidbits to his own satisfaction. Thus, fewer people are tripping over the cook while he is trying to prepare dinner. And, if preparation takes a little longer than usual, no one seems to mind!

Thus, a hibachi actually is a small portable cast-iron stove, or broiling pot, complete with a removable cast-iron grid, and a damper door to regulate the heat of the fire. These little hibachis have become so popular for both indoor and outdoor cooking that a few American manufacturers are offering larger ones, such as the "Charcoal King Broiler" illustrated in Chapter Six. This broiler is available in two sizes, with round cooking surfaces of thirteen inches and eighteen inches in diameter, weighing about twenty-five and thirty-four pounds.

Units like the "Charcoal King" are big enough to be very sensible stoves, with a lower baking section in which potatoes, corn, and other foods can be cooked while meats, birds, or fish are being broiled on top. Hibachis, or similar cast-iron stoves of any size, are not ideal units to transport for use on picnics, but they serve a valuable purpose in preparing toothsomely broiled foods in back yard or patio cooking, as well as for indoor cooking in the fireplace or under the hood in the kitchen.

HOW TO MAKE A FLOWER POT HIBACHI

Hibachis in the smaller sizes are so low in cost that there's little reason to try to improvise one, unless we are in a place where one is unobtainable. However, it's very simple to make a useful hibachi from an old flower pot—and here's how we do it:

These two typical cast-iron hibachis illustrate square and round designs. Cooking surfaces are 10 inches wide. The grill is adjustable for height (more so, in the square design). The sliding door at bottom provides draft control. (Hibachis)

As the illustration indicates, we obtain a fairly large and deep flower pot whose top will fit a round cake rack which can be borrowed from the kitchen. The pot is filled about three inches deep with sand or gravel, so the bottom won't get too hot. On this insulated base we add some charcoal or a few briquettes. A gob of "Sterno Canned Heat," or a "Sterno" charcoal lighter cube gets this fuel going in no time. When the fuel has burned to gray ash, it's time to start the cooking. Since this fire must be a small one,

charcoal briquettes are usually preferable to charcoal, because they burn longer, with more even heat.

HOW TO COOK ON HIBACHIS

The traditional way to handle foods on small hibachis is with bamboo picks, or skewers, which are toothpick-like slivers of bamboo about six inches long, and obtainable where hibachis are sold. You arrange the small bits of food on the grid, and turn them over with a pick until they are done. Then you spear the food and eat it from the pick. Foods broiled on hibachis the oriental way are delicious and, since people are supposed to cook their own, there's no room for complaints.

Slow broiling is best, so avoid adding too much fuel—and wait until the coals have burned down to the correct heat before starting to cook.

RECIPES FOR HOT HORS D'OEUVRES AND OTHER FOODS

We have said that the Japanese cook almost everything on hibachis. They are used for bodily warmth, for keeping foods warm, for preparing hot beverages and, with a pan, for frying and for preparing dishes such as sukiyaki. Here, however, let's merely be concerned with simple foods that can be broiled and served during the Happy Hour before dinner.

Baby Sausages

These are excellent when grilled on the hibachi just as they come from the can or package. So are frankfurters, cut in bite-sized pieces. To spice them up a bit, dip them in one of the barbecue sauces described in this book—or try this one:

In a small skillet on the hibachi, blend together ¼ cup unsulphured molasses and ¼ cup prepared mustard. Stir in 3 tablespoons vinegar, 2 tablespoons Worcestershire sauce, and ¼ cup tomato catsup. Simmer the sausages in this mixture for about 5 minutes. Then remove the skillet from the hibachi and broil the sausages for 5 minutes or so, until done.

Chicken Livers

Wash the livers; cut into bite-sized pieces and drain on absorbent paper. Roll in flour. Cut bacon strips into sections of the proper size to wrap each around a piece of liver. Secure with toothpicks, and broil until the bacon is crisp. Turn them frequently, of course.

Here's a little fancier way of sautéing chicken livers in a skillet on the hibachi. After washing, cutting, and draining them, sprinkle them with monosodium glutamate. Then roll them in ¼ cup flour to which ½ teaspoon salt, ⅛ teaspoon pepper, and ½ teaspoon dried orégano have been added. Heat 2 tablespoons salad oil in the skillet with 1 tablespoon finely minced onion. Sauté the livers in the oil and onion for 5 minutes or so, until they are brown.

Chicken Oriental I

Cut two boned chicken broiler breasts into bite-sized chunks. Put these in a bowl and add ½ cup dry sherry and 2 tablespoons soy sauce. Marinate the chicken pieces in the sauce for about an hour. Then broil them on the hibachi for 5 to 10 minutes.

Chicken Oriental II

Cut two boned chicken broiler breasts into bite-sized chunks. Put these in a bowl and add ¼ cup soy sauce, ¼ cup vinegar, ¼ cup salad oil, ¾ teaspoon monosodium glutamate, ½ teaspoon powdered ginger, 2 teaspoons sugar, and 2 tablespoons minced onion. Marinate the chicken pieces in this mixture for an hour or longer. Then broil them on the hibachi for 5 to 10 minutes.

Kebabs

These are kebabs in miniature size. Alternate the following combinations on small metal skewers, and broil them on the hibachi until done, turning frequently:

A piece of chicken meat, an orange section, and a pitted ripe olive.

Shrimp, pineapple chunk, and a small canned onion.

A cube of cooked ham, a canned peach slice, and a mushroom cap.

A cube of luncheon meat, a canned apple slice, and a small square of green pepper.

A cube of cheese, a canned apricot half, and a stuffed olive.

A small canned sausage, a slice of banana, and a wedge of tomato—or alternate Vienna sausages and thick banana slices.

Luncheon Meat Bits

Cut canned luncheon meat into ¾-inch cubes. Combine in a bowl 2 tablespoons unsulphured molasses and 2 tablespoons prepared mustard. Stir in 2 tablespoons vinegar. Skewer the cubes of luncheon meat; dip in the sauce, and broil until hot.

Meat Balls

Break up a pound of ground beef with a fork and stir in 1 teaspoon monosodium glutamate, ¼ teaspoon salt, and 1 tablespoon minced onion. In another bowl, mash together ½ cup soft bread crumbs with ¼ cup milk. Toss the two mixtures together, and form into small balls. Roll the balls in flour. Dip in a barbecue sauce and broil until brown.

Olives in Bacon

Wrap large stuffed olives in bacon strips cut to the right size. Fasten with toothpicks. Broil until bacon is crisp.

Oysters and Clams

Wash the oysters or clams, and lay them on the hibachi until the shells begin to open. The oysters should be placed on the hibachi with the deep side down, to preserve juice. When the shells begin to open, remove them from the fire and flip off the top shell. Serve on the half shell with lemon juice or other condiments.

Another good way to cook opened clams or oysters is to wrap each in a bit of bacon, as we did with the olives. As soon as the bacon is done, the clams will be. It is preferable to cook the bacon partially before wrapping the shellfish in it, because clams and oysters should be broiled only a minute or two. If overcooked, they will be dry and tough.

Scallops

Fresh Cape scallops (the little ones) need little if any cooking. They are delicious raw. Roll them in buttered bread crumbs and broil them on the hibachi only long enough to warm them up.

The big ocean scallops need a bit more cooking. This recipe is good for either, but the little Cape scallops are so delicious that they are not helped by additional flavoring.

Make a marinade by adding 1 cup soy sauce to 1 cup dry sherry. Soak the scallops in this for an hour or two. Broil them over the hibachi fire until they are light brown. Then dip them in a mixture of half melted butter and half soy sauce. Serve immediately.

Shrimps

Shell and devein raw shrimps, leaving the tails on. Dip them in a mixture of 3 tablespoons melted butter and 2 tablespoons lemon juice. Broil until they turn pink. If you'd like a sauce to dip them in, here's a tasty one:

Combine ½ tablespoon lemon juice with ¼ cup evaporated milk. Stir in 2 tablespoons chili sauce, ½ teaspoon horse radish, and 1 tablespoon dried bread crumbs.

Another way to prepare the shelled and cleaned shrimps is to marinate them for a few hours or overnight in a mixture of ½ cup olive oil, 1 teaspoon orégano, 2 tablespoons lemon juice, and 2 mashed garlic cloves. Add seasoning of salt and pepper. Broil the shrimps on the hibachi until they turn a pink-brown color. Paint them with some of the marinade while they are broiling, if you wish.

Steakettes

Cut a good grade of lean beef into ¾-inch cubes. Make a marinade of 1 tablespoon Worcestershire sauce, 1 tablespoon vinegar, 2 teaspoons of A-1 sauce (or other meat sauce), 2 teaspoons sugar, ¼ cup tomato catsup, ½ teaspoon mono-sodium glutamate, and a dash of pepper. Soak the beef in the marinade for about 2 hours, and broil on the hibachi until browned.

These recipes are typical, but of course by no means complete. They may indicate the fun and the tasty tidbits that can be enjoyed when using a hibachi, particularly while the guests are gathered outdoors partaking of something cooling before dinner.

KEEPING BEVERAGES HOT

A small hibachi is especially useful for keeping beverages hot for serving out of doors. It helps to keep the hot beverage drinkers from bothering the cook, if his pleasant chores remain undone. For this purpose, the ideal heating unit for the hibachi is neither charcoal nor briquettes, but rather a large or small can of "Sterno" (depending on the size of the hibachi and how hot you want it). Just remove the cover, put the can in the hibachi, and light it. A steady, smokeless blue flame will heat whatever is over it until the can cover is dropped on the can to extinguish the flame. When the can has cooled, replace the cover tightly, so the remaining fuel can be used next time.

Since "Sterno" is solidified alcohol, it can be used as fuel for cooking anything that can be prepared on a hibachi. This smokeless "Canned Heat" will not impart a charcoal flavor to foods, but it does have the advantage of instant, steady heat for all frying and boiling purposes.

Chapter Ten

SUGGESTIONS FOR KEEPING THINGS COLD

Since the days in the South Pacific during World War II when we had to live for nearly a year without ice or refrigeration of any kind, I have had great admiration for the highly efficient modern devices for keeping things cold. In those days Uncle Samuel would give us an occasional ration of a few cans of beer—an eagerly anticipated event on hot tropical islands where military vehicles kept the air clouded with volcanic dust of the consistency of talcum powder.

But the problem was how to get the beer cold, and it was one that remained unsolved for months. We buried it deep in the dirt, and in rice paddies and carabao wallows, but every time we'd open a can nearly all of the warm contents would geyser out like water from a hose. Nowadays, on returning to camp after a hot day of hunting or fishing, the icy feel of a cold beverage being removed from a portable refrigerator reminds me how important these conveniences can be to people.

VACUUM BOTTLES

Transportable cooling devices fall roughly into three classes—bottles, jugs, and refrigerators, plus a few ways to rig up reasonable facsimiles thereof. The familiar "Thermos" bottles are too well known to need discussion, and modern ways of shockproofing the doubled glass vacuum shell nearly eliminate entirely any danger of breakage. These bottles come in wide-mouthed models as well as the narrower neck types, and the wide ones are very handy for carrying ice cubes (and water), as well as cold foods like potato salad. But vacuum bottles are suitable primarily for short trips. On camping excursions we'll need something bigger.

INSULATED JUGS

Insulated jugs provide an excellent way to carry a gallon or two of ice water or other cold beverages. A good way is to fill the jug with ice cubes and then to fill it with water. Thus, ice can be removed for other drinks, and a source of ice water is handy for twenty-four hours or more.

These 1- and 2-gallon jugs, as illustrated, are made by several firms. When buying them, their insulating qualities should be the major consideration. Check the ones you like to see how long they should keep things cold. Manufacturers' statements usually can be depended upon, but test the jug with ice cubes and water as soon as it is purchased. If it doesn't do the job properly, return it and select something else. A jug *and* a portable refrigerator should be essential camping equipment, because it doesn't help to open the refrigerator too often whenever someone wants a cold drink.

PORTABLE REFRIGERATORS, AND HOW TO SELECT THEM

The most useful item in the cooling department is a portable refrigerator—and it pays to get the best obtainable. For several years my favorite has been the "Thermos Chillybin," which is a simple box molded from expanded cellular plastic—the lightest and best insulating medium I know of. On deer-hunting trips we have kept

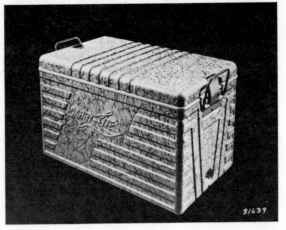

(Carry-Lite)

(Thermos)

(Coleman)

(Skotch Kooler)

(Cronco)

(Cronco)

PORTABLE REFRIGERATORS

At upper left is an example of an ultra-light box with a minimum of gadgets and maximum refrigeration qualities. Box at lower left has a cushioned top, especially designed for use as a seat. Box at lower right is exceptionally long (30 inches) for maximum capacity; excellent for transporting large fish.

(Thermos)

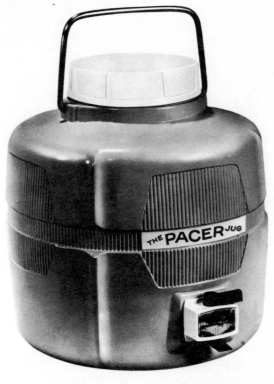

(Hamilton-Skotch)

INSULATED JUGS

ice in this box for as long as a week. We have flown frozen foods from coast to coast, and they seemed as well frozen at the end of the journey as at the beginning. For a reason best known to the manufacturer, I understand that this box no longer is being produced, but the "Carry-Lite" box illustrated here is almost identical. These boxes of expanded plastic are fitted with few, if any, gadgets, and a minimum of metal parts, which eventually could rust. Thus their insulating qualities are high, yet their cost is relatively low.

Other boxes with excellent refrigerating qualities are sheathed with aluminum or other metal or plastic and have smooth interiors easy to keep clean. Between the inside and outside surfaces is an interior of expanded plastic, or something similar. Get a box with trays, bottle openers, and other gadgets, if you want it, but remember that the prime consideration should be how long the box will keep things cold. A tightly fitting cover is very important in this.

The Coleman Company offers a new idea in iceboxes, as illustrated. This "Station Wagon Cooler" is made to stand on end, and the top contains a plastic ice container that will hold a 25-pound block of ice. A push-button faucet in the ice container supplies ice water as the ice melts.

Other boxes, such as the "Cronco" cooler illustrated, are made as long as 30 inches, thus providing extra storage space and the facility to hold extra large fish. Others come with upholstered covers, making them more comfortable when used as seats.

USES FOR PLASTIC BAGS, MILK CARTONS, ETC.

Some readers will raise their eyebrows because trays have been termed "gadgets." Many sportsmen prefer to keep ice and various foods separated by enclosing them in strong plastic bags secured by a knot, a wire-lined tape, or a rubber band. This keeps things from rattling and

Coleman's Station Wagon Cooler

allows the box to be packed more compactly. Sportsmen often discard the trays as superfluous.

These plastic bags are valuable helps in packing a refrigerator, but unfortunately most of them are too thin and inclined to leak. Here and there we may come upon some really sturdy ones in various sizes. If so, lay in a supply, and carry some extras in the refrigerator. When you've caught some fish, sealing them in a plastic bag in the refrigerator will prevent other things from absorbing the fishy odor.

Many sportsmen own two or more portable refrigerators. In addition to the one used for food, the second one is used for a larger supply of ice water than the 1- or 2-gallon jugs can carry. Put a large cake of ice in the second refrigerator and, when it is set in place in camp, fill it with drinking water. A foot or so of rubber hose fastened to the outlet provides a means of withdrawing water. When not being used, the outer end of the hose can be tucked up under the refrigerator carrying handle. A better way, of course, is for the manufacturer to supply a small screw-on faucet, but as far as I know, none have seen fit to do this yet. However, small faucets or spigots are made for other purposes, and readers may be able to find one that could be tapped to fit the refrigerator outlet.

While a chunk of ice in a plastic bag will keep things cold longer than ice cubes, cubed ice may be handier. Fill a waterproof plastic bag with cubes; seal the opening, and put the bag in the freezing compartment of the home refrigerator. There, it's always handy for quick use.

Another very useful idea is to save several of the square-ended paper cartons that milk and orange juice come in. Clean them and fill them with drinking water. Freeze them for a compact way of keeping things cold in the portable refrigerator. When the ice melts, it provides drinking water, and the empty carton (being impregnated with paraffin) makes a very good fire starter.

But suppose we want to keep things cold and don't have these modern conveniences. There are several ways to do it.

COLD STORAGE IN A SPRING

On fishing trips to the famous Allagash region of Maine, I used to stay at a deserted lumber camp, one of whose buildings had been patched up by an old trapper named Dave Howe. For various reasons, Dave was not on the best of terms with the game wardens, but the trout fishing was good in his area, and he was very adept at making sourdough bread and doughnuts. Dave had no ice, but he kept things cold by putting them in a big milk can, weighted with a rock inside, and immersed nearly up to its neck in a cold spring. This, in a limited way, provided as efficient a refrigerator as the ones we have at home.

On outdoor trips to remote areas, springs can offer excellent refrigeration. Usually one is near a cabin, which probably is the reason for the cabin being there. We can sink a wooden box in the cold earth beside the spring and keep food (sealed in plastic bags, jars, or other containers) in the box. If the foods are sealed, water seeping through the box will do the foods no harm. In fact, this constant seepage of new cold water provides excellent refrigeration.

On canoe trips where there is no time to bother with making a refrigerator in a spring hole, foods can be sealed similarly and kept in the cold water. Heavy-duty aluminum foil seals foods effectively, if the drugstore fold described in Chapter Four is used. Remember, though, that raccoons and other animals love to investigate such things, so protect them as well as possible against theft during the night.

HOW TO MAKE AN ICEBOX

If we have access to a farm where there is an icehouse, a block of ice can be preserved for days in an icebox made like the sketch. Sink a large wooden box in the ground in a hole made considerably larger. Pack the space between hole and box with an insulation such as sawdust, grass, or leaves. Put the ice in the box, and cover the box with a secure cover of some sort to keep the top of the box as well insulated as possible. Put a large rock or two on the cover, so animals can't raid the food supply. This "sink-box refrigerator" will do a good job of keeping things cold if it is located in a shady, cool place. In fact, it is much better than nothing even if no ice is obtainable. The ground in a shaded place usually stays surprisingly cool all day—except perhaps in the desert or in the tropics. Sometimes you just can't win!

Chapter Eleven

FISH COOKERY

When the shadbush buds begin to pop in early spring, any fisherman worthy of the name has his tackle ready and is rarin' to go. But the high spot of my year was always later on—in late May or early June—when "The Call" came from Augusta! I knew about when to expect it by following the "ice-out" news from Maine in the local paper, but anticipation of "The Call" made me itchy for weeks. It would be from Warden Supervisor Joe Stickney, summoning me to our annual fishing trip back in the Allagash region of the Maine wilderness.

Joe would be at his log cabin hideaway on Lake Maranacook. When my car bumped down the rocky road through the spruces to the cabin, it was ritual for Joe to appear at the door vigorously wobbling a big shaker of silver gin fizzes. It also was ritual for four lively Maine lobsters to be crawling around in the sink. It was ritual to renew our old friendship with this annual lobster feast at the cabin before the little plane landed at daybreak the next morning to ferry us into the back country.

Joe Stickney passed on to his reward while I was in New Guinea during World War II. I doubt that any man could cook Maine lobster better than he could—or make a better fish chowder, or excel him in preparing a big, pink-fleshed native brook trout over an open fire. Joe was a retired architect who also was a gourmet highly skilled in sportsmen's ways of cooking fish and sea food—and much of what is in these two chapters is the result of his teaching on our annual excursions to the backwoods of Maine. The fact that he also was a warden supervisor was a fortunate coincidence for me. He devoted many years to the job because he loved the woods and everything in them—except people who abused them. I wish there were more Joe Stickneys in this world. Then there would be more true sportsmen, and fewer of the other kind. (Anglers may be interested to know that Joe Stickney was the inventor of the "Supervisor," the "Warden's Worry," and the "Lady Doctor" flies.)

These old days in Maine were the days of the fly rod. They also were the days of the barbless hook, because stream mouths, spring holes, and spruce-shaded pools below old log dams held so many big trout that we just played with them, to be released unharmed—except for one or two we would keep for supper.

"Never waste a trout," Joe would say. "The day will come when there will be too few of them."

Any fish can be wasted, or partially so, if it does not reach cooking time in the best possible condition. The proper care of fish is easy: clean them thoroughly, as soon as possible; keep them dry; and keep them cool, or cold. Fish are at their best immediately after they are killed. From then on, flavor deteriorates, but excellent flavor can be maintained by proper preservation. Since excellence in fish cookery largely depends on this, let's devote a few minutes to learning how it is done. Don't depend on guides. Relatively few know how to do it properly—or perhaps they don't bother.

HOW TO CLEAN FISH

Fish are cleaned by slitting them with a sharp knife from the anus to the gills. After entrails are pulled out, *all* of the gills should be removed. Some dark matter will remain under a membrane beneath the backbone. This membrane should be cut open, so that all of this dark matter can be scraped away. (If the fish is not too large, this can be done by pushing the thumbnail along the cavity.) Then wipe the fish dry, washing it as little as possible.

(*Outdoor Nebraska*)

SUGGESTIONS FOR DRESSING FISH

Keep fish as dry and cool as possible. If fish is to be cooked whole, scrape off scales, if necessary. Slit belly skin from vent to gills, as shown at left.

Pull out all gill matter and innards, holding fish as in picture at right. Scrape out (with thumb or blunt knife) all dark matter under spine. The gill remnants and this dark matter make fish unclean and contribute to spoilage.

Fish now looks as in picture at bottom. Remove head and tail, if desired. Cook the fish per suggestions in the recipes in this chapter.

To fillet fish, it is unnecessary to clean them first. Using a sharp pointed knife, cut around the top of the head to separate cartilage behind the gills from the flesh. (Do not cut into body cavity.) Then make a longitudinal cut along the back from head to tail on one side of and close to the top fins. Work this down to the rib cage. At tail end of rib cage (just back of vent), carry this cut all the way through to separate back of fillet from bones. Now, working forward, cut off the rest of the fillet around the ribs, leaving as little flesh on the carcass as possible. The fillet quickly can be sliced off in one piece, without entering the body cavity. Do the same on the opposite side, thus resulting in two fillets and the carcass (which should have almost no meat left on it).

If you wish to remove the skin, lay the fillet on the edge of a flat surface, skin side down. Beginning at the tail end, work the knife between skin and flesh. Holding this end of skin, slice forward with the knife blade flat against the inside of the skin. The fillet can be sliced off, leaving no flesh on the skin and no skin on the fillet. (If fish are to be filleted, it is unnecessary to scale them.)

NOTES ON TRANSPORTATION

A way to ruin fish is to pack them in ice, if the ice is allowed to melt. A favorite way to keep them properly is to pack dry fish in plastic bags, with as little air as possible. Then they can be iced or carried in a portable refrigerator without getting wet and without spreading the fishy odor to clothing or to foods.

If you have thought to bring along some corn meal, so much the better, as far as smaller fish are concerned. After wiping, roll them liberally in corn meal before packing them away. (Probably you would add corn meal anyway, before frying them in the skillet.) The corn meal helps to keep them dry.

Finally, keep fish as cool, or as cold, as possible. Get them on ice, or in the refrigerator or freezer, as soon as conditions permit. By wiping fish dry and by using the corn-meal method, we have kept fish for several days in cool weather with no refrigeration at all.

This indicates some things *not* to do. Avoid leaving them in a boat where water can slosh over them. Avoid exposing them to sun or warmth. Fish freshly taken from the water are cool. Find a way to keep them so, even if you have to wrap them in several thicknesses of newspaper. The bad thing about newspapers is that they stick to the fish, unless corn meal or plastic bags or something else is used to prevent it.

Fish, when properly fried and drained, are excellent, but too many cooks (and especially guides) stop right there. This is a shame, because no food can be cooked in as many different and delicious ways as can fish. We can bake them, boil them, broil them, or fry them. We can fill them with a variety of stuffings. We can marinate them or serve them with a choice of tasty sauces. We can make them into fish cakes or fish balls. And we can use them as the principal ingredient in a wide variety of soups, chowders, and stews.

The recipes that follow are by no means all, but they are typical of some of the easier ones. Some are ideal for camp cookery. Others (such as those in the section on baked fish) may be more suitable at home. Why not browse through this collection of recipes and mark the ones that seem most interesting? Most recipes, such as the ones for Baked Bass or Baked Salmon, will do for many other kinds of fish as well.

BAKED FISH

Baked Bass I

> 1 or 2 3- to 5-pound small-mouth or large-mouth bass
> ¼ cup olive oil
> 1 tablespoon minced onion
> ½ cup tomato juice
> 2 cups Creole Sauce

Clean the fish and wipe dry. Rub inside and outside liberally with oil. Put the fish in a buttered pan and add the onion and tomato juice. Put this in a preheated 400° oven and bake, not over 12 minutes per pound (weight of one fish). Baste frequently, and do not overcook. Test for doneness by flaking with a fork.

As an alternative for this recipe, try the one for Baked Salmon, which is equally good for bass and other medium-sized fish.

The Creole Sauce is not essential, but it's good. Here's the way to prepare it:

Creole Sauce

> 1½ cups canned tomatoes
> 1 green pepper, seeded and sliced very thin
> 1 medium-sized onion, sliced very thin
> ½ cup mushrooms, sliced very thin
> 1 tablespoon flour
> 1 teaspoon butter, (margarine, or oil)
> 1 beef bouillon cube
> 1 cup hot water

Combine first four ingredients; bring to boil and simmer about 10 minutes. Melt the butter separately, and blend in the flour over low heat until smooth. Dissolve the bouillon cube in a little water, and stir it into the blended flour. Then add the first four ingredients and cook slowly for 2 or 3 minutes. This makes about 2 cups of Creole Sauce.

Put the bass on an ovenproof platter and pour the sauce over them. Sprinkle on about ½ cup fresh buttered bread crumbs, if handy. Put the platter under the broiler for a minute or two, until the sauce is properly browned. (The sauce can be made up in advance, kept in the refrigerator, and heated when needed.)

Baked Bass II

1 4- to 10-pound bass (or other fish)
2 bay leaves
2 slices bacon
2 slices onion

Line a pan with foil and put the bay leaves, bacon, and onion on the foil, so that the fish will be on top of them. (This helps to flavor the fish and prevents sticking.) Lay the fish (cleaned and wiped dry) on the bay leaves, bacon, and onion, adding seasoning on the fish, if desired. Bake at 400° to 425° in a preheated oven, not over 12 minutes per pound. Baste the fish occasionally with whatever juice is in the pan. Test for doneness to be sure the fish is not overcooked.

This is an easy recipe, and is one of the author's favorites for striped bass weighing about 8 or 10 pounds.

Baked Stuffed Fish

1 dressed fish, about 5 pounds
1 rounded teaspoon salt
4 tablespoons melted butter, margarine, or other fat
3 or 4 slices bacon
Stuffing

Clean and dry the fish, and rub outside and inside with salt. Stuff the fish loosely, and fasten opening with skewers (or sew it closed). Lay the fish on a baking pan (lined with foil, if available). The pan, or foil, should be greased. Brush the fish with melted fat. Drape bacon over the fish. (Use of bacon is optional, and should not be used if the fish is of a fatty variety.) Bake in a preheated moderate oven at 350° to 400° for about 12 minutes per pound. Baste occasionally with the drippings, and test for doneness. When done, remove thread or skewers and serve on a hot platter—adding your choice of sauces, if desired. (Also see Chapter Fifteen for more sauce recipes.)

Bread Stuffing

1 cup chopped celery stalks
3 tablespoons chopped onion
6 tablespoons melted butter, margarine, or fat
1 teaspoon salt
4 cups bread crumbs
1 teaspoon herbs (thyme, savory, sage, or herb blend)
Dash of pepper

Sauté the celery and onion in the fat until translucent and tender. Mix all ingredients. Add a little milk or water if the dressing seems too dry, but have the stuffing on the dry side. Stuff the fish loosely with the dressing, and bake, as above.

Vegetable Stuffing

3 medium-sized onions, sliced thin
1 small green pepper, seeded, sliced thin
1 tomato, sliced thin
2 sprigs parsley, chopped
Salt and pepper to taste

Combine the above ingredients and stuff the fish.

Tuna Stuffing

1 7-ounce can tuna
1 tablespoon minced onion
2 tablespoons green pepper, seeded, minced
1 tablespoon lemon juice
½ cup bread crumbs
½ teaspoon grated lemon rind
¼ cup finely chopped celery
1 egg
½ teaspoon salt
⅛ tablespoon melted butter

Rinse and flake the tuna fish, and combine with remaining ingredients. Stuff the fish with this mixture.

Baked Catfish

10 or 12 small catfish, cleaned and skinned
2 tablespoons margarine or butter
1 cup evaporated milk
½ cup flour

Melt the cube of margarine or butter in a baking pan. Dip the fish in milk; roll them in flour, and lay them in the hot margarine. Bake at 350° for 10 to 15 minutes, until golden brown. Remove from the oven and turn the fish over. Return to oven for another 10 to 15 minutes, until golden brown. Serve on a hot platter, garnished with parsley and lemon wedges, if available.

Baked Salmon with Sweet-Sour Sauce

1 5- to 10-pound salmon, or other fish, properly cleaned and wiped dry
2 tablespoons salt
1 large onion, sliced fine
2 cloves garlic, minced
½ cube margarine or butter
6 tablespoons cider vinegar
2 tablespoons brown sugar
2 tablespoons Worcestershire sauce
1 small can mushrooms

Sprinkle the fish with salt, inside and out. Make the sweet-sour sauce by sautéing the onion and garlic in the margarine or butter slowly, until the onion is translucent. (Do not let the butter brown.) Add remaining ingredients.

Lay the fish in a greased baking pan and cover it with the sauce. Bake in a 400° preheated oven about 10 to 12 minutes per pound. Baste frequently, and test for doneness. Serve the fish with the sauce poured over it.

Baked Shad

> 1 shad, about 6 pounds
> 1 tablespoon lemon juice
> 1 tablespoon Worcestershire sauce
> 1 teaspoon salt

Clean and scale the shad, and wipe it dry. Mix the lemon juice and Worcestershire sauce and rub inside and outside liberally with the mixture. Sprinkle inside and outside with salt, rubbing it in thoroughly. (Put a slice or two of bacon in the body cavity, if you wish, but this is not essential.) Seal the fish tightly in heavy-duty aluminum foil and bake it in a very slow oven (250°) for at least 2 hours. Remove the foil and serve the fish on a hot platter.

Shad is notorious for its small bones. Slow—very slow—baking for a long period of time tends to dissolve the bones so they will not be noticed. Some people bake shad more slowly than above—for as long as 6 to 8 hours in an oven set as low as 150° to 200°. By sealing the fish tightly in foil, the natural juices will be retained during the long baking period.

Shad fishermen along the Connecticut River in Connecticut like to catch the female shad for their roe, but they use the male (or "buck") shad for cooking. The preferred method is to broil the fillets very slowly over charcoal, but the above baking method is also used by many people.

Baked Striped Bass

> 1 striped bass, about 8 pounds
> ½ cup flour
> 1 clove garlic, minced
> 1 small onion, chopped
> 1 tablespoon tomato paste
> 1 tomato, sliced thin, or 1 cup stewed tomatoes
> 1 tablespoon vinegar
> 4 tablespoons olive oil

> 1 tablespoon chopped dried mushrooms or 1 small can mushrooms
> 3 lemon slices
> ½ cup water
> Salt, pepper, and rosemary to taste

Clean the fish and wipe it dry. Set it in a greased baking pan and dust it with flour. Combine all other ingredients and pour this sauce over the fish. (Optional: dot the fish with butter, sprinkle with minced parsley and Parmesan cheese.)

Bake the fish in a 400° preheated oven about 10 to 12 minutes per pound. Baste frequently with the sauce. Test for doneness, being sure not to overcook the fish. Serve the fish with the sauce poured over it.

Baked Fish Fillets I

> 2 to 3 pounds fillets
> 1½ tablespoons butter
> 1 tablespoon flour
> 1 medium-sized onion, minced
> ½ bay leaf
> 1 cup chicken stock or 1 chicken bouillon cube dissolved in 1 cup water
> Salt and pepper to taste
> ½ tablespoon lemon juice
> ½ cup bread crumbs

Cut the fillets into serving-size pieces and set them in a greased baking dish. Melt the butter and add flour and onion, blending thoroughly. Add the bay leaf and chicken stock, and simmer for 15 minutes, stirring until the mixture is thickened. Remove the bay leaf. Season with salt and pepper, and stir in the lemon juice. Pour this over the fish, and sprinkle the bread crumbs on top. Bake in a 425° preheated oven for about 20 minutes.

Some people like to sprinkle a little Parmesan cheese over the bread crumbs—to make Baked Fish Fillets au Gratin.

Baked Fish Fillets II

> 2 pounds fish fillets or steaks
> 2 tablespoons lemon juice
> 1 teaspoon minced onion
> 4 tablespoons butter, melted
> 1 teaspoon salt
> Dash of pepper
> Dash of paprika

Cut fillets into serving-size pieces, and salt and pepper them to taste. Put lemon juice, onion, and butter in a skillet and heat slightly. Dip fillets in this mixture and set them in a baking dish. Pour remaining fat over the fish. Bake in a moderate oven (350°) for 20 to 30 minutes—until fish flakes easily when tested with a fork. Sprinkle with paprika and serve.

Baked Fish Fillets III

2 pounds fish fillets or steaks
4 tablespoons butter, melted
1 cup potato chip crumbs (chips rolled to crumbs with a rolling pin or bottle)
Salt and pepper to taste

Cut fillets to serving-size pieces and dip in butter, then roll them in the potato chip crumbs until thoroughly coated. Set the coated fillets in a baking dish; add salt and pepper to taste, and pour remaining butter over them. Bake at 350° until golden brown, about 20 minutes, testing for doneness with a fork. Remember that fish is at its best when not overcooked. Chopped parsley or chives (or other herbs as mentioned in Chapter Sixteen) add to the flavor and appearance of fish dishes such as this, so don't be afraid to "spice it up a bit!"

Baked Fish in Milk

4- to 6-pound fish, cleaned, scaled, and scrubbed, with head removed
1 tablespoon salt
½ teaspoon pepper (white pepper is best)
¾ cup milk
4 tablespoons butter, melted
1 hard-boiled egg, sliced thin
1 lemon, cut in wedges
1½ cups sauce (optional)

Scrub the skin of the cleaned fish and dip it in boiling water. Rub inside and outside with salt. Sprinkle with pepper. Lay the fish in a baking pan and pour the milk over it. Bake about 45 minutes at 350°, then test for doneness. The milk will cook away or be absorbed by the fish, thus making it more moist.

Remove fish to hot platter, using spatulas, so it won't break. Remove skin, and carefully lift out bone. Pour melted butter over it, and garnish with lemon and egg slices.

Instead of butter, try pouring over the fish one of the sauces described in Chapter Fifteen. Also garnish with parsley, or a little paprika, if desired.

Fish fillets can be used instead of the whole fish, but they require less cooking time.

Baked Minted Fillets of Trout

2 or more (depending on size) trout fillets, with skin removed (other fish fillets can be used)
½ cup milk, fresh or evaporated
½ cup flour
½ cup bread or cracker crumbs
2 tablespoons melted butter
¼ teaspoon dried mint or 1 teaspoon chopped fresh mint leaves
Salt and pepper to taste

Dip the fillets (cut into serving size, if necessary) into milk; roll them in flour; dip in milk again, and roll them in the crumbs. Set the fillets in a greased baking dish and baste them with the melted butter, to which the mint has been added. Season with salt and pepper to taste. Bake in a preheated 425° oven for about 10 minutes. If you like them slightly browner, put them under the broiler for a minute or two.

Baked Trout on a Rock

(This one, quite obviously, is to try when out camping without a skillet!)

1 large flat rock
1 trout
Salt and pepper to taste

Heat the flat rock (be sure it's a dry one!) in the campfire until it is very hot. Meanwhile, clean the trout; remove the head, and split the trout down the middle without separating the two sides. Use a stick to poke the rock from the campfire. Use an evergreen bough to sweep it fairly clean. Set the fish on the rock, skin side down. Salt and pepper it. Add a bit of butter or bacon if you have any. Let it bake on the hot rock until the flesh flakes away. The skin will stick to the rock, so you eat it where it is!

Baked Planked Fish

The trick in this recipe is to season the plank properly. Since planked cooking is considered to be something of a "show piece" by many indoor and outdoor cooks, and since planking is used for cooking meats as well as fish, let's take a minute to see how the old-timers did it.

Find a splinter-free, hardwood plank of suitable size—or a bread board, or a wooden platter.

Soak the plank in cold water for about half an hour. Then put it in a moderate oven for 5 minutes or so to warm it up. Then paint it liberally with a good cooking oil. The plank then is ready for use—and it should be seasoned this way each time it is used.

Put the fish fillets on the plank, skin side down; spread melted butter over them, and add salt and pepper to taste. Put this in a very hot oven for about 5 minutes, and then reduce the heat. Cook for 15 or 20 minutes more (depending on thickness of the fish) until flaking with a fork indicates the fish is done. Put it under the broiler for a minute or two if it is not brown enough.

Remove the plank from the oven and garnish the edge with mashed potato and whatever other vegetables are desired. Add a little more melted butter, plus parsley or other herbs.

Some people remove the plank from the stove just before the fish is done. Then they return it to the oven with vegetables added, so everything will brown together. Of course the appearance of the dish is very important.

If the plank has no drain trough and a depression to catch the juices, it should be put in a shallow pan to catch them. Fairly large fish can be cooked by this means—even whole ones that have been cleaned, scaled, and scrubbed. Quite obviously, the use of the plank primarily is for a "conversation piece," but planked fish is a very attractive and tasty dish when properly prepared.

Most of these baked fish recipes are more suitable for fishermen to prepare at home or in camp, rather than outdoors, but they are included here because fishermen want to know how to cook the fish they catch, no matter where they may be. In outdoor cooking, most of these recipes are practical to prepare by using the reflector baker described in Chapter Five—or by using aluminum foil as a reflector, as discussed in Chapter Four.

BOILED FISH

Fish and Potatoes

> 4 or more small fish fillets
> 4 or more medium-sized potatoes, peeled and quartered
> 1 onion, sliced thin

> ¼ teaspoon salt
> 6 cracked peppercorns or equivalent black pepper
> 1 bay leaf (optional)
> 2 whole cloves (optional)
> ¼ cup cream or evaporated milk
> 1 teaspoon flour

Put potatoes, onion, and the seasonings in a skillet and barely cover them with cold water. Cook, covered, until potatoes are half done. Then lay the fillets on the potatoes and cook, covered, until potatoes and fish are done. Remove fish to a platter and keep hot. Scald the cream, and blend the flour into it. Stir this into the potatoes and simmer for a few minutes until the gravy has thickened. Pour this over the fish and serve.

Instead of using the cream and flour, an excellent result is obtained merely by stirring in ½ can of a creamed soup, such as cream of celery or cream of mushroom.

Boiled Fish I

> About 2 pounds salmon fillets or any other suitable fish
> 1 tablespoon butter or margarine
> 1 onion, sliced thin
> 4 cups water
> 1 teaspoon salt
> 1 small bay leaf
> 3 peppercorns or equivalent black pepper

Melt the butter or margarine in a large skillet. Add the onion and cook until it is soft, but not brown. Add water, salt, bay leaf, and pepper. Bring to a boil, and lay the fish fillets into the liquid. Cover, and simmer for about 10 minutes, until the fish is tender. Carefully remove the salmon to a platter and serve hot with melted butter, or allow it to chill, and serve it with one of the fish sauces described in Chapter Fifteen.

Boiled Fish II

> About 2 pounds salmon fillets or any other suitable fish
> 1 cheesecloth bag (such as a large sugar sack)
> 1 lemon, sliced
> 3 bay leaves or ½ teaspoon dried orégano, or other suitable herb (see Chapter Sixteen)
> 1 medium-sized onion, sliced fine
> Salt and pepper to taste

Cut the fillets into fairly large chunks and put them in the cheesecloth bag. Put the bag in a pan and cover it with cold water. Add to the water the remaining ingredients. Bring this to a boil, and boil slowly for about 30 minutes, until done. Remove the bag and drain. Carefully remove the fish from the bag. Serve hot with parsley butter or with one of the fish sauces described in Chapter Fifteen.

Prepare as much fish this way as possible. The leftovers are excellent when packaged in foil and heated over the coals of the fire. If people object to the odor of fish, boiling it this way removes most of the odor. However, it also removes some of the flavor.

Boiled Fish III

About 2 pounds fish fillets (salmon, striped bass, trout, fresh-water bass, etc.)
1 cup finely chopped parsley
1 garlic clove, finely chopped
1 small onion, finely chopped
Salt and pepper to taste

Cut the fish into slices about 1 inch thick and put them in a frying pan. Barely cover them with water. Add remaining ingredients. Cover the pan and allow the fish to simmer for 20 minutes or so, until cooked. Remove fish to a platter and serve with melted butter or with one of the fish sauces described in Chapter Fifteen.

Fish cooked this way is excellent when served either hot or cold. This makes a jellied fish dish when thoroughly chilled.

By scanning the three recipes above, it will be noted that, if we lack certain flavorings, we can get along very well by improvising with something else. Outdoor cooks should carry an herb bag or a variety of herbs and other condiments. The addition of these various flavorings can transform an ordinary dish into a chef's masterpiece.

Poached Fillets

2 or more fish fillets, cut into serving-size pieces
Salt and pepper to taste
2 tablespoons vinegar or lemon juice
4 tablespoons butter, melted
¼ cup minced parsley

Put enough water to cover the fillets into a frying pan, and add the salt, pepper, and vinegar or lemon juice. Bring this to a boil, then slide the fillets into the boiling water. Let them simmer for about 15 minutes, until done. Remove carefully to a hot platter, and add the melted butter and parsley.

Instead of the butter and parsley, this recipe can be varied by adding one of the fish sauces described in Chapter Fifteen.

Poached Fillets, Italian Style

2 or more fish fillets, cut into serving-size pieces
1 tablespoon chopped parsley
¼ teaspoon pepper
2 carrots, diced
1 onion, minced
1 garlic clove, crushed or minced
1 tablespoon olive oil
½ teaspoon salt
3 cups dry red wine
¼ cup butter
1 tablespoon flour

Combine in a skillet everything except the fish, butter, and flour and marinate the fillets in this mixture for 2 or 3 hours. Then bring this to a boil, and simmer the fish in it for 15 to 20 minutes. Carefully remove the fillets to a hot platter and keep warm. Now, strain the vegetables from the sauce and cook the mixture another 5 minutes. Meanwhile, melt the butter in a pan, and stir in the flour until smooth. Add this to the sauce. When the sauce has thickened, pour it over the fish and serve.

This is a favorite recipe for striped bass fillets, but many other kinds of fish are as good.

Blue Trout

This is another "conversation piece," and can be done only when some very fresh small trout are available—preferably live ones. It's a French recipe, called *truite au bleu* because of the unusual blue color imparted to the fish. Kill the trout, and clean them as quickly as possible, tying the head of each to its tail with string. Have enough tarragon vinegar boiling in which to immerse the trout, one at a time. Plunge each trout into the boiling vinegar for half a minute, then immerse each trout in ice water until it turns a rich blue color. Then boil the trout for about 5 minutes, depending on size. Untie the fish and serve them with melted butter and condiments.

Another way to do this is to bring to a boil 3 parts of water to 1 part of vinegar, to which about 6 peppercorns, 1 teaspoon salt, and 1 bay leaf have been added. Plunge the trout in this for 4 to 6 minutes, depending on the size of the trout. One can be tested to see if the meat flakes away from the bone easily.

In this latter recipe, tying the trout is not called for, because fewer steps are taken in the preparation. The reason for tying the fish is to make it easier to remove it from the liquid with a fork. The Eastern brook trout is best for this recipe, although cutthroat and rainbow trout do about as well. If the fish are not quite small (6 to 8 inches) and very fresh, the recipe should not be attempted.

Boiled Trout

After dressing the trout, plunge it in boiling water for 2 or 3 minutes, depending on the size of the fish. Remove from water, and remove head, skin, and bones, trying to keep the flesh unbroken. Put the flesh in a skillet or pan, and add butter, salt, and pepper to taste. Then put the fish under a broiler until the surface starts to brown. Serve at once.

This recipe makes it possible to remove undesirable parts, leaving only the meat. Many people think trout are sweeter and tenderer when prepared this way. In the woods, the browning can be done in a reflector baker, or by using aluminum foil, as discussed in Chapter Four.

BROILED FISH

Fish with Barbecue Sauce

2 or more fillets, cut in serving-size pieces
Barbecue Sauce

Dip the fillets in the sauce and place them on a greased wire grill (or in a hinged wire broiler) about 6 to 12 inches above the coals, depending on the heat of the fire. Turn the fillets in from 5 to 10 minutes, depending on their size, and cook on the other side for 5 to 10 minutes. Brush with the sauce at least twice on each side. When the fish flakes away when being tested with a fork, they are done. Overcooking, or cooking on too hot a fire, will make them dry. Remove from fire to plates, adding more sauce, if desired.

Barbecue Sauce for Fish I

1 jar chili sauce
½ teaspoon garlic salt
½ teaspoon dry powdered mustard
2 tablespoons butter or margarine
2 teaspoons Worcestershire sauce
¼ teaspoon chili powder (optional)

Combine all ingredients and simmer slowly, covered, for at least an hour. This sauce keeps for weeks in a refrigerator, so a large amount can be made up in advance.

Barbecue Sauce for Fish II

1 large onion, minced
½ cup minced green pepper
½ cup dried celery
2 bottles catsup
1 can tomato sauce
1½ cups water
½ cup vinegar
½ teaspoon pepper
1 teaspoon salt

Combine all ingredients and simmer slowly, covered, for at least an hour. This sauce also keeps well, so a large amount can be made up in advance. Long, slow cooking is the secret of these barbecue sauces. When the sauce is nearly done, taste it, and add seasonings to taste, if necessary, but remember that fish need a fairly mild sauce. If a spicier sauce is desired, add a few drops of Tabasco sauce, and perhaps ½ teaspoon or so of powdered mustard.

Fish in Foil

2 or more fish fillets
¼ cup white wine
1 tablespoon lemon juice
1 cube melted butter
¼ teaspoon salt

Combine in a skillet all ingredients except the fish, and bring to a boil. Let the mixture cool, then marinate the fillets in this for about an hour. Wrap each fillet in heavy-duty aluminum foil as described in Chapter Four. A double wrapping is best if the fish is to be cooked directly on the coals. Put the wrapped packages on the grill, or on the coals, for 15 to 20 minutes, depending on the thickness of the fillets and the heat of the fire. Open and serve.

Fish in Pickle Sauce

2 or more fish fillets
¼ cup oil
Salt and pepper to taste
1 egg white
1 rounded tablespoon green pickle relish
1 rounded tablespoon mayonnaise

Brush the fillets with oil and lay them on the grill or on aluminum foil in a pan placed under the broiler. Salt and pepper to taste.

To make the dressing, beat the egg white to peaks. Fold in the relish and the mayonnaise.

When the fillets have browned on one side, turn them over to brown the other side. When done, spread the dressing over the fillets. If the fish is broiled in a pan under a broiler, return it to the broiler after the dressing has been added, to brown the dressing. If broiled over charcoal on the grill, transfer the cooked fish to a sheet of aluminum foil placed on the grill, and lay another sheet of foil over it, tent-fashion, so the reflected heat will brown the top of the dressing.

Broiled Whole Fish

1 or more fish, dressed (and scaled, if necessary)
Salt and pepper to taste
1 or more onion slices for each fish
2 bacon or salt pork slices for each fish

Dry the cleaned fish and add salt and pepper to taste. Put onion slices inside the body cavity. Place a slice of bacon or salt pork on each side of fish, and clamp them in a wire broiler. Broil over the coals for 10 minutes or more (depending on size of fish) until flesh flakes off bones when tested for doneness with a fork.

Grilled Split Fish

1 or more whole fish, about 3 pounds each
½ teaspoon monosodium glutamate (or less, if fish is small) for each fish
Salt and pepper to taste

Clean fish, removing head, tail, fins, and scales. Split the fish, without detaching the two sides. Lay the fish, flesh side down, on the grill (preferably in a wire broiler) and broil until the flesh side is golden brown. Turn the fish over and sprinkle ½ teaspoon of monosodium glutamate over the flesh side. Add salt and pepper to taste. Remove and serve when testing with a fork insures that the fish is done.

This business of "testing with a fork" to insure doneness is included for the benefit of cooks who are beginners. It only takes a little experience to *know* when fish are done, merely by looking at them. The monosodium glutamate is optional and has the purpose of enhancing the flavor of the fish. If the fish is not an oily one, brushing it with butter or bacon fat on the flesh side will help. A little lemon juice always adds to flavor.

Trout in Bacon

6 or more small trout, cleaned and dry
2 slices bacon for each trout

Wrap each trout in bacon, holding it in place with toothpicks or skewers. Put the fish in a wire broiler and broil them about 6 inches above the coals. When the bacon is crisp, the fish should be done. Add salt and pepper after serving. Serve lemon wedges, if available.

Fish on a Spit

Stuff a large, whole fish, as discussed earlier in this chapter under "Baked Fish." Run the spit through the fish, test it for balance, and clamp or wire it in place. The fire in the grill should be made with briquettes, because cooking will take about an hour, and briquettes provide a longer, more even heat than charcoal or wood. Put the spit in place on the grill and start the motor. If the spit does not revolve properly, it may be because the fish is not evenly balanced on the spit.

Push the glowing briquettes toward the back of the grill, and place an aluminum-foil pan under the fish to catch the drippings. Add a new briquette or two (with tongs) from time to time, as necessary, to maintain moderate, even heat.

When the fish is about half cooked, begin occasional basting with one of the barbecue sauces mentioned earlier in this chapter, or with the one that follows. If basting is started too soon, the fish may become more blackened than desirable, because tomato-based sauces tend to burn and become black.

A stuffed fish of 6 pounds or so should take about an hour to cook over moderate heat. When the fish appears to be done, stop the spit and test the flesh with a fork. In this case, it does little if any harm to overcook it a bit.

If the fish is not securely trussed, it may be desirable to bind it with piano wire (leader wire, to fishermen) to keep it properly in place on the spit. The drip pan is recommended because the juices should not drip onto the coals, thus causing flames to flare up.

My old bow-hunting companion, Walter W. Whittum, brought back from the Argentine a recipe for a rather distinctive basting sauce that we like to use on barbecued fish and meats. One of its advantages is that it does not contain anything that will burn to blacken the food, and thus it can be used for basting and seasoning all during the cooking process. This is Walt's recipe, as he gave it to me:

Argentine Chuqui

    2 onions, minced
    2 garlic cloves, minced
    2 teaspoons orégano or marjoram, or both
    2 bay leaves
    1 tablespoon salt
    1 teaspoon black pepper
    1 cup olive oil
    ½ cup vinegar
    ½ cup sherry

Sauté the onions, garlic, herbs, salt, and pepper in the olive oil until the onions and garlic are well browned. Strain, saving the liquid and discarding the solid matter. This should make 1 cup of liquid. If it doesn't, add enough more olive oil to make 1 cup. Add the vinegar and sherry. Pour this into a bottle, such as a liquor bottle, and insert a cork with a hole through it, or some other sort of plug through which liquid can be shaken, like the spout of a bitters bottle.

Since Chuqui is all liquid, it can be shaken onto the cooking food through the small hole in the cork. Shake it on liberally while the food is cooking. More salt can be added, if desired; also 1 teaspoon or so of powdered mustard.

Planked Broiled Fish

Remove the head from a large fish and scale it. Split the fish down its back, leaving the belly skin intact. Remove entrails and dark material under backbone. Wash and wipe dry. Obtain a clean plank of hardwood, or a short split log, and tack the fish, skin side down, to the wood, using nails or pointed green sticks. Prop the fish near the fire, as shown in the illustration. While it is cooking, brush it with bacon fat or with barbecue

(Boy Scouts of America) PLANKED BROILED FISH

horizontal bar or other suitable support where the fish will broil in the heat of the fire or stick the skewers into the ground, as shown. Turn the fillets occasionally, and baste them with bacon fat or with barbecue sauce. The fillets should be done in about half an hour, and then can be slid from the stick onto a platter or a sheet of aluminum foil for serving.

Of course, most of the other methods are easier, but these last two are historic ones often used by old-time woodsmen.

FISH CAKES AND FISH BALLS

Fish Cakes I

　2 cups cooked fish, shredded
　4 medium-sized potatoes, freshly boiled and hot, put through a ricer, or chopped very fine
　Salt and pepper to taste
　1 small onion, minced (optional)
　¼ teaspoon curry powder (optional)
　3 eggs
　1 cup dry bread or cracker crumbs
　½ cup butter, margarine, or bacon fat

Combine the fish, potatoes, onion, and seasoning. Stir in the eggs (stirring as little as possible). Shape into cakes and dip in the crumbs. Sauté in the butter or fat until brown.

The fat should be fairly hot and bubbling, as for any other kind of fat frying. If a food grinder is available, the fish, potatoes, and onion can be put through it, rather than preparing them separately.

If salt codfish is used, first rinse it in hot water and, preferably, soak it in water overnight to remove the salt. Omit salt in seasoning. Canned fish may also be used. In this case, omit salt. Traditionally, in New England, fish cakes are served with tomato sauce or catsup.

Fish Cakes II

　2½ cups canned or boiled fresh fish
　3 tablespoons evaporated milk
　2 eggs, well beaten
　1 teaspoon minced onion (optional)
　Salt and pepper to taste (omit salt if canned fish is used)
　1 cup hot fat

Flake the fish and combine with milk, eggs, onion, and seasoning. Drop by large spoonfuls into a skillet of hot fat. Fry until golden brown. Drain on absorbent paper before serving.

Although this recipe does not call for potato,

sauce. It may be necessary to adjust the plank before the fire occasionally to be sure the fish broils evenly at proper heat. When the flesh flakes from the skin, add salt and pepper, and serve it from the plank, allowing most of the skin to remain adhering to the plank. The cooking time will be from 20 to 30 minutes, depending on the heat and the size of the fish. Of course, more than one fish can be fastened to the plank, if the plank is large enough.

Skewered Broiled Fish

If you have a cooking fire with a dingle-stick bar over it, another way to broil fish is to skewer it, as shown in the illustration. This calls for a large fish, such as a salmon or a lake trout. The fish is filleted and skewered on pointed green hardwood sapling sticks, slightly smaller than broomsticks, from which the bark has been peeled. Try to run the sapling stick directly through the fillet. Lean the skewers against the it can be added, as in recipe above. Also add a dash of curry powder, if you like it.

Codfish Balls

1½ cups salted codfish
3 cups diced potatoes
⅓ cup milk
2 eggs, well beaten
Dash of pepper
2 cups bacon fat or cooking oil

Remove most of the salt from the codfish by soaking it in water for half an hour or so, changing the water at least twice. Combine the fish and potatoes with 1 cup water and boil until the potatoes are tender. Drain, and mash (using the base of a bottle, if a masher isn't handy). Add milk, eggs, and seasoning, and stir until combined. Drop by large spoonfuls into the hot, bubbling (375°) fat. Fry until golden brown. Drain on absorbent paper and serve with catsup.

Fish Balls

1 cup cooked fish, flaked
1 cup mashed potatoes (leftover vegetables, such as peas, can be included)
1 egg, well beaten
1 teaspoon butter, melted
Salt and pepper to taste (white pepper, preferably)
2 cups hot bacon fat or cooking oil

Combine all ingredients except fat. Check seasoning, adding more if desirable. Drop by spoonfuls into hot, deep fat (375°), and fry until golden brown. Drain on absorbent paper and serve while very hot, with tomato catsup or lemon wedges.

FISH CHOWDERS AND STEWS

In these recipes, as in many others, the experienced cook "cooks by the soul," instead of following recipes too closely. We can combine more or less fish with more or less vegetables, and we can use vegetables of many sorts, including leftovers. A pinch or two of herbs, such as sage, marjoram, or thyme, always adds to dishes such as these, whether the recipe calls for them or not. Either bacon or salt pork can be used in which to sauté the onions. Milk and/or cream always is added last, and never should be allowed to boil. Just heat it. Canned milk or powdered milk can be substituted for fresh milk or cream. Even better than these are canned, condensed soups, such as cream of celery, cream of mushroom, or creamed pea soup. The chowder should be quite thick but can be thinned with a little water, if desirable. It helps to blend the flavors to let the chowder set for a few hours, or overnight, in the refrigerator.

Every fall we go to the Rhode Island coast for the striped bass fishing, and frequently catch fish in the 50-pound range on relatively light tackle. We always bring home a few to fillet for the freezer, since striped bass is one of the most delicious of fishes. In doing the filleting, some tidbits of flesh are left on the carcass. These we carefully cut off to store in the freezer for chowder. A big kettle of fish chowder is one of the main events in the hunting camp in the fall. It always is simmering on the stove, ready for cold and hungry hunters.

Some people make fish chowder the easy way, by using just these bits and pieces. Others do it the tastier way, by adding fish heads, fins, and the larger bones, along with whatever meat is on them. These are boiled in a small amount of water until the flesh can easily be scraped from the bones. The flesh is added to the liquid, and of course the undesirable parts are discarded. They have, however, added excellent flavor to this stock from which stew is made.

So—let's look at a few favorite recipes, and prepare whatever kind of chowder or stew we think might be best. The first one is the author's favorite.

Fish Chowder I

- 6 or 8 strips bacon, cut in small pieces
- 2 large or 3 medium-sized onions, chopped fairly fine
- 2 pounds fish fillets or pieces, cut small
- 3 large or 4 or 5 medium-sized potatoes, diced
- 1 teaspoon salt
- ½ teaspoon pepper
- 1 teaspoon dried herbs (marjoram and/or thyme, or herb blend)
- 3 cups water (or stock, if you have made any)
- ½ cup cream or canned milk
- 1 can condensed cream of celery soup (or other creamed soup)

In a skillet, fry the bacon pieces until crisp. Remove from fat and drain. (Diced salt pork can be substituted.) In the fat, sauté the chopped onions until translucent but not very browned. Put the fat and onion into a fairly large kettle or Dutch oven and add the fish, potatoes, salt, pepper, herbs, and water or stock. Let this simmer until potatoes and fish are cooked. Then add the cream or milk and the cream soup. Let this simmer awhile longer before serving, but don't let it come to a boil. Taste it to see if it needs any more salt or condiments.

Serve the chowder in big bowls, with crackers. Sprinkle some of the crisp bacon pieces on top of the liquid in each bowl. Remember that this chowder tastes even better after it has been allowed to stand in a cool place (such as a refrigerator) overnight.

Some chowder addicts chop a green pepper and sauté this with the onion. I have heard of foreigners (usually people from New York State) who make chowder the "Coney Island" way. This consists of adding about ¼ cup tomato catsup and 2 cans tomato sauce, instead of the milk and creamed soup. In New England, we shoot people for doing things like that.

Fish Chowder II

This one will have to be played by ear, as far as the ingredients go.

In a Dutch oven or kettle place a thin layer of diced salt pork or bacon. On top of this place a goodly layer of boned fish. Then add a layer of thinly sliced potatoes and a layer of thinly sliced onions. On top of this put a thin layer of soda crackers. Dot this with butter and add salt and pepper to taste. Repeat the process until the ket-

tle is full, or until you have put in enough to feed all hands. Add enough water to fill the pot about halfway up. Cover the pot and let it simmer until the contents are cooked. The liquid should be allowed to cook away, so that the bottom layers of bacon and fish are browned. Then add cream (or diluted canned milk or—preferably—diluted cream soup) to cover. Heat again until it is steaming hot, but not boiling.

This chowder, of course, can be made in the coals of the campfire, if a Dutch oven is used. If the cook starts it at the beginning of the Happy Hour, it should be ready about the time when people can't wait any longer.

Bullhead or Catfish Stew I

- 6 (more or less, depending on size) fish that have been cleaned and skinned
- 1 pint milk (or more, if needed)
- 2 tablespoons butter
- ¼ teaspoon salt
- Dash of pepper

Boil the cleaned and skinned fish in salted water for 5 minutes. Pour off water, and separate meat from the bones. Cut meat into small pieces. Put the fish in a pan and add other ingredients. Heat, but without allowing the stew to boil. Serve with crackers.

Of course, other fish can be cooked this way. Include a dash of your favorite herbs, if desired.

Bullhead or Catfish Stew II

- 6 small fish, skinned and cleaned
- 4 cups water
- 2 tablespoons chopped celery
- 2 tablespoons chopped onion
- 2 tablespoons chopped parsley (chop the above three together)
- 2 tablespoons butter
- Salt and pepper (and herbs) to taste
- 4 cups milk (1 cup per serving)

Boil the fish in the water until it can be separated from the bones. When fairly cool, separate, and transfer fish to a plate. Strain the stock, discarding the rest. Add to the stock the celery, onion, and parsley. Cook until tender. Add salt, pepper, butter, and milk. Add the fish. Heat until very hot, without allowing the stew to boil. A diced potato or two can be added, if desired. Any kind of fish can be used.

Fish Stew, Italian Style

> 2 or 3 pounds fish fillets, cut in small cubes
> ½ cup flour
> ½ cup olive oil
> 1 onion, chopped fine
> 2 small red peppers or 1 green pepper chopped fine
> 1 tablespoon finely chopped parsley
> 1 clove garlic, minced
> 1 can Italian tomato sauce
> ⅓ cup white wine

Put the fish and flour in a paper bag and shake the bag to coat the fish with flour. Put the olive oil in a skillet and add the fish, onion, peppers, parsley, and garlic. Sauté these until the onion is transparent and the fish is lightly browned. Then add the tomato sauce and wine. Season with salt and pepper. Cover and cook slowly about 30 minutes. Add a little water to thin the stew, if necessary.

Fresh, cut-up tomatoes can be used instead of the tomato paste.

New Orleans Court Bouillon

In the bayou country of Louisiana, sportsmen make a camp ritual of serving court bouillon, which is fish in highly seasoned stock. This recipe is over a hundred years old and is an important gastronomic event in many sporting camps. Let's take it in four easy steps:

Step 1: In a hot Dutch oven, iron pot, or other suitable receptacle, stir 3 tablespoons flour into 3 tablespoons butter, margarine, or vegetable oil until it is smooth and slightly browned.

Step 2: Add and brown slightly:
> 2 medium-sized onions, chopped fine
> 1 garlic clove, chopped fine (with the onions)

Step 3: Add the following, and cook over a slow fire for about 20 minutes:
> 1 teaspoon finely chopped parsley
> 3 green onions, chopped fine
> 1 green pepper, chopped fine
> 2 stalks celery, chopped fine
> (Chop the above together)
> 1 large can tomatoes
> 2 bay leaves
> 1 tablespoon Worcestershire sauce
> 3 lemon slices
> 1 dash Tabasco sauce
> Salt and pepper to taste
> ½ cup claret or white wine

Step 4: Fillet 4 to 6 pounds of fish, and cut the fillets into pieces about 3 inches wide. Put the fish in the sauce and cook slowly, covered, for another 20 minutes, until the fish is done. After the first 10 minutes, carefully turn over the fillets in the sauce, trying not to break them. When the fish is done, serve it with some of the sauce spooned over the top. If the sauce becomes too thick, add a little more water or wine. This dish is excellent with French garlic bread. The fish traditionally used are red fish (channel bass), red snapper, grouper, or snook. My preference is to add the wine about 5 minutes before the dish is done. Court bouillon is very similar to bouillabaise, except that bouillabaise usually contains an equal part of cleaned shellfish (crab, lobster, shrimp, scallops) to an equal part of fish.

Pine Bark Stew

This is another famous fish dish often made in hunting and fishing camps in the South. It does not need an exact list of ingredients, because you use whatever is available. There are two theories advanced for the name: the stew often is cooked in a Dutch oven or a black iron wash pot over pine bark; and the "gravy" is brownish—the color of pine bark.

> 2 pounds fish fillets (such as red snapper)
> 6 slices bacon, cut small
> 1 cup chopped or finely sliced onion
> 3 cups diced potatoes
> 2 cans tomatoes (1 to 1½ quarts)
> 2 teaspoons salt
> ¼ pound butter
> 2 tablespoons Worcestershire sauce
> ½ bottle catsup
> ½ cup chili sauce
> ½ teaspoon pepper
> 1 teaspoon herbs (if available)

In a Dutch oven over a hot fire, add the bacon and try out the fat. Remove the bacon. Fry the onion in the fat until tender. Add hot water to a depth of about 2 inches. Add a layer of fish fillets; then a layer of potatoes and onions. If the pot is a large one, and you are cooking for several people, make two or three times the above recipe, and continue adding layers of fish, potatoes, and onions until the pot is as full as desired. Salt liberally; bring to a boil and let simmer slowly, covered, for 30 to 45 minutes—until testing indicates the stew is done.

While the stew is cooking, melt the butter in a smaller pan; stir in a ladleful of liquor from the stew, and add the Worcestershire sauce, catsup, tomatoes, chili sauce, pepper, and herbs. Simmer slowly, dipping liquid from stew and adding to sauce from time to time.

Serve the stew in deep bowls, with sauce poured over it.

Another way to do this is to add everything to the one pot, without bothering to make the sauce separately. The butter and chili sauce do not seem very necessary, and can be left out, if desirable.

FRIED FISH

NOTES ON FRYING

Since frying fish is so very easy, I often wonder how so many people become so expert in messing it up, with the result either that the food is soaked soggily in grease or that it is burned on the outside and quite raw inside. I frequently make unkind remarks about people who fry foods, and about the results of their efforts. Without doubt, most of us eat too much fried food—especially when out camping. Properly fried food, however, is quite another matter. Fish comes out golden brown, fried at the proper temperature so little fat remains. Most of this is, or should be, drained off by setting the food on absorbent paper for a minute or two—even newspapers. When served golden brown, properly drained, and very hot, with lemon juice or tartar sauce or something else, fried fish can be delicious.

Fish can be fried in deep fat or in scarcely enough to cover the pan. The skillet should be an iron one, because it provides more even heat. Iron skillets are heavy and more suitable to camps than to packsacks. The next choice is a steel one—with a folding handle, if it is to be carried very much. Last choice is aluminum, because aluminum skillets do not hold heat very well.

Fat for frying should be very hot but not smoking. A good test is to have several bread crumbs handy. When the fat seems about right,

drop a crumb in it. If the crumb swims around and bubbles merrily, it's time to put the fish in. But don't put in all the fish at once, because this reduces the temperature of the fat. Add one piece at a time, being sure the pieces keep on bubbling vigorously while cooking. When the fish is a golden brown on one side, turn it over to get the same result on the other. When both sides are golden brown, the fish should be done. Overcooking only makes it dry and tough.

When removed from the skillet, have some absorbent paper napkins or toweling handy to lay it on, so that all excess fat can be absorbed. Then season the fish, and dig in!

Fish does not have to be dipped in flour, egg, crumbs, or something else before frying, but most people like the crispy result. Fish does not have to be seasoned by squeezing a little lemon juice over it, but it helps.

The simplest way is to dip or roll fish in seasoned flour (salt, pepper, dried herbs added to taste) or in corn meal or crumbs. Any kind of flour can be used—regular flour, biscuit mix, pancake mix, or what have you. Any kind of meal or crumbs can be used—dried bread crumbs, corn meal, potato chip crumbs, cracker crumbs, etc. Some people prefer one kind and some another.

If you like a good, crispy coating on fish fillets or sticks, here's the way to do it: Beat up 2 or 3 eggs in a bowl and have them handy. Dip the fish in seasoned flour; then in the beaten eggs, and then roll it in crumbs of one kind or another. This final rolling can be in a mixture of flour and crumbs.

Another way is to dip the fish in milk and then coat it with crumbs. The milk can be whole milk or canned milk. If you use the egg formula, a little water and some salt can be added before the eggs are beaten. Finally, we can make a pancake batter and dip the fish in this, and then in crumbs—or in the batter alone. There are other ways, but these should furnish the idea. Try one way and then try another. You'll arrive at your special favorite, and no one can say what it will be.

So—remember to wipe the fish dry; to sprinkle on a little lemon juice if desirable; to have the fat properly hot; to use whatever coating seems best; to fry to a golden brown; and to drain the fish after frying. The result will be delicious.

Tartar Sauce I

Tartar Sauce goes with fried fish just as surely as ham goes with eggs. There's no set formula for tartar sauce, except that it is a mixture of mayonnaise and finely chopped pickles or olives, plus some finely chopped onion, if you like it, and seasoning. For example, to 1 cup mayonnaise, add about 2 tablespoons chopped dill pickle, 2 tablespoons chopped onion, and 2 tablespoons finely chopped parsley. Add a little lemon juice and salt and pepper to taste. If there's no parsley handy, substitute a dried herb blend, or leave it out. If there's no dill pickle, any kind of pickle will do—or chopped olives, or pickle relish.

While this seems to cover the fried fish problem reasonably well, here are a few recipes people enjoy:

Milk Batter

> 1 egg
> ¾ cup milk
> 1 cup flour
> 1 teaspoon salt
> ⅛ teaspoon pepper

Beat the egg slightly, and stir in the milk, flour, and seasoning until the batter is smooth. This batter recipe and the next one are excellent for pieces of fish fillets, smelts, shrimps, frogs' legs, oysters, and other sea foods.

Beer Batter

> 1½ cups flour
> ½ teaspoon salt
> 3 eggs, beaten
> 3 teaspoons baking powder
> 1 cup beer (or more)

Blend above ingredients and dip sea food in it for frying.

Fried Thin Fillets

This recipe is excellent for fillets of sole, smelt, or any other fairly thin fillets:

> 6 to 8 fillets
> 1 cup flour
> ½ teaspoon salt
> ⅛ teaspoon pepper
> 3 tablespoons olive oil
> 3 tablespoons butter
> Juice of 1 lemon
> ¼ cup chopped parsley

Mix flour, salt, and pepper, and toss fillets in it to coat them thoroughly. Fry slowly in the mixture of oil and butter until golden brown. Transfer to platter. Add lemon juice to the fat; stir, and pour over the fish. Garnish with the parsley.

Fish Croquettes

> 2 cups flaked, cooked fish, such as salmon
> (can be canned)
> 2 eggs
> 1 tablespoon finely chopped parsley
> 1 tablespoon finely chopped onion

Mix the salmon, eggs, onion, and parsley. Roll into cylindrical croquettes or cakes. Roll in cracker crumbs. Fry until light brown. Drain and serve.

Fried Fish Livers or Cheeks

If your party has caught several large fish, such as striped bass, channel bass, or lake trout, remove the livers and store them in waxed paper in a cool place until needed. Roll the livers in corn meal or flour that has been seasoned with salt and pepper. Fry in shallow fat until fairly well done. Any fish livers large enough to bother with can be prepared this way. Many sportsmen consider them the most delicious part of the fish fry—and of course they are loaded with vitamins. The cheeks can be done the same way.

Fried Trout Amandine

> 2 or more small cleaned trout
> Salt, pepper, dried tarragon to taste
> ½ cup milk
> ½ cup flour
> ¼ pound butter
> ¼ cup almonds, shredded
> 1 tablespoon chopped parsley
> Juice of 1 lemon

Wipe the trout with a damp towel and dust them with salt, pepper, and a pinch of dried tarragon. Dip them in milk and coat them with flour. Sauté them in butter until brown. Remove to a hot platter. Put 2 tablespoons butter in a skillet and heat until it bubbles. Stir in the almonds, parsley, and lemon juice, and pour this over the fish.

Hush Puppies I

Hush puppies are Southern corn-meal-based fritters, which should be fried in the fat the fish are fried in, to give them real flavor. Many outdoorsmen think that no fish fry is complete without them. Here is a fancy North Carolina recipe, which is the best one. If you lack some of the ingredients, try the simpler one that follows:

1¼ cups corn meal
¾ cup regular flour
¾ teaspoon salt
6 teaspoons baking powder
1¼ teaspoons sugar
⅓ teaspoon garlic salt
½ teaspoon black pepper
2 cups minced onion
2 eggs
1½ cups milk

Sift and mix the dry ingredients, and stir the onion into the dry ingredients. Separate the eggs and beat the yolks with the milk. Then stir this into the dry ingredients. Beat the egg whites until smooth (not stiff). Add a light sprinkling of baking powder to the egg whites just before you finish beating them. Fold the egg whites into the batter with as little stirring as possible. Make into very small balls, and drop them into the fish fat, frying them until golden brown. Drain on absorbent paper, and serve hot. Leave out the onion, if you prefer.

Hush Puppies II

2 cups corn meal
1 cup flour
½ teaspoon salt
2 teaspoons baking powder
1 large onion, chopped fine
4 tablespoons ham or bacon fat

Combine all ingredients and work in enough water to make a stiff dough. Roll into small balls or into lengths about half the size of your large finger. Fry in the fat with the fish until they are golden brown. Drain on absorbent paper and serve hot with the fish.

Chapter Twelve

PREPARING OTHER AQUATIC FOODS

On trips to California, friends provided these three recipes for cooking abalone. Being a New Englander, I know very little about it, but we have tried these recipes and think they are excellent.

ABALONE

Baked or Broiled Abalone

Remove the abalone from its shell and clean it. Do not slice. Pound it whole until it is limp. Cut several slits in the top side and put small slivers of garlic in the slits. Add some chopped parsley to melted butter or margarine, and pour it over the abalone. (Or mince a garlic clove and add it to the melted butter and parsley, instead of using slivers, as above.) Bake in a preheated oven at 350° for 20 minutes per side, basting occasionally. The abalone may also be broiled instead of baked. This method seems to provide a milder flavor and to make the flesh tenderer than when the abalone is fried.

Fried Abalone

Slice the abalone meat thickly and pound it until it is very limp. Roll in flour and dip in beaten egg. Fry in a skillet with a small amount of vegetable oil until golden brown. Add juice of ½ lemon to 2 tablespoons of melted butter, and pour it over the abalone. Garnish with a few capers, if available.

Boiled Abalone

Slice the abalone in half horizontally and pound it thoroughly on both sides. Flour heavily and season with salt and pepper. Brown on both sides in a small amount of vegetable oil, using a Dutch oven or similar container with a close-fitting lid. Add enough water to cover; put on the lid, and simmer for 2 hours. The combination of flour, oil, and water, plus the flavor of the abalone, makes delicious brown gravy.

CLAMS

Clams on the half shell never seemed as good as when we returned from a cold day of duck hunting and shucked and ate them while perched on a clam bin in a fisherman's shack on Cape Cod. There are many who claim clams taste best just as they come from the shell, fresh and cold from the sea, and filled with flavors no condiments could improve. But at least equal to "clams au naturel" is that delectable New England delicacy called clam chowder.

A duck camp doesn't amount to much without a big covered iron pot of New England clam chowder steeping on the back of the stove, wafting its steamy fragrance invitingly to hungry hunters. No doubt its allure is enhanced by the setting of the shack on the sea, with the boats coming home and the gulls and terns wheeling and crying and the ducks rafting up safely far away—but the secret of good clam chowder is known only to a few and, at its peak of perfection, it is made the way the old Cape Cod duck hunters make it. Let's not risk ruin by trying to list exactly how much of what goes into it. You cook by the soul—not by the book—but here's the general idea:

New England Clam Chowder

Armed with clam rake and flour sack, the first step is to go way out on the flats at dead low tide to find the really big hard-shell clams that lie just under the surface of the sand or mud. Sometimes they can be spotted by a little depression in the sand or mud directly over where they are lying. Usually you rake for them and, when the tines of the clam rake hit something hard, you rake it out or reach down with your fingers and pull it out. Unless you happen to hit a stone you have a hard-shell clam "in hand." While gathering a sackful, don't ignore the smaller clams, because these are delicious for eating raw during the Happy Hour. When the sack is heavy, you come home and go to work—and very pleasant work it is!

You sit on the porch and light your pipe and watch the boats and birds and discuss why it had to be that the ducks that morning mostly were coots. Meanwhile, after the clams have cleansed themselves of grit by resting peacefully in a washbasin of cold sea water, you shuck the clams, of course carefully saving all the juice. These big clams ("quahogs," we call them) are considered better than the smaller ones for chowder because of their extra flavor. You chop the clams fairly small by whatever means are available. For half a dozen hungry men you need about a quart of chopped or very coarsely ground clams, plus the juice that has been drained from them.

If you can get the kitchen help to stop cleaning their guns or to put down their glasses for a minute, they can be peeling and dicing 3 or 4 large potatoes into ½-inch cubes, and they can be coarsely chopping about 4 onions. That's about all these people are allowed to do. The rest is the chef's job and should not be delegated, except that you could let them dice up about ½ pound of salt pork. Lacking the pork, cut about 8 strips of bacon crosswise into thin slivers.

Now you throw some wood into the stove and open the draft a little. You get out the ancient iron pot and its cover, carefully inspecting them, unless you have complete confidence in the last team who did the dishes. You toss the diced pork or slivered bacon into a skillet and let it start sputtering while you put some ice in an old jelly glass and float it with whatever flavor of amber liquid seems reasonable. (This is for inspiration for the cook.)

When the pork or bacon has fried out to crispy golden nuggets, these are removed and put aside on absorbent paper to drain and dry. The chopped onion is put in the hot fat in the skillet and is stirred about a bit until it is transparent and just beginning to be tinged with brown. Drain off all excess fat and set the fried onions aside temporarily. Now you start assembling the chowder. Pour all the clam broth into the iron pot and add the diced potatoes. Let them boil slowly in the broth until they are barely done (which won't take long). Add the chopped clams and fried onions. Add a scant teaspoon of salt, remembering that the clam broth already is slightly salty. Add a vigorous shake of pepper and a teaspoon of a suitable dried herb, such as orégano.

Now we add the milk or cream plus, perhaps, a can or two of condensed cream soup. There's a choice here. My favorite formula is to add ½ pint of cream and 1 or 2 cans of cream of celery soup. This makes a fairly concentrated chowder that can be thinned a bit by adding some milk, if desired. Other versions call only for adding milk or evaporated milk. (Some folks don't add the milk until they serve the chowder. Then they put about 2 tablespoons of evaporated milk into each bowl and pour the hot chowder over it.) The proportions are not very critical, except don't add too much. The clam flavor should predominate.

After adding the milk or soup, the chowder must not be allowed to boil, because boiling will curdle it. Just let it steam, covered, on the back of the stove, safely below the boiling point. Taste it to see what it needs. It's probably delicious as is, and will get even better if allowed to cool and stand in the refrigerator overnight. When freshly prepared, or reheated, ladle it into bowls. Sprinkle some of the crispy salt pork bits over the top, and serve it with pilot crackers. That, my friends, is New England clam chowder —and never let the flavor of tomato come within a mile of it!

Clam chowder can be the mainstay of a cookout on the beach. Make it in a Dutch oven in the coals of a driftwood fire. Let people help dig the clams, and bring along the other ingredients.

Clam Fritters

    3 eggs
    2 tablespoons evaporated milk
    3 cups or more ground or chopped clams
    ½ cup flour
    2 teaspoons baking powder
    ½ teaspoon parsley flakes
    2 teaspoons minced onion
    ½ teaspoon salt
    Dash of pepper

Beat the eggs with the milk. Stir in all other ingredients. Drop by the tablespoonful into very hot (not smoking) fat, and fry until golden brown. Drain on absorbent paper and serve while hot.

Clam fritters go well with clam chowder. Let the chowder stay hot on the back of the stove while making the fritters.

Clam and Noodle Soup

    1 package dry noodles
    1 quart milk
    2 cups or 2 cans minced clams
    1 teaspoon butter
    Salt and pepper to taste

Cook the noodles in salted water until done. Drain, and add the other ingredients. Allow the soup to heat thoroughly, without boiling. If milk is not available, diluted evaporated milk or diluted canned cream soup makes a good substitute and an interesting variation.

Fried Clams

    1 quart medium-sized hard-shell clams
      (shells removed)
    1 egg
    1 tablespoon whole or evaporated milk
    1 scant teaspoon salt
    Dash of black pepper
    2 cups bacon fat
    2 cups ground cracker crumbs or potato chips

Drain liquid from the whole clams. Make a batter by beating together the egg, milk, and seasoning. Dip the clams individually in the batter and coat them with the crumbs. Lay them in a frying pan containing the very hot (but not smoking) fat, and fry until golden brown, turning carefully only once. Drain on absorbent paper and serve very hot, either as is or with a tomato sauce.

Roast Clams

This is a good way to prepare clams if you don't like to shuck them. All you need is the hard-shell clams and melted butter.

Set the whole clams on the grid over a bed of hot coals and let them sit there until they open and are hot. Lift them off (using tongs or gloves); twist off the top shell; add a little butter and serve. (This is another idea for a beach party!)

Steamed Clams

You'll need about a quart per person of the soft-shell type of clams known as "steamers." Wash them thoroughly; if possible leave them in a bucket of cold sea water for a few hours so they will cleanse themselves of grit. Put them in a covered pan containing about a cup, or a little less, of water. Put this over a hot fire until the clams are thoroughly steamed and have opened slightly. Put each portion of clams in a big bowl or soup plate, and let each person shuck his clams and dip them in melted butter. When the clams are removed from the steamer, decant the broth into coffee cups to sip while eating the clams.

To avoid the chance of including a dead clam, discard any with shells slightly open before steaming them. After they are steamed, discard any with unopened shells. While the soft-shell type of clam usually is used for this dish, small hard-shell clams can be cooked in the same manner.

CRABS

Crabbing is a happy summer sport when we're where we can catch crabs big enough to bother with. Soft-shell crabs (those who very recently have discarded their old shells and are beginning to grow new ones) are excellent, shell and all. The meat is extracted from hard-shell crabs to provide a variety of succulent dishes. Giant crabs, such as the West Coast Dungeness variety, are treated very much like lobsters.

If you're so fortunate as to obtain some soft-shell crabs, try preparing them indoors or outdoors this way:

Grilled Soft-Shell Crabs

Dress the crab by cutting off the face just back of the eyes with a pair of strong kitchen scissors. Pull off the apron (the part of the shell that looks like one) and remove all spongy parts (gills, intestines, and stomach). Wash in cold water and drain. Make a sauce by heating the following together:

> ¾ cup chopped parsley
> ¼ teaspoon nutmeg
> Dash of Tabasco sauce
> ½ cup butter
> 1 teaspoon lemon juice
> ¼ teaspoon soy sauce

Baste the crabs with the sauce and fit them close together in a hinged broiler. Broil about 6 inches above a bed of coals for 15 to 20 minutes until lightly browned. Turn and baste about four times. Serve with lemon wedges and Tartar Sauce.

Large hard-shell crabs should be tied up for convenience in cooking. Fold the large claws over the body and tie them there with string.

To prepare hard-shell crabs, plunge them into boiling water for a few minutes until they have changed color. Pour off the water and allow them to cool. Break off the claws and pry off the backs, removing the spongy parts inside. On the belly of the crab will be an apron-shaped section of shell. Pull this off and break the remaining body in two. Using a nut pick and other tools, remove all meat in as large pieces as possible. Feel each body piece, and remove every bit of shell or cartilage. With the resulting plate of crab meat, we are ready for business:

Crab Cakes I

> 1 quart crab meat
> 1 cup evaporated milk, cream, or rich milk
> 2 cups cracker crumbs
> ½ teaspoon powdered mustard
> 1 teaspoon Worcestershire sauce
> ¼ teaspoon pepper
> 1 egg
> 2 cups cracker crumbs, corn meal, or rolled potato chip crumbs
> Deep fat

Blend all ingredients except the cracker crumbs and fat. Fashion the mixture into hamburg-sized patties, roll in cracker crumbs, and fry in very hot (not smoking) fat until golden brown. Drain on absorbent paper and serve.

Crab Cakes II

> 1 pint crab meat
> 1 cup mashed potatoes
> 1 egg, beaten
> ½ teaspoon onion or celery salt
> Dash of pepper
> Deep bacon fat

Blend all ingredients except fat. Fashion into patties. Fry in very hot (not smoking) fat until golden brown. Drain on absorbent paper and serve.

Crab Sandwich

In a skillet, blend a large amount of crab meat with a moderate amount of barbecue sauce. When heated thoroughly, pour over toast or toasted buns.

Recipes for barbecue sauces will be found in Chapter Fifteen. Here's one that goes well with this dish:

> 1 bottle catsup
> ½ teaspoon fresh grated horse radish
> ½ teaspoon sugar
> 1 teaspoon salt
> 1 tablespoon Worcestershire sauce
> ½ teaspoon dried orégano or thyme

Blend all ingredients with a small amount of water and simmer together for a few minutes.

This sauce is for people who like highly flavored food. I do—but not with sea food. Try sautéing the crab meat with a small amount of butter and a dash of salt and of an herb. Don't bother with the barbecue sauce. This will provide the flavor of crab meat—which seems to be the point, in this case.

Crab Salad

> 1 pint crab meat
> ½ cup mayonnaise
> 1 cup chopped celery
> 1 tablespoon minced onion
> 1 tablespoon minced pickle
> 1 hard-boiled egg, chopped
> Salt and pepper to taste

Combine all ingredients; chill thoroughly, and serve on lettuce leaves. Add a dash of paprika to each serving. (This recipe can be cut down to the mayonnaise and seasoning, adding whatever else of the above is handy.)

Crab Sauté

>1 pint crab meat
>1 cube butter
>1 teaspoon finely chopped parsley
>Salt and pepper to taste
>½ lemon, cut in wedges

Melt butter, and add crab meat and parsley. Season to taste. Mix this in a skillet until lightly browned. Serve with lemon.

A variation of this is to add a little white wine to the pan after serving the crab meat. When this is heated, pour it over the crab meat. Another variation is to stir 1 tablespoon chopped chives and 1 tablespoon chopped parsley into the crab meat while it is being cooked.

CRAYFISH

After catching the crayfish, keep them alive in a pail of water. When ready to cook, pour them in a pail of lukewarm, strongly salted water to cleanse them.

Boiled Crayfish

To a pot of boiling water, add:

>2 bay leaves
>1 tablespoon caraway seed
>1 teaspoon celery seed
>2 chili or red peppers, chopped
>1 tablespoon salt
>1 teaspoon vinegar
>½ teaspoon orégano

(Some of these can be eliminated, but the combination helps the flavor.)

Add to the boiling water containing the other ingredients about a gallon (or as many as you have) of the live crayfish. Boil them until they are bright red. Pour off water and serve.

To eat crayfish, break off the tail center fin, which should remove the intestine. Remove from shell and eat as is, or with melted butter.

Fried Crayfish

Boil crayfish as above, and remove meat. Roll the tails in corn meal or cracker crumbs, and fry in bacon fat to a golden brown. Dip in beaten egg before rolling in the crumbs, if you prefer.

EELS

Lots of people don't eat eels, mainly, I suppose, because of their unglamorous appearance. They are slimy things that have to be rolled up in a rag in order to hold them while removing the hook. In frontier times they were trapped in vast quantities, to be salted or smoked as a highly prized food delicacy. Regardless of their appearance, they are well worth eating, and perhaps modern fishermen should learn how to catch and prepare them.

To dress an eel, dip it in boiling water to loosen the skin. Then nail it by the head to a log or something. Cut the skin around the head and work it loose enough to grasp it with one or two pairs of pliers. Then pull it back, down the body. Then cut the body open to remove entrails; wash thoroughly in salted water, and slice in 2-inch sections. Parboiling until the meat is partly cooked will improve texture and eliminate most of the fat, thus improving flavor. This done, we can prepare the following dishes:

Boiled Eel

>2 pounds eel, prepared as above
>3 cups water (or fish stock, preferably)
>1 teaspoon salt
>¼ pound butter, melted
>1 tablespoon minced parsley

Simmer the eel in salted water or fish stock for about 10 minutes, or until flesh flakes off the bone. Serve hot with melted butter garnished with parsley.

Broiled Eel

Remove bones from eel prepared as directed. Season the meat with salt and pepper, and broil on grill until golden brown. Serve with lemon butter. (If the meat might fall through the grating on the grill, lay a section of fly screening or ½-inch wire mesh over it, and broil the eel on this.)

Eel Stew

>3 pounds eel, prepared as directed
>2 teaspoons salt
>1 teaspoon vinegar
>1 tablespoon finely chopped parsley
>2 tablespoons flour
>2 tablespoons butter (or more)
>Dash of pepper

Put the eel sections in a pot with enough water to cover. Add salt, vinegar, and parsley. Cover and cook slowly until tender. Make a paste of the flour in a little cold water, and add this. Also add butter, and season with pepper (and more salt, if necessary) to taste. When the stew thickens, ladle the eel onto hot toast and add some of the gravy.

Fried Eel

Dip eel sections (prepared as directed) in beaten egg. Roll in corn meal or cracker crumbs, and fry in very hot (not smoking) fat until golden brown.

Fried Eel with Onion

1 pound eel (prepared as directed)
6 onions, sliced fine
1 green pepper, sliced fine
1 cup milk
Salt and pepper to taste
2 cups cracker crumbs or bread crumbs
⅓ cup cooking fat

Fry the onions and pepper in the fat in a skillet, adding enough water to prevent them from sticking. Dip the eel sections in milk; dust with salt and pepper; roll in crumbs, and fry in the fat with the vegetables until the eel is browned and the vegetables are done. Serve eel garnished with the vegetables.

FROGS' LEGS

Here is a convenient and inexpensive delicacy that usually gets far less attention than it deserves. (I said "inexpensive"—but did you ever price them in city restaurants?) Frogs' legs are as easy to prepare as trout, and fully as delicious.

The first time I ever had frogs' legs was when I visited a doctor at his camp on a lake in Massachusetts. We went out in the canoe one night to catch a mess of frogs, using old fly rods with small red flannel cloth strips impaled on the hooks. We would spot big frogs in the beam of a flashlight, lower the bait to them, and put them in a sack when hooked. Frogs will jump at red flannel almost every time.

Soon we had enough frogs, and we set the sack in the kitchen temporarily. Unfortunately, the sack tipped over, and the frogs fled to every cor-

ner of the camp. Catching them the second time was far more trouble than the first. A yell from our hostess' bedroom late that night indicated that at least one frog was still at large. It turned out that she had stepped on him while walking barefoot in the dark. Probably the least a guest should do when he parks his frogs in a strange kitchen is to tie the bag securely!

Most people just cut off the hind legs of frogs (like the leg and second joint of a chicken). Some say this is wasteful, because the front leg meat also is good. This school of thought cuts off head and feet, and peels off the skin, which comes off as easily as a glove. Then they clean the frog and wash the meat in cold water. I'll settle for the hind legs, which may be wasteful, but easier. Cut them off at the body; cut off the feet and peel off the skin. Also remember that there are white cord muscles in each of the legs. If you don't pull these out, the reflex action of the legs, when in the heat of the skillet, will make the legs jump. This often makes the ladies nervous and usually ends up with bigger servings of frogs' legs for the men!

Some people recommend soaking the legs for an hour or so in a mixture of equal parts of lemon juice and water, seasoned with salt and pepper. Others just wipe the skinned legs with a damp cloth, on the theory that flavor is lost by washing. Anyway, here are some ways to prepare frogs' legs:

Fried Frogs' Legs

This is the most popular and easiest way to cook frogs' legs:

Frogs' legs (prepared as above)
Salt and pepper
Rolled crumbs (cracker, bread, potato chip, etc.)
Egg(s), beaten
Deep fat

Sprinkle the legs with salt and pepper. Roll in crumbs; dip in egg, and roll in crumbs again. Fry in very hot (not smoking) fat for about 3 minutes, until golden brown. Drain, and serve with melted butter or with Tartar Sauce.

Another way is merely to season the legs, roll them in flour, and fry in hot fat (375°).

Frogs' Legs Newburg

2 tablespoons butter
½ cup white wine
3 egg yolks
½ pint cream
Salt and pepper to taste

Prepare fried frogs' legs as in the above recipe. In a saucepan, boil the butter and wine for 3 or 4 minutes to reduce the wine. Beat the egg yolks and add cream and yolks to the wine and butter. Cook slowly for 2 or 3 minutes more, stirring constantly, until the sauce thickens. Season to taste and pour the sauce over the legs.

Sautéed Frogs' Legs

2 pounds or so of frogs' legs, prepared as
  directed
¼ cup flour
Dash of pepper
¼ cup butter
1 teaspoon grated onion
½ teaspoon salt

Roll the legs in seasoned flour. Sauté the onion in the butter in a skillet; add the frogs' legs, and cook, covered, over low heat about 15 minutes, until the legs are lightly browned and tender.

LOBSTERS

Among all the goodies from the sea, lobster is one of the best—when it is properly prepared. In fact it usually is good even when cooks louse it up—and most of them do, even including some of the very best restaurants. As a New Englander born and raised in lobster country, I find it difficult to understand why so few people and so few restaurants know how to prepare lobsters properly. I shall have the presumption to try to set them straight.

If you have a choice in the matter, selection of lobsters is important. The best ones come from very cold water, where they grow firmer fleshed and more flavorful. This means from the coast of Maine, or farther north. My preference is to select females of about 2 pounds, or slightly larger. The really big ones are tougher, and the very small ones are more trouble to prepare for what you get out of them. Why females? Because, in season, most of them contain roe (or coral), which is an extra added inducement. How do you tell females from males? It's as easy as with people, but ask your lobsterman.

Always select lobsters that are very much alive—and prepare them yourself. Avoid those with soft shells—the "shedders"—which may be foisted off on you during the season. If much time must elapse between buying and preparation, pack them in damp seaweed and keep them cold. They will keep in the refrigerator (in a punctured bag) for several hours, but the sooner they are used, the better.

Southern "lobsters," and those from the West Coast, are "spiny crayfish," without large claws. They are prepared in a very similar manner.

HOW TO CLEAN A LOBSTER

Baked or broiled lobster must be split and cleaned before cooking. It's easy. Put a breadboard or cutting board next to the sink, and use for tools a very stiff-bladed large sharp knife and an ordinary kitchen fork. If you want to cut off all the claws (and I always do, for reasons stated in the recipes), grasp the lobster by the back on the board, and cut them off, flipping them into the sink (for use later). Hold the lobster on its back and drive the knife into him through the chest, continuing the cut down the middle of the tail. Now lay the knife against the head part, on the same line with the lower cut, and split the head open. Put down the knife and break the lobster open, without separating the halves. (You don't cut through the bottom, or back, of the shell.)

With the lobster held open, use the fork to flip out the stomach, which is an oysterlike sac in the head, filled with undesirable matter. Also remove (with your fingers) the anal canal—a brown-red vein running from stomach to tail. Rinse out any discoloration from the body, but don't remove the light green or yellow fat, or the dark green roe. These are delicious. Now the lobster is ready for stuffing, or for baking or broiling without stuffing.

Boiled lobsters are boiled live, without cleaning. But you should remove the stomach and anal vein when you split them after they are cooked.

Baked Stuffed Lobster (a la Stickney)

At the beginning of Chapter Eleven, I mentioned visiting Warden Supervisor Joseph Stickney at his camp in Maine before our annual fishing trips. Joe was the finest lobster cook I ever knew. This is his recipe.

Prepare the lobsters as above, and make a stuffing. The following proportions should be about right for 4 2-pound lobsters:

> 3 *cups "Ritz" crackers, rolled into fairly fine crumbs*
> 1 *rounded tablespoon mayonnaise*
> 2 *tablespoons butter, melted*
> ½ *teaspoon salt*
> 1 *tablespoon Worcestershire sauce*

Combine all ingredients in a bowl, stirring and chopping until the crackers are coated with the mayonnaise and butter. They should be thoroughly coated but not soggy. (This dressing definitely is best when "Ritz" crackers are used.)

Now, remember that we have flipped all the claws into the sink. Fish out the big ones; remove pegs, and rinse them. Lay them aside. The little claws (8 of them per lobster) will be of two types—with double and single jaws. Separate them, and put the two rinsed piles together.

Now poke some of the stuffing into the body cavity, all the way down to the tail. Put 4 double-jawed small claws into the body cavity, chevron-wise. Add more stuffing over them. When each lobster is stuffed, lay it in a pan, arranging them head to tail alternately, side by side. The tails can be allowed to curl up. Put the 2 large claws (for each lobster) between the bodies, all fitted neatly on the bottom of the pan. Sprinkle the remaining pile of small claws over the top of the lobsters. (They are a garnish only.)

If you're cooking indoors, preheat the oven to 500°. Put only enough water in the pan of lobsters to cover the bottom. When the oven is hot, put in the pan of lobsters and bake them until they are bright red. This will take at least 20 minutes—maybe 30 for large lobsters. When they are done, put them under the broiler for a minute if the stuffing is not brown on top.

Set a lobster body on each plate, with a right and left large claw beside it. Crack the large claws before serving, if you wish. Serve with plenty of melted butter—a dish for each person to dunk the meat in. Put a large bowl in the middle of the table for refuse.

Finally, don't overbake the lobsters, or they'll get mushy and lose flavor. Take them out when bright red. The coral (roe) also should be cooked red, but it's very edible even if it isn't. I think you'll find the stuffing delicious, and the meat in the large claws will be moist—not dried up, as with broiled lobsters.

Here are some variations in stuffing—which may be gilding the lily a bit. If you have a can of lobster paste, stir it in with the stuffing. If there is any lobster meat left over from yesterday, dice it up and add it to the stuffing. If you have any fresh scallops, do the same. Some people pour a little melted butter over the stuffing in the lobsters before baking. This may make the stuffing soggy, and it is unnecessary. Some folks like to add a little sherry to the stuffing. This makes it soggy and doesn't seem to contribute anything. Let's not monkey with perfection.

Boiled Lobster

Now you'd think that boiling a lobster is about as simple as boiling an egg—but there's a lot more to it than that. Most people slide the live lobsters into boiling water until they turn red. Whether or not they overcook them isn't the point. Immersing a lobster in boiling water soaks out juices and flavor you probably are paying well over a dollar a pound for. Try it this way.

Put a layer of golf-ball-sized clean stones in the pot to about 2 inches deep. Add water only to the top of the stones. Add 1 teaspoon or more of salt. Bring this to a boil—and then put in the lobsters. They will steam instead of soak, and will be far more flavorful and less soggy than if you had used the dunking method. Split them open and clean them, as previously described, and serve with melted butter, to which a little chopped parsley or other suitable herb could be added. (They also are excellent served cold with mayonnaise.)

Of course it's not necessary to use stones to keep the lobsters above the water if you have a little wire rack or something else that will serve the same purpose. In preparing boiled lobster on beach parties, clean sea water is preferable to tap water.

Broiled Lobster

Split and clean each lobster, as previously described. Spread them open and fit them into a wire broiler. Brush the meat liberally with butter and put the broiler about 8 inches above the coals (depending on the heat of the fire) with the opened lobsters facing upward. Broil until the shells are bright red—about 15 minutes. Brush again with butter occasionally, so the lobsters won't dry out. Season with a little salt and pepper, and serve with more melted butter and lemon wedges.

Optionally, the big claws can be cut off before cooking, and they can be prepared as per Boiled Lobster, above. This makes the claw meat moist instead of dry, and allows it to be removed from the claws more easily.

Lobster Stew

2 lobsters of 2 pounds each or so
(or more smaller ones)
4 tablespoons butter
Dash of paprika
1 pint half milk and half cream
Salt and pepper to taste

Boil the lobsters until barely done. Let cool, and remove meat, fat, and roe. Cut meat into bite-sized pieces.

Put the butter in an iron skillet and melt it over low heat. Add lobster pieces, roe, and fat. Season with salt, pepper, and paprika (for color). Sauté lobster slowly until hot, then add the milk and cream. Heat but do not allow the milk to boil. When hot, serve in bowls, with crackers.

Lobster Newburg

2 lobsters, prepared as for Lobster Stew
2 tablespoons butter
Dash of paprika
Dash of salt
1 teaspoon lemon juice
1 cup cream
3 egg yolks

Put the lobster meat in a chafing dish or double boiler. Add the butter, paprika, salt, and lemon juice (to taste). Beat the cream and egg yolks until smooth, and stir into the lobster. Stir constantly over slow heat until the newburg begins to thicken. Do not allow to boil.

In place of the egg yolks, you can blend 1 teaspoon flour with a little butter and stir this into the newburg with the cream.

Sautéed Lobster

1 pound lobster meat (prepared as for Lobster Stew)
4 tablespoons butter

Salt and pepper to taste
½ teaspoon finely chopped parsley
Lemon wedges

Heat the butter over a slow fire until it melts. Add lobster meat and toss in the skillet. Season with salt and pepper. Add chopped parsley. Cook only until hot. Serve with lemon wedges.

OYSTERS

Broiled Oysters

1 dozen oysters, removed from shells
½ cup white wine
1 garlic clove, sliced
Dash of pepper
6 strips bacon
12 toothpicks

Drain the oysters and soak them for an hour or so in the wine, with garlic and pepper added. Drain them again and wrap each oyster in half a strip of bacon, fastening it with a toothpick. Broil on a grid over coals until the bacon is crisp. (This is a good dish to broil on a hibachi; see Chapter Nine.)

Oyster Chowder

This is a favorite North Carolina recipe.
1 pint oysters
3 tablespoons chopped onion
3 tablespoons butter
1 cup water
⅔ cup diced celery
2 cups diced potatoes
1 teaspoon salt
½ teaspoon pepper
1 quart milk
1 teaspoon chopped parsley

Fry the onion lightly in butter until slightly browned. Add water, celery, potatoes, salt, and pepper. Cook until potatoes are done. Simmer oysters in their liquor only until edges begin to curl. Heat milk very hot, but not boiling. Add milk to vegetables. Drain oysters, and add them to milk and vegetables. Serve in bowls, with parsley sprinkled over the top.

Roast Oysters

Prepare as for Roast Clams.

Oyster Stew

1 pint oysters, removed from shell
2 tablespoons butter
1 pint milk

1 *pint cream*
Salt, pepper, paprika

Sauté the oysters in butter in an iron skillet until the edges begin to curl. Add milk, cream, salt, pepper, and a dash of paprika (for color). Season to taste. Heat but do not allow to boil. Serve in bowls, with crackers.

SCALLOPS

Broiled Scallops

Dry the scallops on absorbent paper and put them in a buttered pan. Add a little salt and pepper, and brush them with melted butter. Put them under the broiler only until they begin to turn light brown. Bay (or Cape) scallops are the very small ones, and will be done in 2 or 3 minutes. Sea scallops are the big (marshmallow-sized) ones, and they will be done in about 5 minutes. No need to turn them. Fresh scallops are excellent to eat when raw, so don't overcook them.

Breaded Scallops

Prepare a buttered bread crumb mixture by putting about 1 quart of bread crumbs in a skillet and adding 4 tablespoons butter and 1 teaspoon herb blend, plus 1 teaspoon salt and a dash of pepper. Melt the butter over very low heat, and stir until crumbs are coated. Don't add enough butter to make the crumbs sticky. They should remain dry. Use slow heat, and stir constantly to avoid burning. These buttered crumbs can be kept in a jar in the refrigerator for use on fish and sea food dishes of several kinds.

Put a pint or so of scallops in a wide pan and pour enough buttered crumbs over them to coat them. Using a spatula, or something similar, toss them about until well coated. Put them under the broiler for a minute (2 minutes for the big scallops), or until beginning to brown. Toss again (or turn) and broil a minute or so more. The object is to brown them and heat them, but not to overcook them. Serve with Tartar Sauce.

Scallop Stew

1 *pint scallops*
Salt, pepper, paprika
1 *pint milk*
1 *pint cream*
2 *tablespoons butter*

Sauté the scallops lightly in butter, adding seasoning. If they are large (sea) scallops, cut each one in bite-sized pieces. As soon as they are heated (about 2 minutes) add the milk and cream. Heat but don't allow the milk to boil. Serve in bowls, with crackers.

SHRIMPS

When possible, purchase shrimps, raw, rather than cooked, because they can be more flavorfully prepared at home. They can be cleaned easily either raw or cooked, merely by breaking off the shells and by removing the black vein with a paring knife or skewer. Hold the shrimp in one hand, and use the other to break off the underbody. Then pull off the top shell. Usually the tail is left on, because this makes them easier to handle. The tail is crispy and delicious when broiled or fried.

Boiled Shrimp I

The easy way is merely to put the shrimp in a quart of rapidly boiling water to which 1 teaspoon salt has been added. When the water comes to a boil again, let the shrimp boil for not over 5 minutes; then pour off the water and let them cool. It is far better to undercook them than to overcook them.

If you want your shrimp to taste a bit more exotic, try this recipe for:

Boiled Shrimp II

3 *pounds fresh shrimp*
½ *jar prepared mustard with horse radish*
3 *tablespoons red pepper*
3 *tablespoons black pepper*
2 *tablespoons paprika*
1 *tablespoon garlic salt*
5 *crushed bay leaves*
½ *cup salt*
1 *can beer or ale*
1 *cup vinegar*

Put all in a kettle. Cover and bring to a boil. Turn shrimp over several times while cooking. Boil 12 to 15 minutes—until tails become pink. Sample to tell if sufficiently cooked. Add more salt, if desired. (This is one of the most popular recipes for boiling shrimp.)

Broiled Shrimp

Clean the raw shrimp; dip them in butter; season, and broil them under the broiler at home or on wire mesh over an open fire. Brush with more butter after turning. Broil only until the shrimp reach a bright pink color. Many people prefer using garlic butter.

Fried Shrimp

Dip in batter and fry as for Frogs' Legs.

Grilled Shrimp

> 2 *pounds large fresh or frozen shrimp*
> ¾ *cup vegetable oil (olive oil is too strong)*
> 2 *teaspoons salt*
> 4 *tablespoons chopped parsley*
> ½ *teaspoon cayenne pepper*
> ¼ *teaspoon dry mustard*
> 1½ *cloves garlic*

Remove shells and devein, leaving on tails. Put the shrimp in a bowl with ¼ cup oil and 1 teaspoon salt. Allow to marinate in refrigerator for a few hours, or overnight.

Mix chopped parsley, remaining salad oil, cayenne pepper, and dry mustard. Crush garlic and stir into mixture. Let this stand in refrigerator also.

About an hour before cooking, combine the two mixtures. Toss together, and allow to marinate nearly an hour more. Then put shrimp on grill over very low fire; brush with sauce, and turn over when the shrimp begin to turn pink. Brush again with sauce, and finish grilling. Serve very hot.

Half-inch wire mesh screening is excellent when placed over the grill or open fire for broiling small foods such as this.

LET'S HAVE A CLAMBAKE!

Clambakes for 4 or more people are easy, so it's a wonder that more people on seaside vacations don't try them. In fact, we can do them almost as well in our own back yards.

Given the eatables, which always are clams, lobsters, and corn, and possibly chicken halves and sweet or white potatoes, plus the traditional beer and watermelon, we can enjoy a clambake almost anywhere with a minimum of equipment. This must include a canvas tarpaulin 8 feet square, or larger, which has no holes through which steam could escape. It also includes the

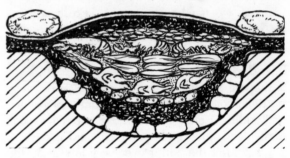

usual paper plates, cups, etc., plus plenty of butter, lemons, salt, and pepper.

Let's talk about a small bake for from 4 to 12 people. This could be expanded to more, but then we begin to get into the commercial type, which usually is handled by professionals.

Find a secluded spot on the beach near which are rocks festooned with rockweed at low tide. (Rockweed is the long, lacy, dark green type of seaweed that has many small egg-shaped pods that pop when pressed.) Assign two people to dig a hole (well above high-tide mark) about 3 feet deep and 4 feet in diameter. Line this with plenty of *dry* rocks. (Use dry rocks, because fire could explode wet ones.) Have another pile of smaller rocks and big pebbles nearby. Also assign another crew to gather dry driftwood—lots of it. Meanwhile, at low tide, other people are gathering rockweed and piling it on the tarpaulin, which is folded over the weed to keep it from drying.

Build a big fire on the rocks in the hole, adding the smaller rocks on top of the wood. When the

A BEACH CLAMBAKE

In this method of preparing a clambake, foods are piled on a square of heavy wire mesh over a pit of hot rocks and coals. They are covered with rockweed and by a tarpaulin to keep heat and steam inside. The tarpaulin is held down by rocks and sand around its edges. (Evinrude) fire has burned down, use a board or big stick to push the out-of-place rocks so all will be in the shape of a rock-lined bowl. Tamp down any embers that remain.

Now, the commissary department should be ready with the food, and we should work fast, before the rocks cool. Throw a layer of rockweed on the rocks to a depth of 6 inches. On this lay a layer of potatoes, a layer of chicken, a layer of corn, a layer of lobsters, and, on top, a layer of clams. Quickly throw another layer of rockweed on top of all this, to make a top layer 6 inches deep. Throw the tarpaulin over the bake and anchor the canvas down with stones and sand, so no steam can escape. With this done, take a swim to work up an appetite for dinner.

In an hour the food should be cooked. If the bake is for more than 10 or 12 people, allow a little longer. Pull up a corner of the tarpaulin and test a potato. If it is done, the bake is ready. The juices from the clams and lobsters have dripped down through chicken and vegetables, flavoring everything nicely. Serve the clams first, with melted butter. Lobster next, with vegetables; then chicken (if you have included it), and finally the watermelon. Between servings, keep the tarpaulin over the food to keep things hot.

There are a few optional refinements, which include removing the silk (but not the husks) from the corn, and putting the clams in individual cloth (sugar sack) bags before putting these things in the bake. The clams are washed before cooking (to remove sand), and the potatoes are washed, perhaps cutting the skin off the ends to help them steam properly. Some people brown the chicken halves over an open fire before putting them in the bake. If everybody likes lobster, the chicken may be superfluous.

This is the basic idea of a clambake—a bed of hot rocks, an insulation of seaweed on top and bottom of the food, and a tarpaulin over the bake to hold in the steam (which does the cooking).

There are other ways to rig a clambake, but this one is the historic and authentic Maine version—and I think it is the easiest and the best. Other ways include doing the steaming in a barrel of one sort or another. Also, we can do small individual bakes on the home grill, using aluminum foil. For each person, use a full-width strip of foil about a yard long, and on it lay a piece of cheesecloth. On this put a dozen or so clams, a lobster, a potato, and an ear of corn. Over this pour a cup of water. Wrap this in the cheesecloth, and wrap the package in foil, using foldovers on the edges to make a tight package. Wrap the packages in a second covering of foil. Put them on the grill, covered with a hood, and steam them for about an hour—until the potatoes are done.

In doing the authentic Maine-type clambake in inland regions where rockweed is unobtainable, we can substitute ferns or green leaves—but this decidedly is a second choice, and the foil method seems preferable to it.

The usual clambake ration for 4 people is:

4 dozen clams
4 white or sweet potatoes
8 ears of corn
4 live lobsters (1½ to 2 pounds)
4 chicken halves (optional)
4 peeled onions (optional)
2 lemons (in wedges)
1 pound melted butter
Salt and pepper

Allow plenty of time to prepare the bake and to cook the food. When on a vacation, time is abundant, and every minute of the process is a lot of fun!

(Boy Scouts of America)

Build a big fire on the rocks in the hole. When the fire has burned down, tramp down any embers that remain. Throw a layer of rockweed on the rocks to a depth of about six inches.

On this, lay a layer of potatoes, of chicken, of corn, of lobsters and, on top, a layer of clams. Quickly throw a layer of rockweed on top of all this.

Throw the tarpaulin over the bake and anchor it down with stones and sand, so no steam can escape.

In an hour the food should be cooked. Pull up a corner of the tarpaulin and test a potato. If it is done, the bake is ready.

Now serve the food for a delicious Maine-style clambake. Keep the cover over the bake to keep food hot until it is served.

Chapter Thirteen

RECIPES FOR FOUR-FOOTED GAME

Sky Lodge, our temporary base in the primeval Jackman region of northwestern Maine, boasted one of the most beaten-up Jeeps still running. This refugee from the junk yard evidently prided itself in always getting there and always getting back—over "roads" so called because once logging sleds had cruised them. This was before saplings and small spruces started growing there; before the log bridges had rotted and washed away; and before the snows and rains had turned whatever was left into rocky gullys. You needed the Jeep to get there quickly, and it was essential for bringing your deer or bear out, because the best hunting country, as usual, is way back of beyond.

Cyril, who was guiding, knew the country well. He knew it well even back in Prohibition days, when he was engaged in the importing of certain bottled liquids toted on his back over the wilderness trails crossing the nearby border of Canada.

While I slipped .44 cartridges into my little Ruger carbine, Cyril gave us the plan of attack.

"You continue down the road," he said to me. "Where she forks, turn left. She poops out in a meadow about three miles down. Go up on the ridge, and turn east. Bear signs there. You'll come to a draw, so start working down before she gets too steep. Pick a spot where you can cover the draw, and wait for me. If you haven't your deer by then, I'll be driving one out to you."

Walking alone, slowly, quietly, and observantly, in the wilderness is an experience more meaningful to me than going to church, because this woodland truly is God's country. A fox looks back inquiringly as he sneaks behind a ledge. A porcupine squeaks and grunts when taken by surprise before he can scramble to safety in his den tree. Here, a buck and two does crossed the night before. Tracks show a moose walked here yesterday. In one of them is a wildcat track, obviously very fresh. A pileated woodpecker flies to a dead spruce, his red head bobbing like a trip hammer while he pecks out a grub. A chipmunk circles around, running along one fallen log and then another, until he draws near enough to satisfy his curiosity. The chickadees know no fear, as they flit nearby, talking to each other. Moss on the rotted logs seems hundreds of years old—a flower garden in miniature on close inspection. Bears have been in the beech trees and ripped off great branches. The leaves are turning. It will be cold tonight. This is God's country—and it will stay so until people put roads through it and drive the wild life away, leaving tin cans and refuse instead. It's long past the time when we should have learned better.

I wanted a young, fat buck, but all I had seen were does. Soon after I reached the draw, Cyril came through. "Ben's got a nice buck," he said. "Let's get the Jeep and get him out tonight."

We managed to get the Jeep so close that we only had to drag the deer about a hundred yards. He was dressed and loaded before sunset.

Cyril eyed the still warm deer liver appreciatively. He pulled his rucksack from the Jeep while I built a fire. Ben dipped water into the blackened pot, loaded it with coffee, and put the pot on a dingle stick over the fire. Cyril got bacon sputtering in the skillet and sliced some onions into it. While these were sautéing in the fat, he cut thin slices from the liver and rolled them in flour. When the onions were nearly done, he pushed them aside in the skillet and added the liver, with a shake of salt and pepper. "Dark outside, pink inside, and fresh from the critter," said Cyril, smacking his lips. "That's the only way to eat liver!"

We made sandwiches with the liver, bacon, and onions, and we ate them, washed down with hot, black coffee. I never have been very partial to liver but, this time, I came back for thirds. Cyril is a guide who knows about outdoor cooking. The liver was delicate and delicious.

ON THE DRESSING AND TRANSPORTING OF DEER AND OTHER BIG ANIMALS

The average hunter risks having two strikes against him before he even starts to cook. He must be selective enough—or lucky enough—to get a good animal. He then must dress it properly and get it to the freezer in prime condition.

Let's take deer, for instance. The opening of the hunting season in the fall usually occurs about the time of the rutting moon—the relatively short annual period when deer fall in love. To make up for lost time, the bucks chase here and there after does, with the result that they grow lean and tough. Their meat may take on a less palatable flavor. The food they eat also affects the flavor of the meat. A deer that has fed on beech nuts and meadow grasses will taste far better than one that has browsed on evergreens —which is why deer from one area often are more flavorful than deer from another.

A game animal must be dressed immediately —and properly. The meat must cool quickly and must be kept cool. It must hang for a reasonable period to tenderize, in the same manner that packing houses treat sides of beef. By no means should it be draped over a car radiator on a long trip home for the flesh to heat and spoil and gather road dust. Treatment of other animals is similar. Proper preparation is more than half the battle. The culinary part is relatively minor.

Thus, if you (or your wife) belongs to the group who "tried it once and didn't like it,"

don't give up the enjoyment of what some may consider to be "far out" dishes prepared from animals such as bear, raccoon, and opossum. Even such borderline quadrupeds as muskrat, porcupine, and woodchuck can be prepared tastefully. I've even had old woodsmen tell me they enjoy eating skunk, but we probably should draw the line somewhere!

There are tricks in the preparation of a "good" animal after you get it. Here are some of them:

RECIPES FOR COOKING BEAR

Bear meat can be excellent when properly prepared. A young bear, taken in the late spring, is considered by many to be superior to pork— and bear meat is cooked very much like pork. A young animal does not need to have its meat marinated, although this helps to tenderize the meat and to remove the gamy taste. Older meat should always be marinated. Much of the gamy flavor of all game animals comes from the fat, which should be removed before preparation. Also cut out all sinews and other undesirable parts. Typical recipes for marinades for all four-footed game are given following these recipes for preparing bear.

Bear Steak

Marinate a bear loin steak overnight or for about 24 hours, and wipe it dry. Meanwhile, make a sauce as follows:

4 onions, sliced
3 tablespoons butter
1 cup water
Salt and pepper to taste
1 garlic clove, mashed
3 tablespoons finely chopped chives
1 teaspoon prepared mustard
2 tablespoons tomato paste
1 dash Worcestershire sauce

Sauté the onions in the water and butter until tender and until the water has nearly boiled away. Season with salt and pepper. Add remaining ingredients (some of which may be left out, if not handy), and simmer for a few minutes, adding a little more water if necessary.

Broil the bear steak to the desired degree of doneness. Transfer it to a platter and pour the sauce over it. Top this with mushrooms sautéed in butter, if available. A sprinkling of chopped parsley also helps.

Bear Steak Casserole

Marinate the steak overnight; wipe it dry, and cut it into 2- or 3-inch squares. Roll these in flour and fry in a little fat in a skillet until well browned. Transfer the meat to a casserole and pour over it the following mixture:

½ cup water
⅛ teaspoon garlic salt
½ teaspoon ground bay leaves
1 onion, chopped fine
Dash of pepper

Cover the casserole and bake for 1 to 1½ hours at 325°, adding a little more water if necessary. (This recipe can also be prepared outdoors in a Dutch oven.)

Braised Bear

Marinate a thick bear steak overnight. Wipe it dry, and sear it on both sides in a Dutch oven with a little cooking oil or bacon fat. When seared, add the following:

½ teaspoon garlic salt
Dash of pepper
½ teaspoon chili powder

Cover and let simmer for about 2 hours. Then add:

3 or 4 large onions, sliced
2 cans tomato soup

Continue cooking until the onions are done. If you desire the sauce to be thicker (like a gravy), stir 1 tablespoon flour with water to make a thin paste, and stir this into the ingredients in the pot until the mixture thickens. Add a little more water if the juices get too thick.

Bear Pot Roast

Marinate a rump roast overnight; dry it, and sprinkle it with flour, seasoned with garlic salt and pepper. Put 2 tablespoons vinegar (or fat) in a Dutch oven, and sear the meat on all sides. Cover, and cook at about 325° until tender— about 30 minutes per pound of meat. Add enough water from time to time to prevent the meat from sticking to the pot. About an hour before the meat is done, add some peeled raw parsnips, carrots, or potatoes.

If you'd like a cream gravy with this, put about 2 teaspoons flour into a little hot fat in a skillet and mix the two together, adding just enough fat for it to be absorbed into the flour. Then add some milk (or evaporated milk and water) and stir until the gravy thickens, adding enough milk to arrive at the right consistency. Add seasoning to taste.

If you have any dried rosemary, thyme, or other suitable herbs, add some to the roast. (You can be a bit generous with it.) If you have a can of pineapple that's not needed for anything else, broil a few slices and serve them with the roast.

Bear Stew

You can use one of the less tender cuts for this. Marinate the meat overnight; wipe it dry, and cut into 1½-inch cubes. Roll these in seasoned flour. (An easy way to do this is to season the flour and put it in a strong paper bag with the meat. Hold the bag closed, and shake.) Sear the meat thoroughly in a heavy skillet to which about 2 teaspoons bacon fat have been added. Then add the following:

2 cups dry red wine (to barely cover)
1 garlic clove, finely chopped
1 small bay leaf
Pinch of thyme

Bring this to a boil, cover tightly, and cook slowly for about 3 hours, until the meat is tender. Add more wine, if necessary. About half an hour before the meat is done, add about 3 carrots and 3 onions, sliced, and sautéed briefly in butter. Include some diced celery, if available.

A stew such as this allows considerable latitude in choice of vegetable ingredients. If the onions are small, put them in whole. Add cubed potatoes if you wish—or a can of peas or chili beans or tomatoes, depending on what you like or what is available.

MARINADES FOR GAME

No one seems to agree on the ideal marinade to tenderize and flavor wild game, and each outdoor cook eventually develops his own recipe, depending somewhat on what is available. We note, however, that most marinades are made up of wine and vinegar, plus an abundant variety of spices. Most marinades also contain chopped or sliced onion, because this seems to draw out some of the gamy taste, while also adding flavor. The meat should be covered by the marinade, and both should be placed in a crock or bowl that is *not* metal. Some cooks float ½ cup oil (preferably olive) on top of the marinade with the idea that this prevents the meat from discoloring and helps the marinade to retain its flavor. How long meats should be kept in the marinade is a matter of judgment. Tender game may not need to be marinated at all. The bear recipes recommended marinating overnight, or for about 24 hours. Very tough meat, or meat that you want to be spiced and very tender, may need to be marinated from 36 to 48 hours. My preference is for no marination, or as little as is necessary, because we like the flavor of properly prepared game. The marinating meat, of course, should be kept in a cool or cold place, such as a refrigerator. The use of so many ingredients may seem a bit wasteful until we realize that the marinade may be reused once or twice, and that some or all of it is used in the preparation of many of the recipes.

Marinade I

> 2 cups claret or other wine
> 2 cups vinegar (or 4 cups of either)
> 1 teaspoon Worcestershire sauce
> 1 bay leaf
> 2 whole cloves
> Pinch of salt

Marinade II

> 2 cups dry wine
> 2 cups white vinegar
> 6 bay leaves
> 12 whole cloves
> 1 tablespoon whole black pepper
> 1 large onion, sliced

Note that this one calls for a good deal more spices than the former one. How much or how little is largely a matter of personal preference.

Marinade III

> Juice of 1 lemon
> ½ cup tarragon wine vinegar
> 2 onions, sliced
> 1 teaspoon chili powder
> ½ cup water
> 2 teaspoons salt
> 2 bay leaves
> ¼ teaspoon black pepper
> ½ cup tomato catsup
> 1 garlic clove, crushed

Marinade IV

> 1 bottle dry white wine
> 1 cup vinegar
> ½ cup vegetable oil
> 1 large onion, sliced
> 2 large carrots, thinly sliced
> 4 shallots, chopped
> 3 sprigs parsley, chopped
> 1 teaspoon salt
> 6 peppercorns, cracked
> 3 to 4 juniper berries
> ¼ teaspoon thyme

In this one, it is best to put the vegetables around the meat and pour the liquids over it. The oil will rise to the top, and serves to retain the flavor of the marinade, as well as to prevent discoloration of the meat. You can leave out the juniper berries and add rosemary or tarragon with or in place of the thyme.

Cooked Marinade V

> 1 pound raw carrots
> 1 pound yellow onions
> ½ pound celery, including tops

Chop these together finely and sauté them in about 4 tablespoons lard or bacon fat without allowing the vegetables to take on color. Then add:

2 quarts vinegar
1 quart red wine
1 tablespoon chopped parsley
3 bay leaves, crumbled
1 teaspoon thyme
1 teaspoon peppercorns, crushed
1 tablespoon whole allspice
1 teaspoon salt

Boil the mixture and allow it to simmer, covered, for half an hour. Allow it to cool before adding the meat.

Note that the meat should always be covered by the marinade. If it is to be marinated for a long time, it is advisable to turn the meat in the marinade occasionally.

VENISON RECIPES

(These recipes also may be used for other antlered game, such as elk and antelope, as well as for domestic meats such as beef and lamb.)

In the following recipes we will assume that the meat has been marinated, if it is desirable to do so. All fat should be removed, as this is what carries the gamy taste. The lean meat then should be larded, or cooked with a small amount of pork fat or oil to replace the natural fat that has been removed.

Chops

Probably I am fortunate in that my last few deer (including an eight- and a ten-point buck) have been so tender that the chops needed no marinating. After most of the fat was trimmed off, the chops were peppered slightly and then broiled as lamb or pork chops are.

If the chops may be a bit tough, after marinating they should be dried with a cloth and placed in a pan with seasoning of salt, pepper, and an herb such as orégano, thyme, or rosemary. The chops then are sprinkled with a tenderizer and with olive oil and are placed in the refrigerator for a few hours. Then they can be rolled in cracker crumbs or flour before broiling or frying —or they can be cooked without this.

Venison is best when cooked on the rare side. Never overcook it.

Deerburgers

Use the lean meat trimmings. Grind 4 parts of deer meat with 1 part of beef or pork fat, or a little of both. Then shape them into patties and fry or broil them as you do hamburg. Basting with barbecue sauce, or serving with one of the venison sauces described at the end of these deer recipes, adds to this dish.

If you prefer non-fat deerburgers, leave out the beef or pork fat and substitute bread crumbs and 1 egg for each pound of meat. Also flavor with chopped parsley and finely chopped onions, if you like them.

Breaded Heart

Slice the heart thin, and add salt, pepper, and a dash of monosodium glutamate. Roll in flour, dip in milk, and then roll in cracker crumbs. Fry in bacon fat or vegetable oil until both sides are golden brown. Then turn down the heat and simmer for a few more minutes. Drain on absorbent paper and serve while very hot.

Heart with Kidney Sauce

Boil the heart and kidneys in water to cover until tender. Allow to cool, and slice into bite-size pieces. While the meat is cooling, sauté minced onion in a little butter until the onion is transparent. Add the meat to the onion, and also add a can of mushroom soup. Salt and pepper to taste, and add 1 cup red wine and 1 cup of the broth in which the meat was boiled. Allow this to simmer for about 15 minutes, and serve on rice or noodles. Wild rice is excellent for this. Saffron rice is a second choice.

Liver

If you're hungry after you kill your deer, you'll probably eat the liver on the spot, as we did in the story at the beginning of this chapter. If you bring it home (in the plastic bag hunters always carry for the purpose), wash the liver carefully, and soak it in slightly salted water for a few hours or overnight. Then cut it in thin slices. Season it with salt and pepper and dredge it in flour. Fry in bacon fat until it is golden brown, preferably removing and draining it while it is slightly on the rare side. The cooking takes but a very few minutes.

A teaspoon of dried orégano or another herb mixed with the flour you dredge the liver in adds to the flavor.

If you like onions, slice them and sauté them in butter with a little water added. When the water cooks away, move the onions to one side of the skillet and fry the liver in it. You may have to add a little more butter (or bacon fat, olive oil, or margarine).

Some sportsmen like to peel off the tissue after soaking the liver in the salted water. Then they slice the liver into shoestrings, like thinly cut french-fried potatoes. They dredge the liver in seasoned flour (shake flour and liver in a paper bag, in this case), and fry it with the onions. They add some sliced mushroom caps, if they have any. They also may add a very thin flour-and-water paste, and 1 cup milk, to make a gravy. When you do it this way, try serving it on toasted English muffins or on toast.

Broiled Steak

Try doing this in the same way recommended for Venison Chops.

Pepper Steak

Use a thick cut of venison from the haunch. Crush a small handful of whole peppercorns with a rolling pin or a round bottle, and press these into both sides of the steak. Put 4 tablespoons butter (or olive oil, margarine, or bacon fat) in an iron skillet and, when the fat begins to smoke, drop in the steak and sear it quickly on both sides. Pan-broil the steak until it is dark brown on each side (but fairly rare in the middle). Remove the steak, and pour 1 cup red wine into the skillet. Scrape the pan and pour the mixture over the steak.

Swiss Steak I

This is a recipe for preparing, pot-roast style, a thick steak you haven't had time to marinate, which might be a bit tough. Select a steak 1½ or 2 inches thick and hammer it well on both sides with a meat hammer or with the edge of a saucer. Add salt and pepper, and dredge it with flour. Let it stand about an hour, adding more flour as necessary to coat it very thoroughly. Then put it in a lightly greased skillet and sear it on both sides. Add a can of mushroom soup, pouring it on the center of the meat. Add enough hot water to the pan to cover the steak. Put a cover on the skillet and cook the meat in a moderate oven (325°) for about 2 hours. If this recipe is being prepared outdoors, a Dutch oven can be used instead of the skillet.

Swiss Steak II

Dry the marinated steak and brush it with garlic butter. Add salt and pepper. Sear it on both sides in a little bacon grease and put it in a Dutch oven. Add the following:

1 onion, chopped fine
½ teaspoon monosodium glutamate
2 tablespoons tomato catsup
2 tablespoons olive oil
4 tablespoons water
Salt, pepper, and paprika to taste

Cover tightly and cook over moderate heat for about an hour, until tender. If the water cooks out, add a little more, or a little dry wine.

The above gives the general idea, but variations add to this recipe, or the previous one. For example, instead of the catsup and water, add a can of tomatoes. Include more onion if you wish —or thickly sliced potatoes, carrots, turnips, or other vegetables. If you prefer the meat a little spicier, drop in a bay leaf or a clove or half a small garlic clove, or a dash of one or a combination of herbs such as rosemary, thyme, basil, etc. (See Chapter Sixteen for information on cooking with herbs.)

Barbecued Ribs I

The ribs of a deer are very tasty when barbecued, and there are several ways to do it. The old lumberjacks and trappers merely cleaned them off and rubbed them with salt and pepper. Then they peeled and pointed a stout sapling about 4 feet long and ran this through the ribs twice, to hold them flat. They stuck the stick in the ground, or leaned it against a support, so it would be at an angle of about 40° over a small fire. They roasted the ribs this way, turning them as necessary to brown both sides. Alder is good wood for a roasting stick, but other sweet woods will do as well. Avoid using evergreens.

If you have barbecue sauce to paint the ribs while cooking, so much the better. If the job is being done where you can marinate them or parboil them for a short time, they will be tenderer. A good way is to cut them in serving-size pieces, parboil them for 20 minutes or so, and then grill them over the coals, adding barbecue sauce. Ribs from any large animal can be barbecued this way.

Barbecued Ribs II

Split the ribs as you would for spareribs, and put them in a roasting pan. Combine the following and pour the mixture over the ribs:

> 1 cup tomato catsup
> ¼ cup vinegar
> ¼ cup Worcestershire sauce
> 1 teaspoon salt
> 1 teaspoon black pepper
> 2 teaspoons chili powder
> ¼ teaspoon cayenne pepper
> 1 or 2 onions, chopped fine
> 1½ cups water

Cover the ribs and bake in a moderate oven (350°) for an hour. Then uncover them and continue baking for another half hour. Turn the ribs two or three times during the last half hour, to brown them well.

Most sportsmen don't bother with deer ribs, but they are very good when properly cooked.

Braised Roast with Vegetables

From 3 to 5 pounds of a less tender cut of meat can be used for this. Rub the meat with salt, pepper, and flour, and sear it in hot fat until it is browned on all sides. Put it in a pot, pinning a strip of salt pork or 2 or 3 bacon slices to the top, using toothpicks. Add ¼ cup hot water and ½ tablespoon vinegar. Cover and cook in a moderate oven for about 2 hours, adding more water if needed. Then add the following:

> ½ cup chopped celery
> 1 apple, cored and chopped
> 1 carrot, diced
> ½ tablespoon lemon juice

Continue cooking for another half hour or so, until the vegetables are tender.

Roast Venison

A 3- to 5-pound piece of meat that has been marinated and trimmed of all fat is used for this. In marinating a roast, it is desirable to puncture the meat in several places with a pick or a narrow knife, to allow the marinade to penetrate. After removing the meat from the marinade, allow it to drain in the refrigerator until it becomes firm.

Season the roast and sprinkle it with flour. Pin a strip of salt pork or 2 or 3 bacon slices to the top. Then put it in a pan and roast it uncovered in a preheated moderate (325°) oven, allowing about 25 minutes' cooking time per pound. This will result in a roast with a crisper surface than in the preceding recipe.

Instead of using the salt pork or bacon, the roast can be basted with salad oil. In any event, baste it very frequently with the juices while cooking. If the roast is a narrow one, or if you like it a bit rare, reduce the cooking time to about 20 minutes per pound.

If the roast is cooked in a hotter oven, such as at 400° to 450°, the cooking time per pound would be about 10 minutes for very rare, 15 minutes for medium, and 25 minutes for well done.

All venison is aided by a currant or grape jelly sauce. Here are two recipes for sauces:

Venison Sauce I

> ½ cup currant or grape jelly
> 4 tablespoons butter
> ½ teaspoon dried herbs

Melt and blend in a saucepan, and serve in a small pitcher to pour over meat after serving.

Venison Sauce II

Heat the following together, stirring occasionally:

> ¼ cup strained marinade
> 1 cup currant or grape jelly
> 1 tablespoon lemon juice
> 1 pinch powdered ginger
> 2 tablespoons whiskey (scotch or bourbon)

After heating and blending, serve in a small pitcher to pour over meat after serving.

Sausage

Mix the following together thoroughly, or grind them together:

> 1 medium-sized square of bacon, ground
> 5 pounds lean venison, ground
> 1 tablespoon rubbed sage
> 1 tablespoon smoked salt

When the above is thoroughly blended, form into small cakes and fry in a hot skillet.

Pot Stew

Cut several pounds of lean venison into 1-inch cubes and dredge them in seasoned flour. In a Dutch oven or heavy kettle, melt ¼ pound of butter and sauté the following until golden brown:

> 1 pound mushrooms, cleaned and sliced
> 1 cup chopped onion
> 1 green pepper, chopped (remove pith and seeds)

Remove the vegetables from the pot and add the meat, searing it on all sides. Add more butter, if necessary. Return the vegetables to the pot, and add enough beef stock (or canned bouillon) to almost cover the meat and vegetables. Let this simmer, covered, for about 2 hours. Then add:

> 1 cup red wine
> 4 or more potatoes, cubed
> 4 or more carrots, thickly sliced
> 1 can whole-kernel corn

Bring this to a boil; turn down the heat, and simmer slowly until the vegetables are done.

You could also add 1 or 2 peeled, cored, and sliced apples, and 1 cup chopped celery. A dash of herbs always helps, but this recipe has the object of providing a tasty stew that retains the flavor of the venison without killing it. When the stew is about done, add more seasoning, if desirable.

Skillet Stew

Cut about 2 pounds of venison into fairly large cubes, dredge it in seasoned flour, and sear it in about 5 tablespoons olive oil or cooking fat. Then add:

> 1 or 2 onions, chopped fine
> 2 cloves garlic
> About 6 parsley sprigs, chopped fine

Sauté these in the skillet with the meat until the onions are slightly browned, taking care that the garlic does not burn. Remove garlic. Add 1 cup water, or ½ cup red wine and ½ cup water.

Cover the skillet tightly and allow the meat to simmer for about an hour, until the meat is tender. Add more water or wine if necessary. Add salt and pepper to taste, with a pinch or two of herbs such as orégano or thyme.

When the meat is tender, stir in 2 tablespoons tomato paste until blended. If this isn't handy, use about half a can of tomatoes, or even some tomato catsup.

This stew can be served over rice or noodles, or with mashed potatoes.

Boiled Tongue

Deer tongue is another part that normally is discarded. Many outdoorsmen consider this a grave error, because they think it is as good as beef tongue, which is a fairly high-priced item at the butcher's.

Wash the tongue and cover it with water in a pan. Add a little salt, a few whole peppers, and a bay leaf or two, or 2 or 3 cloves. Let the tongue simmer until tender. Then remove it from the water and peel it. Serve it plain or with a tomato sauce.

Game Stew

Almost any kind of game can be used for this, such as rabbit, squirrels, raccoon, or cubed meat from big game—even parts that may be tough. Disjoint the game or cut it in serving-size pieces. Dredge it in seasoned flour and fry it in hot fat until it is well browned. Then put the game in a Dutch oven or a large casserole.

In the remaining drippings in the pan, sauté the following:

½ *cup chopped celery*
½ *cup chopped parsley*
½ *cup rice*

Stir this in the hot fat until the rice is evenly browned. Add 2 cups water and boil for about 10 minutes. Pour this over the game. Now you'll need:

6 *medium-sized onions*
6 *whole cloves*
½ *teaspoon dried herbs*
1 *small bay leaf*
2 *tablespoons tomato catsup*
½ *lemon, sliced*
2 *tablespoons butter*

Stick a clove in each onion and add them to the pot. Add everything else. Add enough water to cover. Cover the container tightly and cook over slow heat for 2 or 3 hours, until the meat is tender. Add more hot water (or a little wine) if needed. Make a paste of about 2 tablespoons flour in a cup of water, and stir this into the stew to thicken it slightly. Test for seasoning, and add more if necessary.

MUSKRAT RECIPES

If you call it a muskrat, probably the girls won't eat it, but when muskrat pelts brought prices high enough to bother with, trappers sold the meat as "marsh rabbit," and everybody thought it was delicious. After all, these little animals are strict vegetarians, and there is no reason why they shouldn't be as good as rabbits or squirrels. So, when Junior operates his little trap line, why not let him sell you the meat so you can try these recipes? After skinning and cleaning the animal, be sure to remove all glands and fat. There also will be some white tissue inside each leg, and this should be removed. Then cut the animal into convenient pieces and soak it in salted water overnight.

Baked Marsh Rabbit

Parboil the meat for about half an hour. Drain it, and dredge it in seasoned flour. Put the meat in a pan and add ¼ cup vinegar and ¼ cup water. Lay bacon slices over the meat, and bake until tender.

Braised Marsh Rabbit

Roll the meat in seasoned flour or in a mixture of seasoned flour and corn meal. Fry in hot fat until golden brown. Then add ½ cup water to the skillet; cover it and simmer until done, which will be in about half an hour. Put a few onions, tomatoes or other vegetables in with the meat, if desirable.

OPOSSUM RECIPES

If someone is uninformed on a subject, he might as well admit it—and I must confess lack of experience in preparing and cooking at least three little woodland critters; namely, opossum, porcupine, and woodchuck.

Hunting companions in the South have exposed me to their famous "'possum and 'taters," and their recipes are included here. Maybe one has to be a true Southerner to go into ecstasies over roast 'possum. It is a fat little animal with a rather unusual flavor. We even find them up here in New England occasionally. So, if you'd like to cook an opossum, this seems to be the way to do it:

Roast Opossum

Since this animal usually is roasted with the hide on, it is logical first to remove the fur. This is done by dipping the 'possum in very hot (not boiling) water for a very few minutes. The hair can then be scraped off with a dull knife. If the hair comes off a bit hard, dip the 'possum in very hot water again. Then wash the animal by scrubbing it with soap and water. Slit it, and remove entrails, saving the liver. Remove head and tail, if you like. Some people leave on the head, which they say contains lean, tasty meat. In this case, they put a sweet potato in the mouth, as one decorates a suckling pig.

With the animal so cleaned, soak him for 12 hours or so in cold water to which 1 cup salt has been added. Drain this off and rinse with boiling water. Stuff him with the dressing given below. Sew him up, or fasten the opening with skewers. Put him in a roaster or Dutch oven with a little water, and roast him at moderate heat (350°) for about an hour and a half, until he is tender and richly browned. Baste every quarter hour or more with the drippings. Remove him from the roaster, remove skewers, and put him on a heated platter. Almost an hour before he is done, add sweet potatoes to the roaster, if you wish. Skim the fat from the gravy remaining in the pan, and make a flour and cream gravy with the scrapings.

Opossum Stuffing

1 large onion, chopped fine
1 tablespoon fat
Opossum liver (optional)
1 cup bread crumbs
1 teaspoon chopped red pepper
Dash of Worcestershire sauce
1 hard-boiled egg, chopped fine
Salt to taste

Brown the onion in the fat and add the finely chopped liver. Cook until tender. Add the other ingredients, plus enough water to moisten the stuffing. Mix, and stuff with this dressing.

Some people parboil the 'possum until slightly tender before roasting. Others remove the skin and fat, and cook it as above, either whole or disjointed. Most everybody agrees that sweet potatoes should be served with this dish. Add a little sage to the stuffing, if you like the flavor.

PORCUPINE RECIPE

Up in the north woods there used to be a theory that no one should kill porcupines except in an emergency, because this is almost the only animal that is easy to kill with a stick to sustain people who become lost. Luckily, the author never was in that predicament, and he hopes his readers are equally fortunate.

A porky can be skinned easily by slitting the skin down the belly. The meat is removed and disjointed as you would with a squirrel or rabbit. The meat should be parboiled for half an hour or so to remove the fat and to tenderize the meat. Then the meat is dried, rolled in flour, and fried in bacon fat until browned. People say the liver is good, and I say that those who like it are very welcome to it. For that matter, they also are welcome to the porcupine, even though some say it is as good as young lamb.

RABBIT RECIPES

In going from the ridiculous to the sublime we should observe that more people eat more rabbit than any other game. Rabbits and hares have finely textured, lightly gamy white meat that closely resembles chicken. Young rabbits, with soft ears and paws, need little preparation other

than cooking. Old ones may need to be parboiled a bit, or used in stews or casseroles, rather than in more quickly cooked dishes.

When the rabbit has been skinned and cleaned, if it is to be disjointed, the hindquarters are cut off and divided. Do the same with the forequarters. The back and ribs are less desirable, but often are used, especially in stews, casseroles, and in dishes where the (partly) cooked meat is removed from the bones, such as in a meat pie.

If blood from shot has settled in any part, or if fur has been shot into the meat, dig it out with the point of a knife. With the rabbit(s) thus dressed, here are a few recipes for cooking them:

Baked Rabbit

Clean, and cut in halves, or disjoint. Place in a baking dish and spread lavishly with butter. Season with salt and pepper. Bake in a 400° oven for an hour, basting at least four times. Remove meat from pan. Blend 1 teaspoon flour into the fat in the pan, and add ½ cup boiling water. Stir until boiling. Add seasoning, and pour this gravy over the meat before serving.

Note that in most rabbit recipes the use of herbs and other high seasonings is not recommended, as they interfere with the fine flavor of the meat. Also note that an abundance of good butter is recommended, rather than bacon fat or cooking oils. A secret in cooking rabbit is to use plenty of butter, rather than stronger fats, which would impair the flavor. Rabbit is a lean meat, which needs the addition of butter.

Barbecued Rabbit

1 rabbit, cut into servings
1 cup flour
1 teaspoon salt
¼ teaspoon pepper
¼ cup butter

Soak the rabbit in cold salted water for at least an hour; preferably longer. Drain and dry. Dredge in flour into which the salt and pepper have been mixed. Brown the meat on all sides in the butter, being careful not to let the butter burn. Pour off nearly all remaining fat, and add the following barbecue sauce:

½ cup tomato catsup
1 onion, chopped fine
1 tablespoon sugar
2 tablespoons Worcestershire sauce
¼ cup vinegar

Combine all ingredients and pour them over the rabbit. Cook slowly, covered, for about an hour. If the rabbit is an older one, it may need a bit longer cooking time.

Cottontail Casserole

1 rabbit, dressed and disjointed
8 slices bacon
2 medium-sized onions, sliced
2 medium-sized potatoes, sliced
2 cups hot water
1 teaspoon salt
¼ teaspoon pepper

Let the disjointed rabbit stand in salted water for about an hour. Then remove, wipe dry, and roll in flour. Fry the bacon in a skillet until light brown. Remove the bacon, and fry the rabbit in the bacon fat until golden brown. Arrange the meat in a casserole and arrange over it the sliced onions, potatoes, and bacon. Dust all lightly with flour; add salt and pepper, and pour hot water over all. Bake about 2 hours in a moderate (350°) oven.

Note that this recipe calls for use of bacon fat, which is the second choice if good butter is not available. If butter is available, fry the rabbit in butter and omit the bacon.

Fried Rabbit I

2 young rabbits
2 egg yolks, beaten
3 cups milk
1¼ cups flour
1 tablespoon salt

½ cup butter
2 tablespoons currant jelly
1 tablespoon minced parsley

Wash the dressed rabbits in cold running water; dry, and cut in serving-size pieces. Combine the egg yolks with 1 cup milk, and gradually add 1 cup flour and some salt, beating this batter until smooth. Dip the meat in the batter, and fry in butter until golden brown. Reduce heat, and cook 30 to 40 minutes, covered. Turn the pieces occasionally. Remove the meat to a warm platter and stir the remaining ¼ cup flour into the fat in the pan. When this is blended, add the remaining 2 cups milk gradually, stirring constantly. Heat to boiling, and season with salt and pepper. Pour the gravy over the rabbits, and garnish with jelly and parsley. Grape jelly is a second choice if currant jelly is not available.

You may not need the entire ¼ cup flour, depending on how much fat remains in the pan. Add just enough flour for it to be absorbed by the fat.

Fried Rabbit II

2 young rabbits
2 egg yolks
1 cup milk
1 cup cracker crumbs
Salt and pepper to taste
½ cup (or 1 stick) butter

Disjoint the rabbits and soak the meat in salted water for 12 hours or more. Drain and dry. Beat the egg yolks in milk and dip the meat in this. (You can dip the meat first in seasoned flour, if you like the meat really crusty.) Then roll in cracker crumbs. Season. Sauté the meat in the butter in a hot skillet, turning the pieces until golden brown. Cover, and cook over medium heat for half an hour. Drain the meat on absorbent paper before serving. Note that this is the way chicken is fried, Southern style. If you want a short cut, just roll the meat in seasoned flour and omit the batter and crumbs. This gives a less crusty coating, but some people prefer it that way.

Hasenpfeffer (Sweet-Sour Rabbit)

1 large or 2 small rabbits, cut in serving-size pieces
1 quart vinegar
2 tablespoons salt
1 tablespoon pickling spices

1 tablespoon peppercorns
2 large onions, sliced
2 tablespoons fat
2 tablespoons flour
1 cup cold water
1 teaspoon cinnamon
½ teaspoon allspice

Put the disjointed rabbit in a crock and cover it with the vinegar combined with salt, pickling spices, peppercorns, and one onion. Let this stand in a cool place for 24 hours. Drain, put the meat in a pan, cover with boiling water, and simmer until tender, which will be about 1½ hours. Remove meat and strain broth. Melt the fat in a skillet, blend in the flour, and add water, stirring constantly. Cook until thickened. Add the rabbit, the strained broth, cinnamon and allspice, and the remaining onion. Simmer for 1 hour. Serve the meat with the gravy.

If you're short on vinegar, substitute for the quart of vinegar 1 cup vinegar and 1 12-ounce can beer.

Sautéed Rabbit with Tarragon

1 rabbit, cut into servings
1 rabbit liver (optional)
¼ cup seasoned flour
¼ pound butter
1 cup dry white wine
2 tablespoons minced fresh or 1 teaspoon dried
   tarragon
½ tablespoon meat glaze

Dust the rabbit with seasoned flour. Melt the butter in a skillet; add the rabbit, and brown the meat quickly on all sides, being careful not to let the butter burn. When the meat is a golden brown, reduce heat and add ⅔ cup wine. Simmer the rabbit in the wine, covered, about 45 minutes, or until it is tender. Remove cover and add the tarragon which has been soaked in ⅓ cup wine for half an hour. Increase heat, and turn the pieces of meat to distribute the tarragon. Cook another 5 minutes. Remove the rabbit to a heated platter. Add the meat glaze to the sauce in the pan and pour it over the rabbit.

The liver can be sautéed in butter for 5 minutes and added to the dish just before serving.

Stewed Rabbit

1 rabbit, cut into servings
2 tablespoons butter or fat
1 teaspoon salt

½ teaspoon pepper
Pinch of paprika
4 bay leaves
2 medium-sized onions, sliced fine
1 stalk celery, chopped
3 sprigs parsley, chopped

Brown the rabbit in the fat and add salt, pepper, and a pinch of paprika. Add enough water to cover the rabbit, and simmer for half an hour. Then add remaining ingredients. Cook about an hour more, until tender. Thicken the stew with 1 teaspoon flour stirred into a little water, if desired.

RACCOON RECIPE

Up in the Berkshire Hills of western Massachusetts we have a fall sportsmen's festival known as a Coon Supper. The men hunt the coons a night or two before, sitting comfortably in a convenient cornfield nestled against the shocked corn, waiting for the dogs to "bark up." When the dogs' baying changes to yipping, all hands grab lights, climbing irons, guns, and what have you, and race to the spot where the dogs say they have a coon up a tree. The coon may turn out to be a wildcat, and one of the men may get mired in a swamp or fall off an outcropping in the dark, but this only adds to the excitement.

Coon hunters maintain that if you don't like coon it is because it hasn't been prepared properly, and I'm inclined to agree with them. These fastidious little fur-bearers can be awfully good eating. The combination of the hunt and the dinner was a late fall occasion by which time was set. But I'm sorry to say that the sport has fallen off a bit since they stopped wearing coonskin coats at Yale and Harvard. Obviously the fashion (and the sport) should be revived.

Like rabbits, fairly young animals are the best ones. After they have been skinned and cleaned, all fat must be removed, because this is what makes the meat taste strong. Even more important, the little critters have scent glands, or "round kernels," under the armpits of the front legs. These must be removed from the muscles, because they are exceedingly bitter and will ruin the meat. If you don't like coon, perhaps it's because the person who prepared it neglected to take these precautions. If the coon has been chilled, this is easy. Also, in skinning the coon, avoid letting the fur come in contact with the meat.

From here on, you operate very much as you do with rabbit, and the same recipes can be used. Parboiling the meat for half an hour in salted water (1 tablespoon salt per quart) helps to remove the rest of the distasteful fat and tenderize the meat. The meat can also be put in a marinade (see the Venison recipes) overnight. Baked apples and sweet potatoes go very well with coon. Here's the way the Ladies' Aid of the Congregational Church fixes coon for sportsmen's Coon Suppers in the Berkshires:

Roast Stuffed Coon

After the animal has been skinned, defatted, and deglanded (as above), wipe the coon with a damp cloth, and be sure no hairs remain on the meat. Then dust the outside with baking soda, rubbing it into the meat. Rinse the coon in two or three changes of cold water. Then put him in a turkey-roasting pan or some other deep receptacle, and add the following:

> *Water (to barely cover the coon)*
> *2 or 3 onions, chopped*
> *1 or 2 carrots, chopped*
> *2 or 3 stalks of celery, chopped*

The vegetables can be chopped together. Cover the receptacle and let the coon simmer gently for half an hour. Then remove him from the water; let him cool a bit, and rub him inside and out with a mixture of 2 parts salt to 1 part pepper, plus a dash of paprika.

While doing this, the broth in the receptacle is allowed to cool. Skim off the fat and strain the broth, saving a cup of it for the dressing.

To make the dressing, mix the following:

> *2 or more quarts soft bread crumbs*
> *(depending on the size of the coon)*
> *1 teaspoon salt*
> *¼ teaspoon pepper*
> *1½ teaspoons poultry seasoning*
> *1 egg, beaten*
> *1 onion, chopped*
> *1 apple, cored and sliced*
> *1 cup broth or milk*

Stuff the coon and skewer the opening. Put him back in the receptacle, lying on his back; add a little water; cover him tightly, and roast him in a moderate oven (350° to 375°) until he is tender, which should be about 2 hours. During this time, baste him frequently, drawing off the fat and adding enough water so he won't stick to the pan. When he is about done, remove the cover to let him brown (as you would when roasting a turkey).

If you want gravy, transfer the coon to a hot platter and keep him hot while you make it. Decant the liquid from the roaster and skim off all the fat. In a skillet, melt 4 tablespoons butter and stir in flour until the butter is absorbed. Stir in the skimmed broth and some seasoning. When the mixture thickens, add enough milk to make about 2 cups gravy. Serve this hot with the coon, and carve him about the way you would carve a turkey.

SQUIRREL RECIPES

These are the familiar gray squirrels, although fox squirrels also are tasty in these recipes. If you haven't time to hunt them, just get a bird feeder and they will come to you. Squirrels are fastidious little animals, and more people should enjoy eating them. Perhaps they will when they try some of these recipes.

Brunswick Stew

This is a time-honored sportsman's recipe that actually is a game stew made from squirrels, rabbits, venison, or what have you. Ingredients vary, depending on what is available. A combination of game adds to the dish: any or all of the above, the meat of game birds, or even domestic meats and fowl, such as chicken, veal, or beef. You cook it "by the soul" rather than by recipe, but this is one of the ways it can be done:

> *2 young rabbits (or 4 squirrels, or some of*
> *both), disjointed, parboiled, and separated*
> *from bones; cut meat in eating-size pieces*

2 *pounds venison, diced, dredged in flour, and*
  well browned in hot fat
4 *medium-sized onions, sliced, and sautéed in*
  the above fat
4 *potatoes, diced*
2 *quarts broth, strained (obtained from cooking*
  the rabbits or squirrels)
½ *cup butter*
2 *cans cream-style corn*
2 *cans lima or butter beans*
2 *cans tomatoes*
1 *can okra (if available)*
2 *tablespoons Worcestershire sauce*
2 *bay leaves*
2 *teaspoons salt*
1 *teaspoon peppercorns*
1 *teaspoon dried red peppers*
  (or a dash or two of Tabasco)

Add all ingredients to a Dutch oven or a large pot, and simmer them all together slowly for about an hour, with the pot covered. When nearly done, taste the stew to see if it needs more seasoning. Some of the vegetables can be left out and others added, such as chopped celery, sliced carrots, etc. Include a sprinkling of cloves, chopped parsley, or other herbs, if desired. If the stew is too thick, thin it slightly with water, but leave it fairly thick. Include a can or two of almost any kind of soup, if you like.

This recipe makes a large amount of stew, but none too much for a group of hungry hunters. The proportions can be reduced for small groups.

Fricasseed Squirrel

2 *or more squirrels*
1 *teaspoon salt*
¼ *teaspoon pepper*
1 *cup flour*
6 *slices bacon, diced*
2 *small onions, chopped fine*
1 *apple, peeled, cored, sliced*
1 *tablespoon lemon juice*
1 *cup water, soup stock, or clear soup*

Cut the squirrels into serving-size pieces; rub with salt and pepper, dredge in flour. Fry bacon pieces until crisp, and remove from fat. Fry the squirrel pieces in the hot fat, turning to brown all sides. Add the bacon, onions, apple, seasoning, lemon juice, and liquid. Cover tightly, and simmer for 2 or 3 hours. The addition of a little chopped parsley or a pinch of a dried herb such as thyme adds to this dish. After browning

the squirrels in the fat, some of the fat can be poured off if there seems to be too much.

Fried Squirrel

1 *squirrel*
1 *tablespoon salt*
1 *egg*
1 *tablespoon milk*
½ *cup dried bread crumbs*
Salt and pepper to taste
2 *tablespoons fat or cooking oil*

Multiply this recipe, depending on how many squirrels are to be cooked. Cut the squirrel(s) into serving-size pieces and soak them in cold water containing the 1 tablespoon salt for about an hour. Then remove and wipe dry. Beat the egg with a fork until light, and then beat in the milk. Dip the squirrel pieces in the egg batter and roll them in crumbs that have been seasoned with salt and pepper. Melt the fat in a skillet and, when it is hot, fry the squirrel pieces, turning them until all sides are golden brown. Turn heat down to medium and cook the squirrels, covered, until tender, which will be about half an hour. Remove the meat from the skillet and drain on absorbent paper.

Roast Squirrel

3 *squirrels*
1 *cup cooking oil*
¼ *cup lemon juice*
2 *cups bread crumbs*
½ *cup milk*
½ *teaspoon salt*
⅛ *teaspoon pepper*
½ *teaspoon onion juice or grated onion*
4 *teaspoons olive oil or bacon fat*

Clean the squirrels and wash them in several waters. Wipe them dry. Blend the cup of oil with the lemon juice and marinate the squirrels in this for an hour. Meanwhile, combine the crumbs with enough milk to moisten them, and mix in the salt, pepper, and onion juice. Remove the squirrels from the marinade; wipe them dry; stuff them; skewer body cavities closed; brush them with the olive oil or bacon fat, and place them in a roasting pan. Roast uncovered in a medium oven (325°) until the fork test indicates they are tender, which will be in about an hour. Baste every 15 minutes with the bacon fat. Serve with pan gravy. If a few mushrooms are available, slice and sauté them, and add them to the stuffing.

Squirrel Casserole

    2 squirrels, cut in serving-size pieces
    ½ cup flour
    ½ teaspoon salt
    Dash of pepper
    1 tablespoon butter or 1 slice bacon
    1 small onion, chopped
    6 mushrooms, sliced

Roll the squirrel pieces in seasoned flour. Sauté the onion and mushrooms in the butter until lightly browned. Remove the onion and mushrooms from the skillet, and brown the squirrel pieces in the drippings, turning to brown all sides. Put the squirrel pieces in a casserole and add:

    ½ cup stock or 1 chicken bouillon cube in
       ½ cup water
    ½ cup dry white wine
    1 slice lemon
    6 peppercorns
    1 stalk celery, chopped
    1 sprig parsley, chopped

Cover the casserole and bake in a moderate (350°) oven until the meat is tender, which will be about an hour. Add the mushrooms and onion. Thicken lightly with flour and add ¼ cup sour cream. Return casserole to the oven for about 10 minutes more.

Squirrel Pot Pie

    4 squirrels, cut in serving-size pieces
    ½ cup flour
    4 tablespoons butter

Wash the meat and wipe it dry. Dredge in flour, and fry in butter, turning the pieces until golden brown on all sides. Do not let the butter burn. Transfer the meat to a pot with a cover and add:

    1 quart boiling water
    1 large onion, minced, and sautéed in the
       butter in which the squirrels were cooked
    ¼ lemon, sliced very thin
    1 teaspoon salt
    ½ teaspoon pepper
    ¼ cup sherry or white wine

Cover the above and allow it to stew slowly for an hour. While this is going on, make some dumplings:

    2 cups all-purpose flour
    3 teaspoons baking powder
    1 teaspoon salt
    3 tablespoons butter or shortening
    1 cup milk

Sift dry ingredients together and blend in the melted butter until the mixture resembles a coarse meal. Add the milk and mix quickly with a fork until blended. Roll thickly and cut into small rounds.

Lay the dumplings on the squirrel meat in the pot. Cover, and allow the food to boil for 15 minutes. Put the squirrels in the center of a hot platter and arrange the dumplings around them. Thicken the gravy with 1 tablespoon browned flour that has been browned in 2 tablespoons butter in the skillet. Pour the gravy over the meat and serve as hot as possible.

Stew-Fried Squirrel

    2 or more squirrels, quartered
    ½ cup flour
    ½ teaspoon salt
    ⅛ teaspoon pepper
    4 tablespoons butter

Mix flour, salt, and pepper. Wash the squirrels; wipe dry and dredge in the seasoned flour. Fry in the butter, turning until all sides are golden brown. Do not allow butter to burn. Remove meat from the skillet. Add enough flour to the remaining butter to absorb it, stirring continually. Then stir in enough water to make a thin gravy. Return the meat to the gravy; cover and simmer for about an hour, or until the meat is tender. It may be necessary to add a little more water to the gravy, if it cooks down too much. The addition of a bay leaf or a pinch or two of powdered herbs adds to this dish.

This recipe can also be used for rabbits, game birds, or other game.

WOODCHUCK

Groundhog, or woodchuck, tastes about like squirrel, especially if you get a young one. There's no reason why this tasty little target shouldn't be good, because he enjoys the same grassy diet that rabbits and cattle do. After he has been skinned and cleaned, be sure to remove the glands, or "kernels," on the inner side of the forelegs. All fat should be trimmed off, and the animal should be soaked for several hours in cold salted water. Then he should be parboiled for half an hour to remove any remaining fat. Then he can be cooked in the same ways that have been described for preparing rabbits, squirrels, and other small four-footed game.

The best time to hunt woodchucks for food is in the crisp weeks of the fall before the animals go into hibernation. Woodchucks are the favorite wild meat of many sportsmen.

Chapter Fourteen

RECIPES FOR GAME BIRDS

Preparing game birds is somewhat different from preparing domestic varieties, partly because many wild birds, such as pheasants, quail, and grouse, have almost no body fat. This has to be replaced by using bacon, butter, or other fats in their cooking. Since game birds spend much of their time actively in search of food, the older ones can be rather tough if allowance for their age is not made in their cooking. For example, older birds are usually better when cooked for a long time in dishes such as casseroles, pies, and stews than they would be in dishes more suitable to younger birds, such as pan-fried or barbecued recipes. This (as with all wild game) should be considered in the preparation.

FIELD DRESSING AND HANDLING OF BIRDS

Treatment of the game after it has been shot is also important if we want to minimize the gamy taste. All large birds should be drawn and cooled in the field to insure best taste. Smaller ones, such as quail, should be left undrawn until after plucking. This means that these birds should be plucked and then dressed the same day they are shot. After being prepared for cooking, game birds can be kept in cold storage for several days, or can be securely sealed and kept frozen for six months or more.

But it never did make much sense to me to hang undressed game birds for several days, only to allow undesirable juices from their innards to penetrate shot holes in the meat during this time. An old sportsman friend of mine heartily disagrees with this. I think he has been reading too many English books, written before the days of refrigeration, when a very gamy taste was considered desirable because it was almost impossible to serve game any other way, unless it was served almost at once.

This same gentleman is of the cult who prefers undercooking to the extent that some pink blood juices should be seen when the bird is carved at the table. While this might be debatable with very young and tender birds, older ones never should be served rare or medium, because they will be sure to be tough.

HOW TO PLUCK AND DRESS BIRDS

If the skin of game birds is to be left on in cooking, the birds should be plucked as soon as possible, because quill feathers stiffen into the skin after the birds have been cooled. It is, of course, easier to skin birds, and this has little if any effect upon their flavor, although it would impair appearance for certain cooking methods, such as roasting. To skin game birds, chop off the wings close to the body. The meat on the wings is usually tough, and there is too little to bother with. Also remove the legs at the knees. Then slit the skin under the tail and skin back over the breast and up the body toward the neck. Break the breast away from the back. The breasts of game birds are very plump and usually very tender. Except for stews and other long-cooked dishes, they are the only parts on most skinned game birds that seem worth bothering with.

To simplify plucking of game birds, dip them (before cleaning) in hot paraffin or in a kettle containing both paraffin and almost boiling water. This makes it easy to peel off the feathers, and it helps to prevent tearing the skin. If the paraffin has been allowed to cool and harden, the feathers will stick together and can be pulled off easily. When the bird has been plucked, cut off the head and the legs at the knees. Then dress the birds, saving the giblets, if desirable. If any fuzz remains (and it usually does) this can be singed off over a flame. The handiest way is to light a can of "Sterno Canned Heat" and use this flame for the singeing. Pin feathers can be removed with tweezers or with a small knife. When thus cleaned and plucked, put a few slices of onion in the body cavity. This seems to help remove some of the gamy taste. (The onion is discarded before cooking.) Thus prepared, the birds can be kept under refrigeration for several days, until they are to be cooked. When ready to cook them, ducks should be placed in a salt-water brine (about 2 tablespoons salt per quart of water) and left in a cold place overnight. This removes strong flavors and blood clots. We don't do this with upland game unless the birds are old or badly shot up, although many sportsmen consider it a good practice with all plucked birds. In any case, the birds should be washed thoroughly before cooking.

The following recipes are listed under the species of birds to which they seem best suited. However, the fact that a recipe is listed for one kind of bird does not mean that it is not suited to another. Many of these recipes are fairly general in type and will serve admirably for several species. For example, many of the recipes for pheasant are equally suited to grouse, woodcock, quail, or doves. Some recipes are very easy and are ideally suited to outdoor cooking, while others are a bit more detailed and could be handled more easily in the home kitchen or in a camp. These are included because outdoor cooks usually are sportsmen—and sportsmen like to know how to cook their game wherever they may be.

COOTS (MUD HENS)

We do not include the coot among the ducks because the coot is not a duck at all, but a member of the Scoter family. When coots feed on plant life their flesh can be excellent, but when they have been feeding on shellfish (which they often do) it can be quite the opposite. However, the flesh can be made palatable (or even delicious) by using breast and leg meat only and by marinating the meat for 24 hours or so.

Baked Coot Breasts

Skin 2 coots with a boning knife and fillet the breasts from the bone. Also cut off the legs, which are not disjointed. Save the livers and gizzards if you wish. Wash the meat in fresh water and soak it for 2 hours in fresh water to which 1 teaspoon salt has been added. Drain, and put the meat in a non-metal bowl with the following marinade, which is mixed and poured over the meat:

    2 teaspoons salt
    1 teaspoon pepper
    1 bay leaf, crushed
    2 garlic cloves, chopped
    6 whole cloves
    2 small red chili peppers
    1 medium-sized onion, sliced
    1 pint sherry or vinegar
    ½ pint vinegar
    ½ pint water

Let the meat stand in a cool place in this marinade for about 12 hours. Then cook it as follows:

    ¼ cup bacon fat
    1 cup water
    1 cup marinade
    2 cans tomato sauce
    Salt and pepper to taste
    1 cup rice

Brown the meat in the fat and put it in a Dutch oven or a heavy baking pan with a good cover. Remove the onion slices from the marinade and sauté them in the fat until light brown. Add the water, marinade, tomato sauce, and seasoning. Cover and bake in moderate heat (300° to 350°) for 2 hours. At the beginning of the last half hour, add the rice and enough more water to cover ½ inch deep over the rice. When cooked, test for doneness, and adjust seasoning, if necessary. (The rice may be steamed separately, if desired, and served with the pan gravy.)

Fried Coot Breasts

Skin 2 coots with a boning knife and fillet the breasts from the bone. Also cut off the legs, which are not disjointed. Save the livers and gizzards if you wish. Marinate the meat for about 24 hours in a mixture of 2 quarts water and 1 cup salt to which 1 tablespoon vinegar or cooking wine has been added. Then cook it as follows:

1 cup flour, seasoned
¼ cup bacon fat or cooking oil
2 cups milk
¼ teaspoon garlic salt
½ medium-sized onion, grated
1 can cream of mushroom soup

Roll the meat in seasoned flour and fry it in the bacon fat or cooking oil until golden brown. Make a smooth paste with ½ cup of the remaining flour and some milk. Pour remaining fat out of the pan and stir in the flour paste. Then stir in the remaining milk and add the garlic salt, onion, and the mushroom soup. Cover the pan and allow the meat to simmer in this sauce over low heat for 2 hours.

Stewed Coot

2 coots
½ cup flour, seasoned
4 tablespoons butter or ¼ cup fat

Remove breasts and legs; wash and dry them, roll them in flour, and fry them in the fat until browned.

In a Dutch oven or other pot, combine the following:

4 onions, sliced
4 carrots, sliced
1 can tomatoes or 4 fresh ones, peeled and
  segmented
2 teaspoons salt
1 teaspoon pepper
2 bay leaves
½ tablespoon parsley flakes
½ teaspoon marjoram, thyme, or other
  suitable herb
1 quart water
1 cup white wine

Bring this to a boil and add the coots and the gravy in which they were braised. Cover, and cook slowly for about 1½ hours. Test the meat for doneness and simmer longer, if necessary. At this point, add 2 or 3 diced potatoes, if desired. If a flour thickening is desired, mix 1 tablespoon flour with ½ cup water to make a smooth paste, and stir this into the stew. Continue slow cooking until potatoes are tender and gravy has thickened. Add a little more water (or wine) if necessary to make gravy of the right consistency.

DOVE RECIPES

Doves (including squab and other small game birds) should be plucked, cleaned, and heads and lower legs removed. Many sportsmen consider this too much trouble for so small a bird, and they prefer to skin rather than pluck them. Others just remove the breasts, and perhaps the legs. Many save the hearts and livers for use in the recipes. The meat usually is soaked in cold water, to which a little vinegar has been added, for an hour or two, or even overnight. Then the birds are wiped dry and are ready for the recipes that follow. Two doves usually are allowed for each person, although hungry outdoorsmen can often eat more. Proportions in these recipes are about correct for the number of doves specified. For a different number, the recipes can be varied accordingly.

Broiled Doves

10 doves
½ cup sugar
1 cup soy sauce
2 garlic cloves, crushed

Mix the last three ingredients in a large bowl and marinate the birds in this mixture for 3 or 4 hours. Then broil the birds over a coal fire, basting them occasionally with the marinade. When the leg bones can be twisted away from the meat, the birds should be done. Cook them very slowly over moderate heat. (This recipe is good for most upland game, if you like the flavor of this marinade.)

Doves in Casserole

10 to 12 doves
2 small green apples
¼ cup chopped chives
1 or 2 stalks celery
3 tablespoons parsley
½ teaspoon salt
⅛ teaspoon pepper
¼ teaspoon poultry seasoning
¼ teaspoon sage
1 can mushroom soup
1 can small peas
½ cup cream
½ cup water
¾ cup dry vermouth
1 tablespoon butter
Dash of paprika

Arrange the doves in a casserole. Chop together the next four ingredients until very fine, and sprinkle them over and around the doves. Add the next four seasonings, varying the amounts according to taste. Mix together the remaining ingredients except the butter and paprika, and pour this mixture over the doves and vegetables. Dot with butter and sprinkle lightly with paprika. Bake in a moderate oven (350°) for about 2½ hours. Add a little thickening to the gravy, if desired.

Doves with Rice

    10 doves
    ¼ cup oil
    1 onion, sliced
    1 can tomato paste
    1 can tomato sauce
    1 can stewed tomatoes
    ½ cup red wine
    Salt and pepper to taste
    Pinch of thyme
    Pinch of sage
    1 cup uncooked rice (or more)

Brown the doves in the oil. Add the onion and sauté it until slightly brown. Then add the three tomato ingredients and as much water as is needed to barely cover the doves. Add remaining ingredients, except for the rice. Simmer this over low heat for from 45 minutes to an hour. Prepare the rice in a separate container according to directions on the package. When the doves are cooked, use the sauce to pour over the rice. If fewer doves are used, decrease the tomato ingredients accordingly. If more than 4 people are to be served, increase the rice to 1½ or 2 cups.

Doves on Toast

    10 doves
    1 cup water
    ½ teaspoon salt
    ⅛ teaspoon pepper
    ½ cup wine (optional)
    1 tablespoon butter
    1 tablespoon olive oil
    2 tablespoons flour
    2½ cups milk
    5 slices toast (cut in halves)

Put the doves in a skillet and partly cover them with water. Add salt and pepper. Add the wine, if desired (it cooks out, but helps to tenderize the birds). When the liquids cook out, fry the doves to a golden brown in the butter and olive oil. Remove doves from the skillet and stir the flour into the remaining fat until the flour is browned and smooth. Gradually stir in the milk, to make a gravy. Put the doves on toast, and pour the hot gravy over them.

Doves in Wine Sauce

    10 doves
    1 cup burgundy wine
    1 teaspoon vinegar
    1 tablespoon sugar
    2 garlic cloves, minced
    1 tablespoon celery salt
    ½ cup flour
    ¼ cup cooking oil
    1 cup fresh or canned mushrooms, sliced

Marinate the doves overnight in the next four ingredients. Drain and dry them; rub them with celery salt and roll them in flour. Sauté the birds in the oil until brown. Drain off the oil and add the marinating sauce. Add enough more wine to cover the birds. Add the mushrooms. Cover the skillet and cook over low heat for about 2 hours. Thicken the sauce with a little flour-and-water paste, if desired.

Grilled Doves in Foil

    10 to 12 doves
    3 apples
    10 to 12 slices bacon
    Salt and pepper to taste

Clean the doves and soak them in vinegar-water for about an hour. Rinse in cold water, and wipe dry. Salt the inside of each bird. Core and quarter the apples, and put one segment in the cavity of each bird. Wrap a slice of bacon around each bird, fastening it with a wood sliver or a toothpick. Wrap two doves to a package in aluminum foil (see Chapter Four) and grill slowly over charcoal (or in an oven) for an hour or so.

Roast Doves

    8 doves
    8 slices onion, ¼ inch thick
    4 cups seedless grapes
    1 teaspoon salt
    ½ teaspoon pepper
    ¼ teaspoon monosodium glutamate
    1 cup butter, melted
    ½ cup white wine
    2 cups stock (chicken soup or bouillon)

Stuff a slice of onion into the neck opening of each bird. Stuff each bird with about ½ cup grapes. Fasten body cavities. Mix the salt, pepper, and monosodium glutamate with half the butter, and roll the birds in this mixture. Place them on a rack in an uncovered roaster. Pour over them the remaining butter, wine, and stock. Roast uncovered in a moderate (300°) oven for 2 hours. Baste occasionally. Make a gravy with the drippings, if desired.

DUCK RECIPES

Let's remind ourselves that the estimated age of all game indicates the ways in which it should be cooked. Young game can be cooked by all methods, but obviously older birds and animals should be cooked by moist heat (as in stews, etc.) rather than by dry heat (such as in broiling). This, of course, is the way we cook chickens, for example. The younger birds are preferred as broilers, young and middle-aged birds as fryers—but the older birds are reserved for longer cooking methods where moist heat is used, such as in stews.

If ducks and geese are cooked over open fires, they should not be cooked directly over the coals, because the dripping and burning fat will cause too much flame. Set a foil pan under the bird to catch the drippings, after pushing the coals back where dripping fat will not cause flare-ups.

Ducks usually are plucked (as described in the beginning of this chapter) rather than skinned. After plucking and cleaning, wash the ducks in cold salted water and dry them thoroughly. Ducks in the fall usually have fine-flavored meat, and any stuffing can be used with them. At other times of year they may be more strongly flavored and are improved by soaking the cleaned birds for 2 or 3 hours in fairly strong salted water to which 1 teaspoon baking soda has been added. If ducks so prepared are to be kept under refrigeration for a few days, after wiping them dry put a few slices of onion in the body cavity. This helps remove the excess gamy taste, and the onion is discarded before the ducks are cooked. In the following recipes we shall assume that the birds are prepared according to the above suggestions. Duck should not be overcooked, because the meat will become dry and crumbly.

Baked Duck with Barbecue Sauce

This recipe calls for skinning and disjointing the ducks, which many old-timers and gourmets won't agree with. It also calls for a barbecue sauce, which some people will think overpowers the flavor of wild duck. However, the recipe is good, and equally suitable for geese, pheasants, and other game birds.

> 2 ducks
> 1 cup wine vinegar
> Salt and pepper to taste
> ½ cup flour
> ½ cup fat

Skin the ducks and cut into serving-size pieces. Cover the pieces with water to which the vinegar has been added. Let stand in liquid for several hours or overnight. Drain the duck pieces and dry them. Salt and pepper each piece and roll it in flour. Brown the pieces in a skillet in hot fat and put them in a baking dish. Pour over them the barbecue sauce, made as follows:

> 1 large onion, minced
> 1 garlic clove, minced
> 4 stalks celery, chopped fine
> 4 tablespoons salad oil
> 2 cups consommé
> 1 bay leaf
> 1 cup tomato juice
> 2 teaspoons Worcestershire sauce
> 4 peppercorns
> 1 sprig parsley, minced

Cook the onion, garlic, and celery in the oil until tender but not brown. Add remaining ingredients and simmer for 30 minutes.

Bake the duck pieces in the barbecue sauce at 350° for about 3 hours, or until tender.

Baked Duck with Wine

> 2 ducks
> Salt and pepper to taste
> 2 apples
> ½ cup butter or margarine
> 1 cup sherry

Rub the whole ducks inside and outside with a little salt and pepper. Put an apple, unpeeled and quartered, in each duck, and fasten the body cavity. Sauté the ducks in the butter until light brown. Put them in a baking pan and add the sherry. Cover and bake in a hot (425°) oven for about 45 minutes. Make a flour gravy with the drippings, if you wish to. Serve with a fruit jelly.

Duck with Mushroom Gravy

    2 ducks
    1 onion, sliced
    ½ cup butter or margarine
    Salt and pepper to taste
    1 bay leaf
    2 cups water
    1 cup fresh mushrooms, sliced
    2 tablespoons flour
    ⅛ teaspoon thyme

Disjoint the ducks into serving-size pieces. Brown the meat and the onion in the fat until the onion is transparent and the duck is golden brown. Pour off the drippings into another skillet. Season with salt and pepper, and add the water and the bay leaf. Cover, and cook over moderate heat for 1½ hours.

In the other skillet containing the drippings, sauté the sliced mushrooms and stir in the flour and the thyme until the mixture is smooth. Add this to the ducks and continue to cook slowly for about 30 minutes longer. Use ½ cup wine instead of the same amount of water, if desired. If you lack fresh mushrooms, omit the flour and substitute a can of mushroom soup. Serve with rice, preferably.

Roast Duck (Basic Recipe)

If you dislike gamy taste in ducks, soak them overnight in salted water (¼ cup salt to 1 quart water) to remove most of the gamy taste. If you like the taste of game, don't bother with this. The gamy taste is further diminished by using a simple stuffing which also helps to flavor the duck but which is discarded after cooking. To make this disposable stuffing, use chopped celery leaves; or quarters or slices of an apple, an onion, some chopped celery, and a little parsley; or a whole orange, an onion, and some celery, all chopped together. If you don't mind the gamy flavor and want to eat the stuffing, use a fancier stuffing, such as one of those suggested in this section.

Stuff the birds with whatever is desired, and sew or pin the opening. Tie the birds, if it is desired to keep legs and wings close to the body. Sprinkle a little paprika over the breasts for added color while roasting, if you wish.

Put the birds in a roasting pan, breast side up, and put them in the oven while it is heating to 450°. Leave the roaster uncovered until the breasts are browned. Then turn the birds breast-side down and cover. At the end of the first hour, turn the oven down to 350°. The ducks will need to cook from 1½ to 2 hours, depending on how big they are, how old they are, and how many you have in the oven. To be sure they do not get dry, baste them with the drippings every 10 or 15 minutes. The exact temperature for the oven and the time the ducks should be left in also depend upon how rare or how well done you like them. If the oven is at a constant temperature of about 425°, the ducks should be done in 1½ hours—slightly less for rare. As we have said, they should not be overcooked.

A very good basting sauce, which adds to the flavor of the ducks, is made as follows:

    1 cup fruit jelly (apple, grape, currant, etc.)
    3 tablespoons prepared mustard
    1 cup port or sherry
    Salt and pepper to taste

Bring this to a boil and baste the ducks with it and with the drippings.

In serving wild ducks, most people like to bring them to the table whole, garnished with parsley, water cress, or something else. They are cut into halves with a knife and game shears. Another way is to cut them in halves in the kitchen and remove the breastbones. Then put the stuffing, or ½ cup wild rice, on each duck half. They are excellent when served with a fruit jelly; with a basting sauce made as above; with a flour gravy; or with a fancy sauce such as this one:

Apricot Sauce

    1 No. 2 can (2½ cups) apricots
    1 tablespoon grated orange peel
    2 cups red wine
    2 tablespoons butter
    ¼ teaspoon pepper or to taste
    Duck livers (as many as you have)

Drain the apricots and rub them through a sieve into a saucepan. Add the orange peel, wine, butter, and pepper, and bring to a boil. Put the livers through the sieve, and stir them into the sauce along with the juices (or some of them) remaining from cooking the ducks. Serve hot with the ducks. If apricots are not handy, use peaches, applesauce, or some other canned fruit.

Glazed Apple Slices

This is another good dish to serve with any roasted game birds:

2 pounds green apples
2 cups brown sugar
Juice and grated rind of 1 lemon
¼ tablespoon nutmeg
⅛ tablespoon ground cloves
½ tablespoon cinnamon
1½ cups water

Peel, core, and slice apples. Arrange slices in a shallow baking dish. Combine 1 cup sugar with the rest of the ingredients, and pour over the apples. Bake for 25 minutes at about 375°. Sprinkle the rest of the sugar over the apples and set the dish under the broiler until the sugar caramelizes. Serve either warm or cold.

Stuffing with Apples

6 bacon slices, cut in small pieces
3 cups apples, pared, cored, diced
1 onion, minced
2 stalks celery, chopped
8 tablespoons sugar
1 tablespoon dried parsley (or other herbs)
2 cups bread or cracker crumbs

Fry bacon pieces crisp and remove from skillet. To the fat add all remaining ingredients except the crumbs. Cook, covered, slowly until apples are partly done. Add bacon and crumbs. Blend well, adding more crumbs, if it seems necessary.

Stuffing with Bread Crumbs

3½ cups stale bread crumbs
1 tablespoon butter
¾ cup boiling water
1 tablespoon sage or poultry seasoning
1½ teaspoons salt
¼ teaspoon pepper
1 onion, minced
½ cup finely chopped celery

Put the crumbs and butter in a bowl and pour the boiling water over them. Let stand until the water is absorbed. If still too wet, add more crumbs. Stir in remaining ingredients. Stuff the birds lightly, because the stuffing swells a little. Add ½ cup chopped chestnuts and/or chopped giblets, if they are handy.

Stuffing with Chestnuts

4 pounds chestnuts
½ cup finely chopped celery
¼ cup melted butter
1 cup heavy cream
2 cups soft bread crumbs
2 teaspoons salt
¼ teaspoon pepper

Drop chestnuts in water and discard any that float. Cut cross slits in the others; cover with water and boil for 20 minutes. Drain, and peel off shells and skin. Chop finely or press through a coarse sieve. Sauté the celery in butter until tender. Combine all ingredients and mix lightly.

Stuffing with Pecans

This makes enough for 2 or 3 ducks and is an excellent stuffing if the ingredients are handy:

4 cups soft bread crumbs
1 cup finely chopped celery
1 cup finely chopped onion
1 cup seedless raisins
1 cup pecan meats, chopped
½ teaspoon salt
½ cup milk, scalded
2 eggs, beaten

Mix the first six ingredients together. Add the scalded milk to the beaten eggs, and stir this into the dry mixture. Fill the ducks with this stuffing; truss and roast as above.

Stuffing with Potato

3 potatoes, cooked and mashed
¼ cup cream or reconstituted milk powder or evaporated milk
1 tablespoon fat or cooking oil
Seasoning to taste (salt, pepper, minced onion, herbs, etc.)
2 eggs, beaten

Stir the cream, fat, and seasoning into the potatoes. Then stir in the beaten eggs. Add a few sliced mushrooms or chopped nuts, if available.

Ducks in Foil

In outdoor cooking we can prepare the duck for roasting and seal it in heavy-duty aluminum foil, as described in Chapter Four. Wrap the breast with 2 strips of bacon or some thinly sliced bits of salt pork. The duck can then be roasted in the hot ashes or on a grid over the coals. Turn the package frequently and the duck will baste itself. Cooking time over moderate heat will be about an hour. A double package of foil (one within the other) is recommended because when the duck seems to be cooked it is well to open the package to be sure the bird is done. The doubled package helps prevent puncturing the foil and keeps ashes out of the food when the package is opened.

Duck on a Spit

Prepare the duck for roasting, as described above, and balance it on a spit. Put a foil pan under it to catch the juices, moving the coals in the grill back far enough so that they will not be in the way of the juice pan. As the duck turns on the spit it will baste itself, but basting with the following marinade sauce helps the flavor. In the woods, a 1-inch-thick green peeled straight sapling, pointed at the end, will serve as a spit. It can be rested at the right distance over the coals and can be turned by hand occasionally. Some outdoorsmen wrap the spitted bird in foil to help retain the juices and to prevent ashes from getting on the meat. Others prefer the slightly smoky flavor obtained when cooking without foil.

Duck Marinade Sauce

> ¼ cup vinegar
> ¼ cup salad oil
> 2 teaspoons salt
> ¼ teaspoon dry mustard
> ½ garlic clove, crushed
> Dash of herbs, such as mace, nutmeg, clove

This mixture can be used to marinate the duck and also for basting it while cooking.

Roast Duck Breasts

This is a good method when equipment is lacking. Remove the breast and cut the two sides from the breastbone. Impale them on a stick over the fire; roast them on a grid, or cook them in foil, until well browned. Add salt and pepper, or baste them with a sauce such as the one above while they are cooking.

Another quick trick is to slice the breast meat very thin across the grain, to obtain several bite-sized pieces. Sprinkle these with condiments and fry them for about 10 seconds on each side in a lightly greased skillet. Serve them with a sauce, if available. (This is a Japanese method, often used when cooking on hibachis.)

GOOSE RECIPES

Since geese are big birds, they are usually roasted. Hunters who want a quick meal like to fry the breasts, as described in the next recipe. In any event, save the giblets for spaghetti sauce.

Fried Goose Breasts

> 1 pair (or more) of goose breasts
> ¼ cup flour
> Salt and pepper to taste
> ¼ cup bacon fat
> Water or milk

Skin the goose and slice out the whole breasts. Slice about ¼ inch thick, across the grain. Dredge in seasoned flour, and pound, to tenderize. Fry in hot fat for 1 minute on each side. Remove the meat from the pan and stir in 1 tablespoon flour for each 1 tablespoon fat remaining. When smooth, stir in water or milk to make gravy of the right consistency. Add salt, pepper, or other condiments to the gravy, and pour it over the fried goose breasts.

Goose Giblet Spaghetti Sauce

> Giblets from about 6 geese or 10 ducks
>   (reduce recipe accordingly for less)
> 2 tablespoons olive oil
> 2 medium-sized onions, diced small
> 2 garlic cloves, diced small
> ½ green pepper, diced small
> ½ cup chopped parsley
> 1 tablespoon dry marjoram
> ½ tablespoon dry thyme

Grind the giblets; combine all ingredients and brown them slightly in the oil. Then stir in:

> 2 cans tomato sauce
> 1 can mushroom sauce

Simmer the sauce slowly for about 1 hour, adding a little water if it gets too thick. Pour the sauce over well-drained spaghetti and sprinkle with Parmesan cheese.

Roast Goose

Prepare the goose for cooking. If it is an older bird, soak it in cold-water brine overnight. If it shows any blood marks from shot holes, do this anyway. Rinse and wipe dry. Rub the goose inside and out with butter, salt, and pepper; or with salt, pepper, and vinegar; or with salt, pepper, white wine, and a little nutmeg. Stuff the goose with one of the stuffings recommended for ducks, or, if you want to give it the full treatment, with one of the two stuffings that follow. Sew up the cavity, and tie legs and wings to body. Sprinkle with flour. Set the goose on a low rack in a roasting pan and prick the skin all over with a sharp fork to allow fat to run off. Roast, uncovered, in a 325° oven, allowing 25 minutes per pound. Baste the goose with juices from the

A SUSPENSION ROTISSERIE   (Boy Scouts of America)

Large birds can be roasted by being suspended over a reflector fire from a dingle stick, as shown in the photo at right, which is made clearer by the drawing. Run a green wood skewer through the body below the wing joints, and another through the body below the legs. Loop a strong cord or light wire around one of the skewers, as shown, and suspend the bird a few inches above a drip pan by tying or hooking it to the dingle stick. When the bird is half done, reverse it by suspending it from the other skewer. This method allows the bird to be rotated while being cooked.

pan and drain off some of the fat if there is too much.

If the goose seems to be getting too brown on top before it is cooked, put a piece of aluminum foil or a cloth soaked in salad oil over the breast.

Another way to do this is to set the goose in the roaster, breast side down, with enough water in the pan to cover the breast. When half cooked, remove most of the water and turn the bird breast side up until it has browned. Keep basting frequently after turning the bird. An older bird will require a little longer cooking time than a younger one.

For a simple stuffing, merely fill the cavity with quartered onions, apples, and celery. As we have said, this flavors game birds and reduces some of the gamy taste. This stuffing can be discarded, or the goose need not be stuffed at all. A good stuffing, however, adds immeasurably to the dish.

In outdoor cooking, geese can be cooked on a spit over an open fire, in a Dutch oven, or wrapped securely in aluminum foil, as recommended for ducks and other game birds.

Another good basting idea, especially suitable for geese, is to baste frequently with a mixture of ½ cup gin, ½ cup water, and 3 or 4 juniper berries. Juniper berries grow wild in many places. They add to the basting liquid but are not essential. Incidentally, try serving wild goose with the Glazed Apple Slices mentioned earlier in this chapter (see Index).

Prune Stuffing for Geese

½ pound dried prunes
1 cup white wine
½ pound sausage meat
6 apples, cored, peeled, chopped
6 onions, chopped
1 bay leaf
½ teaspoon dry thyme
½ teaspoon dry marjoram
Salt and pepper to taste
1 tablespoon minced parsley
1 cup soft bread crumbs

Soak the prunes overnight and cook them until tender in enough white wine to cover them. Let cool, remove pits, and reserve the juice. Cook the sausage meat in a skillet until brown, breaking it up with a fork. Take out meat and reserve. In the sausage fat, sauté the apples and onions. Add the herbs, and salt and pepper to taste. Add the parsley and the wine the prunes were cooked in, plus enough more wine to just cover. Cook until the apples are tender, and rub the mixture through a coarse sieve into a bowl. Add the sausage, prunes, and the bread crumbs to make a dry stuffing. If the stuffing is not dry enough, add more bread crumbs. Let cool, and stuff the goose. Sew or skewer the opening. Rub the bird with melted butter seasoned with salt and pepper and a pinch of powdered ginger, if you have it.

Now, since we're doing a fancy job on this, let's make a gravy. In this case, don't use the juice the prunes were cooked in, in the above recipe, but add enough more wine to make up for it. When the goose is half cooked, drain off the fat and add the prune juice plus enough more wine to make 1 cup. Add 1 cup water. When the goose is cooked, thicken the gravy with 1 tablespoon flour rubbed smooth in ½ cup water. Stir this into the gravy. Also add 1 ounce gin, 1 teaspoon brandy, and 1 tablespoon currant jelly. Serve the gravy hot.

Liver Stuffing for Geese

> *Goose liver*
> *3 chicken livers*
> *3 tablespoons seedless raisins*
> *3 large mushrooms, chopped*
> *1 cup white wine*
> *1 pound chestnuts*
> *½ cup cooking oil*
> *1 cup consommé*
> *½ pound sausage meat*
> *¼ teaspoon each of dry mace, basil, and rosemary*
> *¼ clove garlic, minced*
> *Bread crumbs (if necessary)*

Marinate the livers, raisins, and chopped mushrooms in the wine overnight. Score the chestnuts, and heat them in the oil about 4 minutes, shaking the pan constantly. Remove nuts from the oil; remove shells and skin, and simmer them in the consommé until tender. At the same time, fry the sausage, breaking up the meat with a fork. While this is being done, transfer the livers, mushrooms, raisins, and wine into a saucepan and bring it to a boil. Remove livers and chop them. Remove chestnuts and chop

them. Combine all ingredients; season with salt and pepper, and add the herbs and garlic. If the mixture is too moist, add enough bread crumbs to make a dry dressing. Stuff the goose, and sew or skewer the opening. Cook the goose as above.

To make a gravy, remove the goose to a hot platter; pour off the fat, but not the juices, and stir into the pan 1 cup white wine and 1 cup sour cream, added to the juices in the pan. Blend, bring to a boil, and serve hot.

GROUSE, PARTRIDGE, AND WOODCOCK RECIPES

Those who are so fortunate as to have shot a few grouse should do them the honor of special treatment in the kitchen. They deserve fancy cooking, but they certainly don't need it. As we said earlier in this book, they are especially delicious when broiled over an open campfire. One way to do it is to remove the skin; split the bird into two sections; season it with salt and pepper; and broil it slowly on a forked stick over hardwood coals. Since grouse are lacking in fat, it is always well to baste them with bacon, salt pork, or other fat.

As with pheasant, ducks, and other game birds, we may wish to soak them in salt brine for a few hours to remove blood marks from shot holes. Back in camp, a favorite and easy way to prepare them is to remove the breasts, salt and pepper them, and brush them with fat. Put them in a greased broiler and broil them for 15 minutes or so in a moderate (350°) oven. An added touch is to pour a little bourbon over them and return them to the oven for a minute or two more.

If only the breasts (and legs) are used, don't throw away the other eatable parts. Wash the back, wings, etc., and cook them up for soup stock. Here are some other ideas:

Fried Grouse

This is done in the same way we do chicken. Cut the birds into frying-size pieces, salt and pepper them, and fry them until golden brown in enough bacon fat to cover the bottom of the skillet. Turn the pieces to brown them on all sides. Then cover the skillet and cook slowly over moderate heat for about 30 minutes.

A little fancier way is to put the following in a paper bag:

Some tasty woodcock about to be broiled with bacon in a basket broiler. (Michigan Conservation Department)

½ cup flour
¼ teaspoon baking powder
½ teaspoon salt
¼ teaspoon pepper
½ teaspoon paprika

Cut one or more grouse into serving-size pieces, dip them in a small bowl of cream or evaporated milk, and then drop them in the bag. Shake the bag to coat the pieces thoroughly. Put ½ cup shortening, oil, or fat in a skillet and get it almost smoking hot. Brown the meat in the fat until all sides are coated. Then cover the skillet and let the birds cook over moderate heat for about 30 minutes.

If you do this on a kitchen range, preheat the skillet to 400°. When the meat is browned, cover and finish cooking at 225°.

Roast Grouse

4 grouse
Salt and pepper to taste
Celery leaves
4 tablespoons butter
8 slices bacon

Pepper and salt the cleaned grouse inside and out, and stuff with celery leaves. Add 1 tablespoon butter to each body cavity. Skewer the cavities closed; cover each breast with bacon slices, and roast the grouse uncovered in a 350° oven for about 25 minutes.

The celery leaves are discarded, but they help to flavor the bird and to remove the gamy taste. Sections of apple and/or onion can be substituted, or the birds can be stuffed with one of the fancier dressings mentioned earlier. In serving birds such as this, carve the breast beside the breastbone, down as far as possible. Then separate the two halves with game shears. Here's a couple of good sauces to go with this:

Red Wine Sauce

2 teaspoons minced onion
1 cup red wine
1 cup beef stock

Sauté the onion in the pan with the juices remaining from cooking the birds. When the onion is golden brown, add the other ingredients. Bring to a boil and cook for 5 minutes, stirring occasionally.

Jelly Sauce

3 *tablespoons fruit jelly (grape, currant, apple, etc.)*
3 *tablespoons butter*
½ *teaspoon herbs (such as marjoram)*
Salt and pepper to taste

Combine above in a saucepan and heat, while stirring until blended. Thin with a little wine if you wish.

Rotisseried Grouse

This is a fancy back yard recipe to serve when you want to make an impression on somebody!

2 *or 3 grouse (save the livers)*
2½ *cups bread crumb stuffing*
½ *cup butter*
⅓ *cup brandy*
2 *tablespoons grated orange rind and pulp*
1 *cup finely chopped celery*
1 *egg, beaten*
½ *teaspoon herb blend*
Pepper and salt to taste
½ *cup French (oil and vinegar) dressing*

Chop the livers and sauté them with the bread crumb stuffing in half the butter. Sauté the celery in remaining butter until transparent. Combine all ingredients except half of the brandy and the French dressing, and stuff the grouse. Fasten body cavities and balance the grouse on a spit. Cook over a medium fire of scattered briquettes. Baste every few minutes with the French dressing. Cooking will take about an hour, if the fire is right. When cooked, set the birds on a platter and pour the remaining brandy over them. Garnish the platter and serve the birds cut in halves at the table. Serve with Glazed Apple Slices and wild rice.

Skillet Grouse

Prepare the grouse by using the floured recipe for Fried Grouse above. When the grouse pieces have been browned in the skillet, add all the following except the wine:

1 *cup soup stock (or mushroom soup)*
1 *teaspoon lemon juice*
1 *onion, chopped fine*
4 *carrots, chopped fine*
1 *tablespoon finely chopped parsley*
2 *cloves*
2 *bay leaves*
Pepper and salt to taste
½ *cup red wine*

(Boy Scouts of America)

Roasting a bird on a spit

Cover, and cook until vegetables are tender. Add the wine, and continue cooking, covered, for a total of about 30 to 40 minutes after adding the vegetables.

Spitted Grouse

This is an easy recipe for cooking birds on a spit over a campfire—or a much simpler one than the recipe above for doing them on a rotisserie at home.

4 *grouse, cleaned and plucked*
2 *oranges (or apples, or whatever is available for stuffing)*
2 *onions, chopped*
1 *cup butter or margarine*
½ *teaspoon herbs (such as sage, savory, marjoram)*
Salt and pepper to taste

Rub each bird outside and inside with salt. Stuff with orange wedges and onion. Skewer or sew body cavities closed.

Erect a spit over the campfire by resting a 1-inch-thick debarked sapling on two forked sticks driven into the ground so the sapling spit is about a foot over the tamped-down coals of the fire. Spit the grouse and set them over the fire. Turn, and baste occasionally with the butter to which the herbs and seasoning have been added. Cooking should take about an hour, but test for doneness by inserting a fork between the body and leg, or twist a leg to see if it can be separated from the meat, which should indicate that the birds are done. (If the stuffing is for eating rather than for flavor, use your choice of the dressings previously mentioned.)

PHEASANT RECIPES

This beautiful inhabitant of cornfields, hedgerows, and swamps can be cooked exactly as one cooks chicken—but since it is a wild bird, more flavorful than domestic fowl, we add a few embellishments to the recipes to provide distinctive outdoor flavor. Since pheasants are relatively lacking in fat, this must be added when cooking the birds to prevent dryness. These recipes are suitable for preparing all species of upland game birds, and the recipes given for grouse are equally suitable for pheasant, except that, since the pheasant usually is a bigger bird, it should be cooked a little longer.

Glazed Pheasant

Let's start with a fancy one again! Prepare the bird for cooking as you would a roasting chicken. Here's how to make the stuffing:

¼ *cup butter or margarine*
½ *cup finely chopped onion*
¼ *cup finely chopped almonds*
1½ *teaspoons salt*
2 *teaspoons sugar*
¼ *teaspoon thyme, marjoram, or poultry seasoning*
1 *tablespoon grated orange rind*
1½ *cups cooked rice*

Combine the first three ingredients and sauté until the onion is soft. Add remaining ingredients; blend, and stuff the bird with this. Tie legs and wings. Now, make an Orange Glaze, as follows:

1 *cup orange juice*
2 *teaspoons grated orange rind*
¼ *cup honey*
¼ *cup salad oil*

Mix above ingredients. Put the stuffed pheasant on a rack in a roasting pan, breast side up, and pour the glaze over it. Roast in a slow (325°) oven for 2 to 2½ hours, or until the bird is browned and the leg meat feels soft. Baste frequently. About half an hour before the bird should be done, slice 2 oranges. Remove the rack from under the pheasant and lay the orange slices around the bird. Continue roasting and basting until the bird is done. Serve on a platter with the orange slices around the bird and the glaze poured over it.

Pheasant in Cream

1 *dressed pheasant*
½ *cup flour*
½ *teaspoon salt*
¼ *teaspoon pepper*
½ *teaspoon paprika*
½ *cup shortening or oil*
1 *cup coffee cream*

Cut the pheasant in serving-size pieces and put them in a paper bag with the next four ingredients. Shake the bag to coat the pieces with flour. Put the cooking oil in a skillet and, when it is almost smoking hot, fry the meat in the oil until golden brown. Pour the cream over the meat and continue cooking slowly, covered, until all the cream is absorbed. This will take about an hour. When the meat is tender, remove it from the skillet to a hot platter and make a milk gravy with the drippings. (To make the gravy, stir 1 teaspoon flour into ½ cup milk until smooth, and stir this slowly into the drippings. Continue cooking for a few minutes, adding a little more milk if the gravy gets too thick.)

In place of the cream, you could add a can of mushroom soup and about ¼ cup milk. In this case, there's no need to make any more gravy.

Pheasant in Dutch Oven

This is the same as the recipe above, except that you do it over an open fire in a Dutch oven, and you add a small can of drained green peas a few minutes before the bird is done.

Pheasant in Foil

    2 pheasant breasts
    4 pineapple rings
    4 tablespoons sherry

Take a square pan or skillet and lay the pineapple rings in it. Season the pheasant breasts and lay them over the pineapple. Add the sherry (or other wine). Crimp a large doubled sheet of heavy-duty aluminum foil over the pan or skillet so no steam can escape. Bake on the grill or in a moderate oven (350°) for about an hour.

This can also be done by making two Hot Dinner Packages (Chapter Four). Wrap a breast and 2 pineapple rings, plus 2 tablespoons wine, securely in a double package of foil. Make two packages this way, and cook them in the moderate heat of the campfire for about an hour, turning the packages every 15 minutes.

Pheasant Pie

    2 pheasants, skinned and cut in pieces
    1 quart water
    ½ teaspoon salt
    2 carrots, diced
    1 onion, sliced
    1 bay leaf
    Dash of pepper

Simmer the pheasant meat with the other ingredients in a pot until the meat can be removed from the bones. Remove the meat from the bones

and put the meat in a well-buttered casserole. Pour in 1 cup canned, drained peas and 1 cup White Sauce (see Index). Cover the casserole with biscuits and cook in a 475° oven for about 15 minutes, until the biscuits are nicely browned. (The broth in which the birds were cooked can be saved for stock for use in another recipe, or it can be discarded.)

Roast Brandied Pheasant

    3 pheasants
    6 slices bacon
    ¼ cup butter
    2 tablespoons minced onion
    1 garlic clove, crushed
    ½ cup brandy
    2 cups chicken stock
    ½ teaspoon black pepper
    1 teaspoon salt
    1 pint heavy cream
    ¼ cup prepared horse radish

Cover each bird with 2 strips of bacon and tie them so they won't lose their shape. Brown them in the hot butter with the onions and garlic. When the birds are browned, put them in a baking pan with the juices from the frying pan. Pour the brandy over the birds and light it. When the flame dies, add the chicken stock, pepper, and salt. Roast uncovered in a 375° oven for half an hour, basting frequently. Pour the cream and horse radish over the birds, and continue roasting for 15 or 20 minutes, still basting frequently. Put the birds on a hot platter and pour the sauce over them. (Serve this with rice and currant jelly.)

QUAIL RECIPES

Quail should be plucked, dressed, and eaten as soon as possible after killing. Like most game birds, they are lacking in fat and should be well larded to prevent the flesh from drying out. They are so small that usually we do not bother to stuff them, but any of the stuffings for game birds can be used, and some recipes call for them. In spite of their small size, they are among the most flavorful of game birds.

Broiled Quail

Split the plucked and dressed quail in halves through the back, and broil them slowly on a grid over a coal fire. Baste frequently with butter. (Or put them on a well-greased pan and broil them in the kitchen range.) When browned, season lightly and serve on buttered toast with currant or grape jelly.

Fried Quail

Dust the birds with seasoned flour and fry them in butter. When well browned, lower the heat; cover the pan, and let them simmer for about 20 minutes. If you want gravy, remove the quail to a hot plate and stir into the drippings enough flour to absorb them. When stirred smooth, gradually add milk until the gravy is of the right consistency.

Quail in Dutch Oven

6 to 8 dressed quail
⅓ cup olive oil or butter
¾ cup chopped parsley
½ cup chopped green pepper
2 cloves garlic, minced (or garlic salt)
1 medium-sized onion, minced
¾ cup sauterne or other white wine
2 cans tomato sauce
1 can mushrooms
Pinch of thyme
Pinch of rosemary
Salt and pepper to taste

Pour the oil or butter into a hot Dutch oven and fry the birds, turning them in the hot fat until they are a red-brown color on all sides. Then add the parsley, green pepper, garlic, and onion. When these are tender and golden, add the wine, and cover, removing the Dutch oven to a spot on the fire where the ingredients will simmer. In a few minutes add the tomato sauce, mushrooms, and seasoning. Simmer slowly for about 1½ hours. This dish is very good when served over noodles.

Quail on Toast

Pluck and dress as many quail as needed. Wash and wipe, and stuff the birds with your favorite dressing. Truss carefully, letting the legs stand up (instead of down, as with a chicken). Wrap or tie half a bacon strip around the legs. Roast in a hot oven (450°) for 15 or 20 minutes, basting frequently with a mixture of butter, hot water, salt, and pepper. Serve on toast that has been moistened with broth from the quail. Garnish with parsley and serve with grape or currant jelly.

Quail in Wine

6 quail, cleaned and trussed
½ cup butter or other fat
2 onions, minced
2 cloves
1 teaspoon peppercorns
2 garlic cloves, minced
½ bay leaf
2 cups white wine
½ teaspoon salt
⅛ teaspoon pepper
1 teaspoon minced chives
2 cups cream or evaporated milk

Melt the fat, and add the onions, cloves, peppercorns, garlic and bay leaf. Cook several minutes. Add the quail, and brown on all sides. Add wine, salt, pepper, and chives. Simmer until tender, which will be about 30 minutes. Remove quail to a hot serving dish. Strain the sauce and add the cream or milk. Heat almost to the boiling point but do not allow to boil. Pour the sauce over the quail.

Roast Quail

Dress, but do not skin, as many birds as you wish. Stuff body cavities with buttered bread crumbs mixed with chopped pecans. Roll the birds in flour. Place the birds in a casserole and pour over them some browned butter that has been mixed with a little hot water. Add ⅛ cup sherry for each bird. Cover and bake in a slow (300°) oven until tender, which should be in about 20 minutes.

WILD TURKEY RECIPES

Since wild turkeys are native to some parts of the United States, and are being introduced successfully into others, it seems appropriate to include this recipe, which is a favorite of many turkey hunters:

Roast Wild Turkey

Dress the bird as you would a native turkey or chicken. Also have on hand:

1 cup butter
Salt and pepper to taste
Bacon
1 cup white wine

Rub the turkey inside and out with ½ cup butter and with pepper and salt. Stuff him with one of the stuffings previously mentioned, or

(George X. Sand)

Writer George X. Sand exhibits a wild turkey shot in Florida. At right, it is being prepared for the camp oven.

one of the two that follow. Skewer or sew the body cavity closed. Put the turkey in a roaster and drop several small strips of bacon over the breast. Cover the breast with a cloth and pour the wine and the remaining (melted) butter over the turkey, so the cloth will be soaked. Add a little salt and pepper. Roast in an oven set to 350° for 20 minutes to the pound, basting frequently with the juices. When the bird is about done, remove the cloth to brown the bird a little more, if necessary.

The traditional stuffing for wild turkey is made with peanuts. Here are two ways to do it:

Peanut Stuffing I

    12 slices bread, toasted and cubed
    2 cups salted peanuts, crushed or ground
    ½ cup chicken stock or bouillon

Mix the toast cubes and crushed peanuts, and add enough stock to make a fairly dry dressing.

Peanut Stuffing II

    3 cups roasted peanuts
    ½ cup white wine
    4 cups dried bread crumbs
    1 egg, beaten

    1 onion, finely chopped
    3 teaspoons butter, melted
    ½ cup chicken stock
    ½ teaspoon black pepper

Brown the roasted peanuts in the oven and chop them fine. Combine these with remaining ingredients and toss together lightly. (This should be enough for a 10-pound bird.)

Wild Turkey, Camp Style

My old friend George X. Sand, who is one of the best outdoor writers in the business, sends along this method for preparing turkey in a turkey hunters' camp:

Use aluminum foil, a heavy skillet with a lid, or a Dutch oven. Cut up the bird as you would a chicken. Salt and pepper the parts, and dredge them in flour (using the paper-bag method). Place the pieces on a large, doubled strip of heavy-duty aluminum foil (or in the pan or oven) and add 4 tablespoons butter. Fold up the edges of the foil to make a platter, and pour over the turkey ½ cup sherry. Fold the foil to make a tight package and put an outer wrapping around this, so no juices can leak out. Put the package on the grill or in a moderately hot part of the campfire. Cooking time will take from 1 to 1½ hours, depending on the heat and the size of the bird. Turn the package every 15 minutes, so that all parts will be evenly cooked and basted.

Another camp method is to cut up the bird and boil the bony parts in a little water, with seasoning and a bay leaf. Remove the meat from the bones and add it to the boneless meat, which has been cooked as above. Also cook some rice, using the stock the bones were cooked in. Serve the meat and rice together.

In writing these chapters on how to cook various kinds of fish and game, I have included recipes for marinades, stuffings, and sauces wherever they seem most appropriate. Some are elaborate, while some are very simple—as are the recipes themselves. Recipes for one kind of bird, or for its stuffings, marinades, and sauces, often are adaptable to another kind if allowance for the size of the bird is made in cooking time and in proportions. Readers who expect to go on trips where some of these recipes will be used should check in advance the ones they prefer to be sure that the needed ingredients will be included in the list of provisions.

Chapter Fifteen

SAUCES AND GRAVIES

One of the main things that separates the men from the boys in outdoor (and indoor) cooking is whether or not they think to make gravies and sauces for the dishes that need them. Variations in gravies and sauces provide variations in menus and help to prevent the "sameness" that could make outdoor cooking seem dull and ordinary.

It's a shame that camp cooks don't use gravies and sauces more often, because their preparation is very easy. For example, we can make a basic white sauce merely by blending and cooking butter, flour, and milk, plus some seasoning. This just takes a few minutes, and it can be made in a skillet. With this made, we can transform it with any number of tasty variations, of which eight of the very easy ones are included in this chapter. We also can make brown gravy somewhat similarly, and can vary it by adding mushrooms (fresh, canned, or dehydrated) and other partially cooked or leftover vegetables, if we wish to do so. We also can pep it up with various condiments and herbs, or with bottled sauces such as Worcestershire, A-1, Maggi, and many others.

Since these gravies and sauces are so very easy to prepare, it seems unnecessary to fall back on the canned varieties, most of which are very good, however. Canned or dehydrated soups also provide the bases for excellent sauces and gravies and, if these are available, they should not be neglected.

Sauces are made separately from the main dish, while gravies are made as a part of it.

GRAVIES

Basic Gravy (for Meats)

Gravy made from drippings from a roast needs only salt and pepper for seasoning and, if you have seasoned the roast well, it may not need even that. Just skim off most of the fat; add seasoning, if necessary, and serve. If the juices are of insufficient quantity, add some water, and bolster the flavor with bouillon cubes, Worcestershire or A-1 sauce, tomato soup or sauce, meat-based soups, and/or cooked vegetables such as onions, carrots, and peas. Juices from other vegetables also can be blended in.

Bacon Grease Gravy (for Meats or Game Birds)

This really should be called "Meat Fat Gravy," because almost any kind of fat, such as chicken, beef, or ham, will do. To about ¼ cup of the grease, add in the skillet about 3 cups milk—or similar properly diluted proportions of evaporated or powdered milk. While this is heating in the pot or skillet, blend about 4 tablespoons flour in a little milk or water until the mixture is smooth. Then slowly add the flour mixture to the milk and fat, stirring all the time until the gravy has thickened properly, which should take only 3 or 4 minutes. Do this over a very slow fire, because gravies are best when slowly cooked. Test it for flavor and add whatever condiments seem advisable. If the gravy is too thin or too thick, bring it to the desired consistency by adding a little more milk or more of the flour mixture.

Brown Gravy (for Meats)

Remove the meat from the pan it was cooked in and pour off some of the fat, if there is more than 2 or 3 tablespoons. Then stir into the remaining drippings about 1 tablespoon flour for each 1 tablespoon drippings. While stirring, scrape up all of the crusty fragments in the bottom of the pan. When this is all stirred to a rich brown, slowly add about 1 cup water or beef stock. Then add about ½ teaspoon salt and a little pepper to flavor it as you like it. When the gravy has thickened and become smooth, it is ready to serve.

Some people like to strain off the undissolved crusty meat fragments, but outdoor cooks usually think these are better left in. As variations to this simple recipe, stir in with the flour a small onion minced very fine. Also add a shake of Worcestershire or A-1 sauce, if you like.

Note that in making all of these floured gravies we add about as much flour as we have fat in the pan. If the drippings are almost entirely of fat, we add enough flour to absorb the fat. The flour should be stirred in until no lumps remain, and the gravy should be cooked very slowly, so that there will be no taste of the flour when the gravy is cooked.

Cream Gravy (for Fried Chicken or Game Birds)

After having fried the chicken, there will be some fat and scrapings in the pan. Estimate the number of spoonfuls of the fat and measure an equal amount of flour. Blend this thoroughly with water, to make a thin paste. Add this to the fat and scrapings in the pan, and stir all together until well blended. Then add about 1 cup milk. Cook this over low heat, stirring constantly until the gravy has thickened and is creamy. Then season to taste. Down South, they don't like to strain this gravy because the scrapings add to the flavor.

Giblet Gravy (for Chicken and Game Birds)

Wash the giblets and boil them in 3 cups water to which you have added a finely sliced onion and 1 teaspoon celery salt (or regular salt and green celery leaves or dried celery). When this has come to a boil, put the covered pot over low heat and simmer the giblets until they are tender. Remove the giblets and strain the broth. Chop the giblets.

Pour all but about 4 tablespoons (¼ cup) drippings from the pan the bird was roasted in, and stir into the remaining drippings an equal amount of flour. When this is blended, add the strained broth and the giblets, and cook until thickened, stirring frequently.

WHITE SAUCES

The following simple sauces are as easy to make as the gravies were. First, let's memorize the simple formula for Basic White Sauce because, having made this, we can add many variations for all sorts of dishes.

Basic White Sauce

Use equal amounts of flour and butter, such as 2 tablespoons of each. In a skillet over a low fire, blend the flour and butter until smooth. Then remove the skillet from the fire and very slowly add ½ cup milk for each 1 tablespoon flour you used. Pour the milk in, a small amount at a time, stirring until completely blended. Then put the skillet back over low heat and cook and stir until the sauce thickens and is smooth. Season to taste with salt and pepper. Of course you can add a little more flour if you want the sauce a little thicker, or you can add a little more milk if you like it thinner.

This sauce is excellent for all sorts of dishes, such as creamed potatoes, onions, peas, and other vegetables; creamed dried beef, creamed chicken, leftover fish, hard-boiled eggs; as a basis for cream soups—and so on. It is also the basis for numerous excellent sauces made by adding other ingredients to the Basic White Sauce. Here are a few of them:

Cheese Sauce

Stir into the Basic White Sauce until melted and blended about half as much shredded cheese as you have sauce.

Cream Sauce

In making the Basic White Sauce, use half milk and half heavy cream instead of all milk. When the sauce is completed, stir in an egg yolk to provide a yellow sauce instead of a white sauce. (Do not cook the sauce any more after adding the egg, or it may curdle.) If you like the sauce to be slightly pink, add a dash of paprika, with or without the egg yolk. More than one egg yolk can be added for more pronounced egg flavor and a yellower sauce. To prevent the egg yolks from curdling the sauce, it is safer to add a little of the sauce to the egg yolks, blending completely, and then to stir this into the remaining sauce. This sauce is excellent with potatoes, croquettes, fish, chicken, and some meat dishes.

Curry and Egg Sauce

For each cup of Basic White Sauce stir in 1 teaspoon curry powder and 1 or 2 sliced hard-boiled eggs. Add 1 tablespoon chopped parsley or ½ teaspoon parsley flakes, if you like. This sauce is especially good with fish or shellfish, such as shrimps and scallops.

Egg Sauce

For each cup of Basic White Sauce stir in a finely chopped hard-boiled egg and 1 tablespoon minced parsley. A dash of Tabasco sauce can also be added. Try this over any kind of broiled fish, or with boiled potatoes.

Horse Radish Sauce

For each cup of Basic White Sauce stir in ½ cup drained horse radish and a little lemon juice. This is excellent when served with meat; especially with boiled beef, boiled corned beef, or tongue.

Mustard Sauce

For each cup of Basic White Sauce stir in 1 teaspoon prepared mustard (or ½ teaspoon dry mustard) and 2 finely chopped hard-boiled eggs. Taste this, and add more mustard if you like it really hot. This sauce is very good with corned beef hash or with fish fillets.

Parsley Sauce

For each cup of Basic White Sauce stir in about ⅓ cup finely chopped fresh parsley and 1 tablespoon grated onion.

Wine Sauce

For each cup of Basic White Sauce stir in ½ cup white wine and 2 egg yolks. (Remember not to cook the sauce after the egg yolks have been added.) This sauce (and the Parsley Sauce above) are excellent with fish fillets or with boiled fish.

BARBECUE SAUCES

Barbecue Sauce I (for Meats and Birds)

This is the author's favorite. We make up a large amount of it because it will keep in jars in the refrigerator for weeks—always ready to baste on meats and chicken while being grilled over an open fire.

2 cans tomato juice
2 bottles catsup
1 cup brown sugar or honey
1 cup minced onion
1 cup cider vinegar
½ cup chopped fresh or 2 tablespoons dried basil
1 tablespoon coarse cracked peppercorns
2 tablespoons celery salt
1 tablespoon chili powder
2 slices lemon
1 garlic clove, crushed to a paste
1 teaspoon dry mustard
½ teaspoon Tabasco sauce
2 tablespoons Worcestershire sauce

Put all ingredients in a pot and bring it to a boil, stirring frequently. Then turn down to low heat and let the sauce simmer, covered, for at least an hour. One secret is to let it simmer—simmer—simmer. Another secret, as told to me by an old Negro cook at a camp down South, is to include the lemon. When the sauce is done, you fish out what remains of the lemon. It would be difficult to overcook this sauce if it is cooked very slowly and tightly covered.

In barbecuing meats and chicken, the sauce should be painted on the food with a brush fairly late in the cooking, because tomato-based sauces like this one will turn black when burned. The above sauce is fairly elaborate but is easy to make if the ingredients are available—and it is well worth it. After you have made the first batch you may wish to change the proportions of some of the ingredients, because quantities are a matter of taste.

Here are some sauces that require fewer ingredients:

Barbecue Sauce II

1 cup soy sauce
1 cup catsup
1 tablespoon dry mustard
½ cup white wine
½ cup honey
2 pieces candied ginger, sliced

Mix all ingredients and allow to simmer, covered, for a few minutes. This is very good with spareribs or other meats. For added flavor they can be marinated in the sauce before cooking, and then the sauce can be used for basting.

Barbecue Sauce III

2 tablespoons dry mustard
⅓ cup chili sauce
1 cup brown sugar
¾ cup pineapple juice
1 teaspoon lemon juice

Mix all ingredients and allow to simmer, covered, for a few minutes. This sauce is especially recommended for ham.

Barbecue Sauce IV

⅓ cup butter
⅓ cup salad oil
⅔ cup water
2 teaspoons A-1 sauce
2 tablespoons lemon juice
¼ teaspoon Tabasco sauce
2 teaspoons sugar
1 teaspoon salt
Dash of pepper
2 teaspoons flour

Melt the butter; add liquid ingredients, then stir in dry ingredients. Stir and cook about 3 minutes, until slightly thickened. This sauce is recommended for basting chicken and game birds.

Barbecue Sauce V

2 teaspoons paprika
3 tablespoons Worcestershire sauce
2 tablespoons olive oil
3 tablespoons catsup
2 tablespoons sugar
¼ cup sherry
Salt and pepper to taste
Garlic salt to taste

Combine all ingredients and simmer for a few minutes. This sauce is recommended for venison and other meats. After basting the meat while it is being cooked, some of the sauce can be added as a gravy.

Barbecue Sauce VI

¼ cup salad oil
1 onion, minced
2 tablespoons vinegar
3 tablespoons lemon juice
1 cup water
1 teaspoon salt
1 teaspoon celery salt
1 tablespoon prepared mustard
2 tablespoons brown sugar

Sauté the onion in the salad oil until it is transparent. Add remaining ingredients and simmer about 30 minutes. This sauce is especially good for basting chicken and game birds.

SAUCES FOR FISH

Black Butter Sauce

¼ cup butter
1 tablespoon lemon juice
Salt and pepper to taste

After frying fish, melt the butter in the skillet or pan containing the drippings in which the fish was fried. Stir and simmer until the butter mixture turns a dark brown. Then stir in the lemon juice and season to taste. Pour this over the fish. (You can substitute margarine or vegetable oil for the butter, if necessary.) Avoid burning the butter, because it then will be bitter. Vinegar can be substituted for the lemon juice. Both fish and sauce should be served hot.

Chili and Mustard Sauce

¼ cup butter
¼ cup minced onion
1 clove garlic (minced with the onion)
1 teaspoon Worcestershire sauce
2 tablespoons chili sauce
1 teaspoon prepared mustard (or ½ teaspoon, or more if desired, dry mustard)
½ teaspoon salt
Dash of pepper

Sauté the minced onion and garlic in the butter until transparent but not browned. Stir in remaining ingredients, and serve hot. This sauce is very good for shrimps.

Cocktail Sauce I (for Shellfish)

1 cup catsup
½ cup chili sauce
¼ cup horse radish
1 tablespoon Worcestershire sauce
Dash of Tabasco sauce
½ teaspoon salt (use celery salt, onion salt, or garlic salt, if you have it)
1 teaspoon finely chopped green pepper

Blend all ingredients and serve cold for a dip for cold shrimps or for a sauce on crab meat or other shellfish.

Cocktail Sauce II (for Shellfish)

½ cup mayonnaise
⅓ cup chili sauce
1 teaspoon dry mustard
4 tablespoons vinegar (use tarragon vinegar if you have it)

1 teaspoon salt
½ teaspoon pepper
Pinch of garlic powder
2 teaspoons capers

The last two ingredients are optional, but they add to the sauce. Combine ingredients and let them stand in a cold place long enough for them to blend. Use as dip or sauce for all shellfish.

Bacon Sauce

¼ pound bacon, sliced and diced
1 medium-sized onion, chopped fine
2 tablespoons flour
1 cup boiling water
2 tablespoons vinegar (or 1 of vinegar and 1 of lemon juice)

Fry the bacon pieces until crisp. Remove and drain. Sauté the onion in the bacon fat until transparent. Pour off all but about 2 tablespoons fat. Stir in the flour until cooked and blended. Add the boiling water and the bacon pieces. Let these simmer for a few minutes, then add the vinegar. Season with pepper (and salt, if needed). Pour this over cooked fish fillets.

Sweet-Sour Sauce

4 ginger cookies
½ cup brown sugar
¼ cup vinegar
¼ teaspoon onion powder
1 cup hot meat or fish stock (or water)
2 slices lemon (peel left on)
½ cup seedless raisins

Combine all ingredients in a saucepan and stir the sauce over low heat until it bubbles. Pour over fish, and serve warm or cold.

Tartar Sauce II

½ cup mayonnaise
2 tablespoons chopped small pickles
2 tablespoons minced onion
2 tablespoons chopped pimento-filled olives
1 tablespoon minced parsley
½ tablespoon chopped capers
Salt and pepper to taste

The olives, onion, and pickles can be chopped together and stirred into the mayonnaise along with the other ingredients. Salt and pepper are added to taste. Dried herbs (about ½ teaspoonful) can be substituted for the green parsley. If capers are not handy, leave them out—although they add greatly to the sauce. We don't always use olives, and we frequently include chopped pickle relish, which often is called "pepper hash." The recipe for Tartar Sauce, as explained in Chapter Eleven (see Index), is variable, and basically is a mixture of mayonnaise, chopped pickles and onions, and seasoning—but the formula above is a very good one if all ingredients are available.

Fish Sauce (for Cold Fish)

½ cup mayonnaise
½ teaspoon prepared horse radish
½ teaspoon prepared mustard (or ¼ teaspoon dry mustard)
½ teaspoon lemon juice
Dash of pepper
1 tablespoon milk or cream

Blend all ingredients, and serve the sauce over cold fish, such as cold boiled salmon.

Cucumber Sauce I

1 cup sour cream
3 tablespoons water
2 tablespoons lemon juice
½ teaspoon salt
¼ teaspoon paprika
1 teaspoon finely chopped chives
1 cup pared and sliced cucumber, finely chopped
1 teaspoon finely chopped parsley

Combine all ingredients and pour over the cold boiled fish. This sauce also is very good when poured over barbecued (broiled) fish, such as salmon.

Cucumber Sauce II

2 cucumbers, peeled and grated or chopped fine (save the juice)
1 onion, peeled and grated
4 cooked beets, grated
1 tablespoon prepared horse radish
4 tablespoons mayonnaise
1 teaspoon salt
¼ teaspoon pepper
1 teaspoon sugar
Dash of garlic powder (optional)

Blend all ingredients, including the juice from the cucumbers. Chill and serve with any kind of fish.

SPAGHETTI SAUCES

Spaghetti Sauce I

4 tablespoons butter, margarine, or oil
4 tablespoons flour
2 cups tomato juice
1 onion, chopped fine

1 teaspoon dried parsley (or other herbs)
1 teaspoon sugar
1 teaspoon salt

Over a slow fire, stir the flour and fat until blended and smooth. Then stir in the tomato juice. Add remaining ingredients and simmer until the sauce has thickened. A can of tomato paste adds to this. Substitute a can of tomatoes or a bottle of catsup for the tomato juice, if you wish. Also add a little garlic, if desired.

Spaghetti Sauce II

1 pound mushrooms, cleaned and sliced very thin
4 tablespoons olive oil
4 tablespoons butter
1 tablespoon salt
1 teaspoon pepper
2 tablespoons lemon juice

Sauté the mushrooms in the oil and butter. Add the seasoning. Remove from fire, and stir in the lemon juice. (Note that this sauce contains no tomato.)

SOME OTHER SAUCES

Curry Sauce (for Meat)

4 tablespoons flour
2 tablespoons curry powder
2 tablespoons salad oil
2 cups canned pineapple juice
2 tablespoons lemon juice
1 small onion, grated or chopped fine
2 teaspoons salt
½ teaspoon powdered ginger

Combine the first three ingredients and stir them together in a saucepan over low heat until the mixture bubbles. Then stir in the remaining ingredients, and cook and stir until the sauce has thickened. This sauce is especially recommended for barbecued spareribs.

Horse Radish Sauce (for Roasts)

4 tablespoons melted butter or fat
2 tablespoons flour
1 cup milk
6 tablespoons prepared horse radish
¼ teaspoon salt

In a saucepan, blend the butter and flour until smooth. Then stir in the milk until smooth. Then stir in the horse radish, and cook slowly until the sauce has thickened. Add salt and test for seasoning. Serve in a sauce dish with pot roasts and sliced beef.

Mushroom Sauce (for Meats and Fish)

1 onion, sliced or diced fine
2 tablespoons butter or margarine
1 can condensed cream of mushroom soup
1 cup milk
½ teaspoon salt
¼ teaspoon dried herbs, such as thyme, if available

Sauté the onion in butter until transparent. Gradually stir in, over a low fire, the undiluted soup, then stir in the milk. Add the seasonings. This sauce is a popular North Carolina recipe for use with fish dishes.

Mustard Sauce (for Meats and Fish)

½ onion, minced fine
3 tablespoons butter
2 tablespoons vinegar
2 teaspoons dry mustard
1 cup Brown Gravy (see Index)

Sauté the onions in the butter until transparent. Make a paste with the vinegar and mustard, and stir this into the onions and butter. Then stir in the Brown Gravy, and let the sauce simmer for a few minutes. (Canned or dehydrated gravy can be substituted.) This sauce is excellent on hamburg patties, as well as on other meats and fish.

Roquefort Sauce (for Steaks)

3 tablespoons Roquefort or Bleu cheese
3 tablespoons mayonnaise
3 tablespoons Worcestershire sauce
3 teaspoons dry mustard

Mix all ingredients until they form a paste. Just before the steak is done, spread the sauce on the top side, so it will melt and run into the steak. (You may not want to use this on the best cuts of steak, but it is well worth trying on cheaper cuts, such as London Broil.)

Tomato Sauce I (for Meats and Fish)

2 tablespoons butter
2 tablespoons flour
2 cups canned tomatoes
1 teaspoon Worcestershire sauce
½ teaspoon salt
¼ teaspoon pepper

Blend the butter and flour in a skillet over low heat until smooth. Stir in remaining ingredients. Cook until the sauce thickens. If you want a smooth sauce, the tomatoes can be strained, or tomato juice can be used instead. You also could add 1 teaspoon sugar, 1 small minced onion, and/or ½ teaspoon dried herbs.

To make this into a tomato curry sauce, stir in 1 tablespoon of curry powder. This is very good over chicken, fish, or rice.

Tomato Sauce II (for Meats and Fish)

Bring to a boil 1 can condensed cream of tomato soup and season it to taste. When it simmers, it is ready to serve over meat loaf, croquettes, chops, fish, and many other dishes.

Chapter Sixteen

LET'S SPICE IT UP A BIT!

We beached the canoe at the fork of the streams and walked into the spruce from where wisps of blue smoke were curling. A trapper was building a bark teepee shelter there for a stopover on his trap line. We pooled our food supplies and stayed for lunch.

Without doubt this chance meeting would long since have been forgotten except for my surprise to note that among his very meager possessions the trapper had included one of the lightest, smallest, and most essential—his spice bag.

"The beans, the bread, the fish, the meat—they taste all the same all the winter, except for the spice," the bearded man explained. "With the spice, she peps him up; she tastes different—very good!"

A TRAPPER'S SPICE BAG

This French Canadian planning to winter in the wilderness was no exception to the rule that a spice bag is an essential element of equipment for outdoor cooks. A hundred years before, in this very place, Indians doubtless used whatever spices they could find—just as they did everywhere else. Wagon trains traveling westward in the old days used spices, as do modern pack trains today. The use of spices, herbs, and condiments in cooking is as old as civilized man, and always has been an important element of trade with foreign countries. No matter how modest the cabin or where it may be, one usually finds a patch of green herbs growing nearby. The seeds needed to grow them, once rare and expensive, now can be bought at any seed store for pennies. Spices, herbs, and condiments add ever changing new experiences in aroma and flavor, even to the most ordinary dishes. Their uses are essential not only to celebrated French chefs but also to the Queen of the Kitchen and her peripatetic mate—the outdoor cook.

A spice bag is merely a collection of small containers of whatever aromatic and flavorful roots, seeds, and dried leaves the roaming chef desires to accumulate. Salt, pepper, and dry mustard, of course. Poultry seasoning, cinnamon, and garlic powder, probably. Vinegar (perhaps concentrated), oil, and a sauce or two, if there is room. And something special like dried basil, bay leaves, marjoram, or tarragon, if the outdoor cook really knows his business.

When travel restrictions do not permit carrying as many spices, herbs, and condiments as desired in their original containers, the needed amounts can be carried compactly in small plastic envelopes, all of which will take little room in the spice box. These envelopes can vary in size, depending on the bulk required. Labels to identify contents can be slipped inside each envelope, which then can be secured with a rubber band.

HOME-GROWN HERBS

At this writer's base of operations there are always some herbs growing back of the house —mint, parsley, chives, and basil; plus a few others occasionally. Just before flowering time the tips of green-leafed herbs can be picked and dried on racks in a warm oven, then crushed by stripping the leaves for storage in tightly sealed jars for winter use. If one has a freezer, the green herbs can be frozen singly or in blends for use in all cooking purposes. If these methods seem impractical, dried herbs in wide variety can be bought at grocers for pennies.

THE VALUE OF HERBS IN COOKING

Many herbs, such as basil, marjoram, parsley, savory, and thyme, are good to flavor most anything. Others have more specialized uses. We don't need them all. It's fun to try one or another, and ultimately to settle on a few that seem to suit us best. Certain herbs, such as bay leaves, rosemary, and sage, are quite powerful and should be used sparingly. Most can be used quite freely, but the best way is to experiment cautiously, and never to use so much as to overpower the main flavor of the food. Start with no more than ½ teaspoon to 1 pint or 1 pound, and add a bit more later if it seems best. Tastes vary so much that there can be no rules.

Experts in herb cooking will agree that dried herbs are three or four times more powerful than the same measure of green herbs. They will agree that, in preparing stews, soups, and other foods that take over an hour to cook, the herbs should be added about an hour before the dish is done, in order to obtain maximum flavor. They will agree that, in preparing cold sauces, salad dressings, and juices, the herbs should be added when these are being prepared, to assure proper blending. They will also agree that the flavors of many herbs are released in full volume by simmering them in a little water or wine before adding them to such dishes as soups and stews.

TABLE OF VARIOUS HERBS, AND HOW THEY ARE USED

Disregarding certain common condiments, such as salt and pepper, the following table of twenty popular herbs or spices and the uses to which each is best suited may be of help. The table is not as accurate as it could be but is as accurate as it can be set down briefly. For example, fourteen of these herbs or spices are recommended for meats. Some of these are more appropriate for certain meats, less so for others. Certain ones not mentioned for meats may be appropriate in specific dishes. But this table should be of some help and, when a little common sense is used, it is difficult to make bad mistakes. To reduce all possible chances for error here, a few brief notes are included.

	Birds	Eggs	Fish	Meats	Salads	Sauces	Soups	Stuffings	Vegetables
BASIL Wonderful with tomatoes and with dishes containing tomatoes.	X	X	X	X	X	X	X	X	X
BAY LEAVES Use sparingly, especially in marinades, stews, and boiled meats. Alternate part of a leaf here and there on Shish Kebab skewers.				X					
CHILI POWDER Often used in Mexican-type dishes, sea food stews, and vegetable chowders.				X	X				X
CHIVES Use where you would use onion.		X	X		X		X		X
CINNAMON Excellent mixed with sugar on camp breads and hot cakes.									
CURRY Very good in rice and meat or game-bird combinations and in egg dishes.	X	X		X					

	Birds	Eggs	Fish	Meats	Salads	Sauces	Soups	Stuffings	Vegetables
DILL Mix a pinch or two in potatoes, sauces, tomatoes, and sea food salads.			X	X	X	X	X		X
GARLIC Use very sparingly wherever you would use onion.									
MARJORAM Very good in almost everything.	X	X	X	X	X	X	X	X	X
MINT Especially good with lamb.			X	X		X			X
MUSTARD (DRY) Make paste with vinegar and use very sparingly instead of prepared mustard.			X	X	X	X			X
NUTMEG Ideal in rice puddings.									
ORÉGANO Used mainly in Italian-type dishes; in pot roasts and in green salads.		X		X	X	X	X		X
PAPRIKA Is milder than cayenne. Used mainly for adding pinkish color, especially in sea food stews. Sprinkle over meats and fish for darker color.	X	X	X	X	X	X	X		X
PARSLEY Used as a garnish for fish, salads, etc.; also in soups and stews.			X	X	X	X	X	X	X
ROSEMARY Use sparingly with lamb, beans, and greens. Primarily a meat herb.	X			X	X	X	X		X X
SAGE Excellent in stuffings for birds and in veal and pork dishes. Use very sparingly.	X			X	X	X			X
SAVORY Perfect for flavoring peas and beans. Can be used in stuffings in place of sage.	X	X		X	X	X	X	X	X
TARRAGON Use sparingly in marinades, pot roasts, fish, sea food, and egg dishes.	X	X	X		X	X		X	X
THYME Especially good in soups, stews, and tomato dishes.	X	X	X	X			X	X	X

The ancient Greeks were the first civilized people to prefer outdoor to indoor cooking. They considered that foods cooked outdoors were flavored by their gods, and that outdoor cooking provided them with additional health and strength. Outdoor cooks who learn the simple facts about the choices and uses of herbs and spices will find that their foods also are provided with additional tempting flavors and more fragrant aromas.

Chapter Seventeen

VEGETABLES AND SALADS

In addition to the recipes for preparing vegetables in a skillet (Chapter Three) and in foil (Chapter Four), here are several simple ones to add the gourmet's touch to outdoor dinners:

VEGETABLES

Boiled Asparagus

Allow nearly a pound of fresh asparagus per person. In season, try to select bunches with stalks of the same (and as large as possible) diameter, with little or no white showing at the ends, and with compact buds. Cut off the tough ends, which can be used in soup. Wash the stalks in cold water to remove grit. Put them in a skillet containing barely enough boiling salted water to cover them, and cook only until tender—10 to 15 minutes. Remove from water immediately; drain, and serve with melted butter or with mayonnaise thinned with a little lemon juice. If any asparagus is left over, serve it cold as a salad, with Vinaigrette Sauce (French Dressing) (see Index).

Asparagus with Cheese

For something really delicious and unusual, try this:

> 3 bunches (pounds) fresh asparagus
> ½ cup flour
> 1 egg
> 2 ounces white wine
> 1 cup cracker or dry bread crumbs
> 2 tablespoons grated cheese
> 1 teaspoon garlic salt
> Dash of pepper
> ½ cup salad oil

Roll asparagus in flour and then dip it in the egg, which has been beaten with the wine. Combine crumbs, cheese, garlic salt, and pepper, and coat the asparagus with this. Fry in oil until golden brown and tender (about 10 to 12 minutes). Dry on absorbent paper and serve immediately.

Asparagus in Foil

Prepare asparagus for cooking as for Boiled Asparagus. Wrap loosely in a doubled sheet of aluminum foil, adding a little water, a pat of butter, and salt and pepper to taste. Seal packet with the drugstore fold, and cook it over or in the coals of an open fire for 20 minutes or so, until tender. Avoid puncturing the foil, because the juice should be served with the asparagus.

Baked Beans

> 1 pound large white beans (dry)
> ½ pound salt pork or bacon
> ½ tablespoon salt
> 1 tablespoon dark molasses
> 1½ tablespoons sugar
> 1 tablespoon powdered mustard
> 4 small or 2 medium-sized onions, sliced

Pick over the beans; wash them and cover with 3 inches of water. Bring to a boil, pour off water, and bring to a boil again with fresh water. Pour this off and add fresh water a third time. Cook about 40 minutes or until, when you remove one or two beans and blow upon them, they will split their skins. Cut the salt pork in half and score the skin with several deep cuts. Put a piece of the pork in the bean pot (or Dutch oven, or other suitable container) and pour the beans over it. Mix and add all the other ingredients except the onions and remaining pork. Bury the onions and remaining pork near the top of the beans. Add enough boiling water to just cover the beans. Cover the pot and bake for 8 hours at 300°. Inspect occasionally, and add a little more water if necessary. Remove the cover during the last hour of cooking, so the top of the beans will be brown and crusty.

BAKING BEANS IN A BEAN HOLE

Cooking in a bean hole actually is pit cooking, and many foods such as stews and pot roasts can be prepared this way—in a fireless cooker in the ground.

The container for the beans or other food should be a Dutch oven or some similar heavy pot that can be covered tightly. I've seen Maine guides use lard pails very successfully but, with such a thin container, care must be taken not to burn the food. If a tin pail is used, punch two or three small holes in the cover so steam can escape, and surround the pail and cover with green leaves or some other insulation to prevent the foods from burning.

If the hole is to be lined with rocks, dig it about 3 feet wide and 3 feet deep. If no rocks are used, 2 feet wide and 2 feet deep should be enough. Rocks hold heat and thus are preferable, but if no rocks are used the ground can be heated thoroughly and the food can be cooked in the coals and hot ashes.

Remember to dig the fire hole in dirt or sand —never in peaty soil that might allow the fire to spread underground.

With the hole prepared and the pot of beans being made ready according to the preceding recipe, we build a big fire over the hole, allowing hot coals and ashes to drop into the hole. The fire should burn for several hours to heat the earth around the hole thoroughly. Many cooks start the fire the night before and let it burn all night, rekindling it in the morning to be sure the area is very hot. Others put the pot of beans in one or more wet burlap sacks. This keeps out dirt and helps to prevent food from burning if the container is thin.

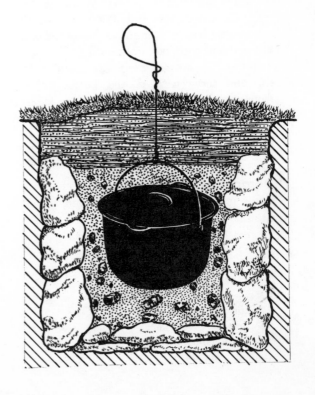

Lower the pot into the bean hole, leaving the bail sticking up, so the pot can be pulled out easily when the beans are done. Poke ashes and coals around the pot and tamp them down with a stick. Put a big rock on top of the pot to hold the cover down tightly. With the hole nearly filled thusly, rake dirt over the hole and pack sod on top to seal the hole tightly. A layer of green leaves over the top of the pot helps to prevent dirt from getting under the pot cover.

With the hole thus sealed, it can be left alone all day or all night to be uncovered about 12 hours later. Pull out the pot, brush it off, and enjoy bean-hole beans as old-time woodsmen have made them for many years!

Beans with Cheese

1 can beans
½ cup diced or grated cheese

Heat the beans and cheese together until the cheese melts. This makes a good hot sandwich when served with toast.

Beans with Onion

1 can beans
2 slices bacon, minced
½ onion, chopped
1 garlic clove, crushed
¾ cup tomato sauce
1 teaspoon Worcestershire sauce
¼ teaspoon dry mustard

Sauté the onion and garlic with the bacon. When the bacon is crisp, discard the garlic, add other ingredients, and heat.

Another version of this that peps up the taste of beans is to fry a sliced onion in bacon fat until the onion is transparent. Pour off excess fat and add the beans and a little brown sugar.

For sweet-sour beans, add a little vinegar to this.

Bean Salad I

1 pound green beans (any kind)
French Dressing (Vinaigrette Sauce) (see Index)

Cook beans until tender. Drain, and allow to cool, adding a little salt. When cold, mix with French Dressing. (This salad can also be made with other beans, such as black, white, red, pink, or pinto.)

Bean Salad II

1 can red kidney beans
1 onion, minced
½ cucumber, peeled and diced
½ cup diced celery
1 tomato, peeled and diced
Dash of curry powder
Dash of salt
½ cup mayonnaise

Combine all ingredients and serve on lettuce, if you have it handy.

Bean Soup

1 pound dried beans, washed and picked over
1 ham hock
1 onion, chopped
4 tablespoons butter
Salt and pepper to taste

Put the beans and ham hock in a pot with water to cover. Sauté the onion in the butter and add this to the pot. Cook for about 2 hours, or until beans are tender. Remove hock, and scrape off and dice the meat, adding this to the soup. Season with salt and pepper, adding more water if necessary. Mash the beans a bit. (If you don't have a ham hock, substitute diced sliced ham or crisp chopped bacon.)

Succotash

To make succotash, we can do it the easy way by adding 2 parts canned or frozen corn to 1 part canned lima beans, seasoned to taste. If fresh vegetables are available, let's do it this way:

6 ears of corn
1 quart lima beans
2 tablespoons flour
2 tablespoons butter
Salt and pepper to taste

Cut the corn off the cobs (not too closely). Boil the beans and the corn cobs in enough lightly salted water to barely cover, adding a little more water from time to time, if necessary, until the beans are almost tender. Remove the cobs. Add the corn. Make a thin paste with the flour and a little water, and stir this slowly into the succotash until it has thickened slightly (you may not need it all). Add butter, salt, and pepper. After adding the corn, do not cook the succotash more than 5 minutes.

Boiled Beets

The trick in cooking beets is not to let them bleed. Leave on at least 1 inch of the stems; wash them but do not peel them, and boil them in lightly salted water, covered, for about 20 minutes. Avoid testing them until nearly done. When done, peel and slice, and serve with melted butter or, if cold, with French Dressing (see Index).

If the beets are young, the greens are excellent when cooked. Wash them and steam in very little water until they are tender. Then cut them up, season with salt and pepper, and serve with butter or a little vinegar.

Boiled Cabbage

Remove outside leaves and core. Wash and drain, slicing the cabbage if you wish to. Boil in salted water until tender, which will be in 15 or 20 minutes. Season with salt and pepper, and add a little melted butter.

Some cooks leave the core on, as this keeps the leaves together. In this case, cut the cabbage in quarters or eighths so each section contains a little of the core.

Cabbage with Cheese Sauce

Chop the cabbage fairly fine and put it in a skillet or baking dish with alternate layers of cheese sauce. Add bread crumbs on top, and bake until they are brown. Use a sheet of aluminum foil to reflect heat on the top if you are doing this in a skillet over an open fire.

Carrots

Wash and scrape the carrots, and cut them into slices or slivers. Boil in slightly salted water until tender. Season with salt, pepper, and butter. Also try them with Cream Sauce or Cheese Sauce (see Index), or fry them in butter to which some sugar or syrup has been added.

Creamed Vegetables

Remember that many cooked vegetables are delicious in Cream Sauce or Cheese Sauce (see Index). These include beets, cabbage, carrots, cauliflower, celery, corn, onions, peas, potatoes, etc. Cream Sauce is very easy to make, and it adds a tasty touch to vegetables cooked outdoors.

Cucumbers

Since these are most always served in salads, why not make an impression on your guests by serving them fried? Peel them, and slice ¼ inch thick. Soak the slices for an hour or so in salted cold water to which a little vinegar has been added. Dry the slices, and dip them in milk and then in beaten egg. Then dredge them in dry bread or cracker crumbs, and brown them in deep fat. Drain, and serve hot.

Mushrooms

Those who are tempted to pick and eat wild mushrooms should be sure of their varieties, because there is no guide to safety except identification beyond all shadow of doubt. However, there are at least four varieties that are easy to identify and are delicious. One is the common puffball, which is large, white, round, and without a stem. If it is white all the way through, it is safe. Peel it, slice it, and sauté it in butter.

Another is the meadow mushroom, which is the usual commercial variety. I wouldn't trust myself to identify this one surely, but anyone can be sure of the morel (which we mentioned finding in Wyoming in Chapter Four). If you have morels locally, get an expert to show you the true variety from the false. The false morel is very dangerous, but the two are easy to tell apart. Fourth is the oyster mushroom, which grows on logs or stumps—it is connected to the wood or one side and has gills that run into the stem. Wild mushrooms are so delicious that outdoorsmen should learn to identify a few safe varieties—but unless you are sure, it is much safer to leave them alone.

Capped mushrooms are washed with the caps removed from the stems. The caps can be sautéed in butter or cut up and used in soups, gravies, and stuffings. When sautéing the caps of large mushrooms, put a dot of butter in each cap and add some seasoned bread crumbs, if you wish. These make an excellent garnish for steaks. Slice the stems for soups and gravies.

Creamed Mushrooms

½ pound mushrooms, washed and sliced
¼ cup butter
2 tablespoons flour
1 cup milk
Salt and pepper to taste

Sauté the mushrooms in the butter for only 2 or 3 minutes. Blend in the flour until smooth. Add the milk slowly, stirring until the sauce has thickened. Season with salt and pepper. Serve on toast, over meats and vegetables, etc.

Onions

My favorite way is to roast onions in foil, as described in Chapter Four. Another is to peel and slice them, and to sauté the thick slices in butter. After turning each slice, sprinkle on some dry bread crumbs. Turn them carefully, so the rings won't separate, and use them for a garnish on meats.

Fried Onions

Fried onions are equally easy. Peel and slice them into the skillet; add 2 tablespoons of butter, a cup or so of water, and seasoning. Let them boil slowly, covered, until they are transparent. Then remove the cover and cook them until the water has cooked out. Use a spatula to turn them, and let them brown as much as desired.

Creamed Onions

For creamed onions, we should use the small ones. Peel them, and boil them in salted water until tender. Pour off the water and add Cream Sauce (see Index). Garnish with dry bread crumbs. If the onions are large, fry them as above. When the water has cooked away, but before the onions begin to brown, add the Cream Sauce and serve them when the sauce is hot.

Peas

Boil peas in a very small amount of slightly salted water to which some butter has been added. Taste them occasionally, and stop cooking as soon as they are done, because they are better underdone than overcooked. A trick here is to add 1 teaspoon sugar for 1 quart peas. If you're cooking the frozen variety outdoors, try this:

Peas in Foil

1 package frozen peas
2 tablespoons onion soup mix
2 tablespoons butter
2 tablespoons crisp chopped bacon

Blend the onion, butter, and bacon. Take the peas out of the package and spread them with the mixture. Wrap the frozen peas in foil and cook them on the rack over the coals for 15 minutes.

Remember that cooked peas are very good when mixed with Cream Sauce (see Index).

Stuffed Green Peppers

If fairly large ones are available, a tasty way to use them is to cut off the tops and scoop out the insides, leaving only the shell. Stuff this with beef hash or hamburg, and set the stuffed peppers in a skillet. Add about ¼ inch of water; cover the skillet and cook the peppers until they are tender, which should be in about 20 minutes.

Sautéed Green Peppers

6 peppers
½ cup olive oil
1 garlic clove, minced

Slice the peppers into slivers, discarding interior parts. Sauté these in the olive oil with the garlic until tender, which should take about 15 minutes. Stir frequently.

Potatoes

Try the recipes for Potato Pancakes and Mountain Potatoes in Chapter Three, and for potatoes baked in foil in Chapter Four.

Buttered Potatoes

Peel and wash several medium-sized potatoes, and boil them gently, covered, in a cup or so of lightly salted water. In about 25 minutes, test them with a two-tined fork for doneness. When done, pour off the water and put the pan back on the fire, uncovered, until remaining water evaporates. Add some butter, and roll the potatoes in it to coat them. Sprinkle on chopped parsley, if available, or serve them with Cheese Sauce (see Index).

Hashed Brown Potatoes

Hashed brown potatoes are another favorite. Slice the peeled potatoes into shoestrings or rub them through a very coarse grater. Heat ¼ cup of bacon fat in a skillet, and add the potatoes, using a spatula to keep them in a flat cake away from the sides of the pan. Cook very slowly, and turn them with the spatula when they are browned on the bottom. When brown on both sides of the cake, add salt and pepper, and serve. Here are two variations:

One or 2 sliced or diced onions can be added to the potatoes while they are cooking.

Just before the potatoes are done, pour about ½ cup cream over them, and let this be absorbed by the potatoes while cooking.

Pan-Fried Potatoes

Pan-fried potatoes are cooked similarly, except that the peeled potatoes are cut in fairly thin slices and cooked slowly in a little bacon fat until they are nicely browned on both sides. Then drain them, if necessary, and season with salt and pepper. For variations, onions can be cooked with them, or grated cheese can be sprinkled on them after they have been turned.

Rice

Nowadays the rice sold in packages usually is so clean that washing it is unnecessary, but it is well to wash it through two or three waters to rid it of excess starch, if this seems necessary.

Boiled Rice

To boil rice, put 2 quarts water and 1 tablespoon salt in a kettle and bring it to a brisk boil. Add the rice gradually so the water will continue to boil. Boil it, uncovered, until the rice is done. This should take about 15 minutes. If you overcook it, it will be mushy. Pour off all water and dry the rice over very low heat, stirring occasionally with a fork to make it fluffy. Avoid drying it for too long, because it may get tough.

Fried Rice

My hunting companions have an easier way, which can be called fried rice. Put 3 tablespoons cooking fat in a skillet and add 1 cup rice, cooking this over moderate heat until the rice is golden brown. Then add 1 teaspoon salt and 4 cups hot water. Cover, and let the rice simmer until tender, which should be in about 15 minutes.

You could use chicken or game-bird stock instead of water, if the rice is to be served with birds.

Boiled Wild Rice

Wild rice can be boiled like domestic rice. After washing and inspecting the rice, slowly add 1 cup rice to 4 cups rapidly boiling salted water. Keep it boiling for about 20 minutes, until testing indicates that it is done. Then drain it and serve it with butter.

Popped Wild Rice

Popped wild rice is an excellent dish to serve with game birds. Wash and inspect, then dry 2 cups rice on a towel. Heat deep fat to 375° (just below smoking) and drop the rice gradually into the fat. Let it cook until it pops. Then drain it on a paper towel and salt it lightly. If the popped rice is not to be served immediately, store it in a covered container and warm it in the oven before serving.

Spaghetti (and Other Pasta)

Pasta comprises all extruded starchy foods, such as noodles, macaroni, and spaghetti. All are cooked similarly, in boiling salted water that covers the food to about twice its depth. Let the water boil for about 10 minutes, until the pasta becomes soft. Stir while cooking. Then drain, and rinse by running hot water over it. Serve it with one of the spaghetti sauces recommended in Chapter Fifteen, or with a garlic and oil sauce made by sautéing 2 peeled and crushed garlic buds in ½ cup olive oil, seasoned to taste with salt and pepper.

Spaghetti or macaroni also is delicious when served mixed with Cheese Sauce (see Index). If you're fond of cheese, add a little more than the recipe calls for.

Wild Greens

No outdoor cooking book would be complete without calling attention to the many wild greens that nature provides in season. There are so many that an entire book could be written about them, so we can only touch upon them here. Where the dandelion grows lushly, gather a mess of the succulent leaves and steam them in a little water, with a piece of salt pork, until they are tender. Then serve them seasoned, with butter or vinegar.

Plantain, or pokeweed, milkweed, water cress, curly dock, lamb's quarter, wild mustard, cowslips, sorrel, mouse-ears, fireweed, and many other common weeds and plants provide excellent greens for salads or for cooked greens. The American Indian was adept at locating and roasting many varieties of roots and distinguishing edible berries. Stalks of several young plants, when properly prepared, taste as good as asparagus. Even the inner bark of many trees can keep a man from starving. A favorite dish in Maine is fiddlehead greens—the curled fronds of ferns just emerging. Some of these foods of nature must be prepared in one way and some in another. Some parts are edible and some are not. Some must be cooked, while others are delicious when raw. I hope that someday someone will write a complete book about it. When this happens, I shall be one of the first to buy it!

Many wild and domestic greens can be combined with ham, cheese, onions, peppers, hard-boiled eggs, and cold vegetables to make excellent salads—and salads are very necessary to a balanced diet indoors or outdoors.

SALAD DRESSINGS

The cookery of vegetables and the preparation of salads have been described so many times in so many cookbooks that it seems rather needless to dwell upon them in much detail here. But, given the ingredients for a salad, there are several simple dressings of special value to the outdoor cook. Here are a few of them:

Bleu Cheese Dressing

The French Bleu cheese, the American Blue cheese, and Roquefort cheese are equally good for this one. Merely mash up some of this cheese with enough (domestic) brandy to make it into a spreadable paste. Use this for spreading on crackers at cocktail time. If the mixture seems too tart, include some cream cheese to make it milder. To transform this into an excellent salad dressing, thin it with some mayonnaise and perhaps a little lemon juice. The proportions are varied according to taste.

Celery Seed Dressing

> ½ cup sugar
> 1 teaspoon dry mustard
> 1 onion, grated fine
> 1 teaspoon salt
> ⅓ cup vinegar
> 1 cup olive oil
> 2 teaspoons celery seed

Mix sugar, mustard, onion, salt, and part of the vinegar. Beat thoroughly. Alternate oil and the rest of the vinegar. Beat until thick and clear. Add celery seed. Cover, and chill.

Dr. Burke's Dressing

My old friend Edgar Burke gave me this one. Dr. Burke was a renowned author and sportsman whose name is familiar to anglers, gunners, pigeon fanciers, and decoy makers—as well as to surgeons. He was also a notable gourmet. This is his favorite salad dressing. It's a bit complicated in ingredients, but more than worth the effort.

> 6 tablespoons olive oil
> 2 tablespoons vinegar (stir in slowly)
> 2 teaspoons Worcestershire sauce

(Star-Lite)

Modern dehydrated or flash-frozen and dried foods can be stored almost indefinitely without refrigeration, (as in above) or on a boat (below). They are prepared for cooking merely by immersion in water for a few minutes, per directions on the packages.

¼ *teaspoon garlic salt* (*more, if you like*)
¼ *teaspoon dry mustard*
1 *teaspoon each dry basil and Dash*
¼ *teaspoon pepper*

Merely mix the ingredients. Since they are inclined to settle, the bottle must be shaken before using. It is best made up in advance to allow the ingredients to blend.

French (Vinaigrette) Dressing

This is the basic French Dressing, which also is called Vinaigrette Sauce. It is simply a combination of good olive oil, vinegar, salt, and pepper. Proportions depend upon taste, but it is usually made by mixing 4 parts oil to 1 part vinegar, with salt and pepper added as desired.

Dehydrated Dressings

Since it may be impractical for campers to carry so many of the above ingredients, let's remember that very good salad dressings in many varieties are obtainable from grocers in moistureproof envelopes. These dressings can be made up on the spot merely by mixing them with salad oil or vinegar, or both.

DEHYDRATED SOUPS AND

VEGETABLES

Finally, while we're talking about vegetables, let's remember that very excellent soups and vegetables can be obtained in moistureproof packages that weigh almost nothing, will keep almost indefinitely, and can be reconstituted merely by adding water. Famous firms like Maggi and Lipton provide dozens of varieties of delicious soups whose ingredients come in light, tough, moistureproof envelopes. All that is needed is to add the prescribed amount of water, bring them to a boil, and let them simmer for a few minutes to provide soups that few people could make as well at home.

Armour and Company has made a notable advancement in the revolutionary development of their "Star Lite" freeze-dried foods, which include meats, fish, and complete packaged dinners, as well as vegetables. By this flash-freezing and drying process, about 98% of water is removed, while normal shape, size, and nutritional values are retained. Upon being immersed for a few minutes in water, "Star Lite" foods recover the appearance, taste, and texture of the foods before they were dehydrated. A man could carry a complete dinner in his pocket for months and, whenever he wished, bring it very nearly to its original perfection merely by adding water and warming it over a fire.

While these dehydrated delicacies temporarily may rob an outdoor cook of his culinary attainments, they are a real boon to sportsmen when weight becomes a problem or when ice is unobtainable.

Chapter Eighteen

EGGS AND CHEESE

The young husband who accused his wife of not even knowing how to boil an egg undoubtedly was more nearly right than he realized. There are ways to cook eggs properly, but most cooks prepare them otherwise. Since the right methods are as easy as the wrong ones, this is a subject that deserves discussing.

First, however, let's ease the transportation problem, since eggs broken before their time do not add to the neatness of an icebox. One way is to pack the fresh eggs separated slightly from each other in a bed of corn meal, or flour, or something similar. Another is to break the eggs into a wide-mouthed bottle, such as an olive bottle. Then it is only necessary to pour out the required number of eggs for whatever cooking is to be done.

While fresh eggs are to be preferred when available, dehydrated eggs are much tastier than they used to be, and are especially handy when combined with other foods in egg dishes —thus conserving the fresh ones for frying, boiling, or other purposes. Dehydrated eggs need no refrigeration and are light and compact to transport. At this writing perhaps the most notable advance in this has been made by Armour and Company, whose packaged "Star Lite" cooked scrambled eggs are very nearly equal to fresh ones in taste and texture.

Boiled Eggs

The way not to boil an egg is to boil it, because boiling makes it tough. One way is to put the eggs into cold water and let this come slowly to a boil. When the water begins to boil, remove it from the heat; cover the pan, and let the eggs stand in the hot water for from 2 to 4 minutes more, depending on how well set the whites are desired to be. For hard-boiled eggs, leave them in the hot water for about 15 minutes. Another way is to bring the water to a boil, add the eggs, and remove the pan from the fire. In this case, let the eggs stand in the hot water for about 5 minutes, if you want the yolks soft and the whites well set.

In either case, when the eggs are removed from the hot water, let cold water run over them for a few seconds. This helps prevent the whites from discoloring and makes it much easier to remove the eggs from the shells.

Bull's-Eye Fried Eggs

All we need for this are eggs, bread, and butter. Remove crusts from one or more slices of bread and cut out a large circle in each slice, using a can cover or something similar. Fry these bread rings in a little butter until they are golden brown on one side. Turn the rings over and drop an egg into the hole in each slice of bread. Fry this slowly until the eggs are set, turning them over once, if desirable.

For variations, add a little minced onion to each egg after it has been put into the bread ring. Or add a little cheese, so it will melt on top—or a sprinkling of curry powder.

Creamed Eggs

  4 eggs
  3 tablespoons butter
  3 tablespoons flour
  ½ teaspoon salt
  1½ cups milk

Hard-boil the eggs as described above. When they have cooled, remove shells and quarter the eggs lengthwise. Prepare a cream sauce by melting the butter in a skillet and stirring in the flour and salt, blending until smooth. Then gradually stir in the milk, cooking the sauce slowly until it is thick and creamy. Pour the sauce over the eggs, which may be on toast, on cooked spinach, on fish fillets, or something else.

If there are any leftover peas or other suitable vegetables, or some diced ham, this can be added to the dish. So can a little grated cheese. A favorite trick of ours is to stir into the sauce a tablespoon or so of cold Welsh Rabbit. This makes an excellent cheese sauce. (The recipe comes later in this chapter.)

Egg Salad

6 eggs
2 tablespoons mayonnaise
½ teaspoon dry mustard
1 teaspoon chopped chives and/or parsley, if available
Salt and pepper to taste

Hard-boil the eggs and allow them to cool. Remove shells and mash the eggs in a bowl with the other ingredients.

This makes an excellent filling for egg salad sandwiches. It can also be mixed with diced ham, tuna fish, crab meat, and many other foods for serving as a salad on lettuce.

To make stuffed eggs, cut the hard-boiled eggs in halves and remove the yolks. Mash the yolks with the other ingredients, and fill the egg whites with this mixture. Include a little curry powder, if you like it.

Egg-Vegetable Salad

1 can beets, diced
3 hard-boiled eggs, sliced
1 tablespoon minced onion
2 tablespoons mayonnaise

Combine first three ingredients and stir in enough mayonnaise to bind them. Serve on lettuce leaves, if available. Include chopped chives or chopped green onion tops, if you have any.

French Toast II

8 slices bread
6 eggs
¼ cup milk
Dash of salt
1 teaspoon bacon fat

Remove crusts from the bread (which should not be too fresh). Beat the eggs with the milk and salt, and soak the bread slices in the egg mixture. Add the bacon fat to the skillet and get it moderately hot, pouring off all but enough fat to grease the bottom of the skillet. Set the soaked bread slices in the skillet and fry them on both sides until golden brown. Since the idea is to soak the bread with the egg mixture, care must be taken to prevent the bread from breaking apart when it is being lifted into the skillet. If any egg batter remains, pour it onto the bread slices in the skillet, but not enough to make it run off the bread. Serve the French toast with butter and maple syrup, or with whatever kind of jam or jelly may be handy, or with cinnamon and sugar.

Fried Eggs

This also sounds easy, but there is a trick to it if the cook is to do his job right. Use only enough bacon fat (or butter) to cover the pan, because too much grease will harm the flavor of the eggs. Have the pan only moderately hot, because eggs fried in too hot fat become tough and indigestible. Break each egg carefully into the pan. If the white runs too much, fold the edges over with a spatula when the white begins to set. The pan may be covered to aid in cooking the tops. If cooked uncovered, spoon a little of the fat over the eggs, or turn them over, if desirable. The tricks are not to use too much fat and not to fry the eggs over too hot a fire. When cooked, we like to drain the eggs (and bacon) on absorbent paper to remove excess fat.

Omelets

4 (or more) eggs
4 teaspoons water (1 for each egg)
Salt and pepper to taste
1 tablespoon bacon fat or butter

Combine eggs, water and condiments, and whip them together with a fork only until the colors are combined. Chronic omelet makers use a special skillet with a rounded bottom, and they take care that the skillet never is scratched, because this may cause the omelet to stick. Add the fat to the skillet and, when it is hot, pour in the eggs. Do not stir or puncture the bottom of the omelet. When it has begun to set, use a fork to push the edges of the egg inward so that, when the pan is tilted, egg mixture will fill the spaces. Do this around the pan until nearly all of the egg liquid becomes set. If the pan is a smooth one, a little shaking will free the omelet and let it slide around in the pan. If necessary, use a spatula to free it.

Now, while the omelet is setting, you can add jelly, cheese, mushrooms, cooked chopped spinach, or whatever else is desired to fill the omelet.

Then use the spatula to fold one third of the omelet over. Slide the omelet from the pan to a cutting board, at the same time flipping over the opposite side, so the omelet will be folded in thirds (with opposite edges overlapping each other). Cut the omelet into the desired number of pieces and serve.

We could use a little milk instead of water, but people who know their omelets prefer to use water, as they think this makes a lighter omelet. The trick is to use low enough heat so that the top of the omelet is cooked when the bottom remains golden brown.

A fluffy omelet can be made by beating the whites and yolks of the eggs separately. Beat the whites stiff and stir in the beaten yolks. Do not add milk or water. Pour the fluffy mixture into the pan and cook it very slowly until the top has begun to set. Then serve, as above.

Poached Eggs

Pour about a quart of water into a skillet and add about 1 teaspoon salt and 1 tablespoon vinegar. (The vinegar helps to keep the egg white from spreading.) Bring the water to a boil and keep it just under the boiling point. Break each egg into a cup, and carefully pour it into the water. Cover the pan and allow the eggs to simmer for a few minutes, until they are firm. Then lift them out with a skimmer and serve them on buttered toast.

In Chapter Four we discussed a simple method of poaching eggs individually in egg poachers made of aluminum foil.

CHEESE

The outdoor cook need be concerned with only a few types of hard cheeses such as grated Parmesan and Provolone, and with a few types of semi-soft cheeses, such as American, Bleu, and Swiss. If kept dry and cool, the hard cheeses can be kept almost indefinitely in their original containers. The semi-soft cheeses also keep very well unopened, and nearly as long after being opened if they are tightly wrapped in aluminum foil and are kept dry in a cool place.

Since this book has discussed the many uses of cheeses in outdoor cooking in other chapters, little more need be said about them here. However, it seems appropriate to pass along my fa-

vorite recipe for a very excellent Welsh Rabbit, because this dish is delicious in itself and because it can be used as the basis for a very good cheese sauce, for cheese spreads, for toasted open sandwiches, and for other purposes. Outdoor cooks may prefer to make this rabbit at home and carry a jar of it on outdoor excursions. In any event, make all the double boiler will hold. It will keep in the refrigerator for weeks, ready for a tasty snack whenever needed.

Welsh Rabbit

About 2 pounds American (sharp) cheese
1 cube butter
About ½ pint milk
1 egg
1 heaping teaspoon cornstarch
1 rounded teaspoon dry mustard
1 tablespoon Worcestershire sauce
½ teaspoon salt

Cut the cheese into ½-inch cubes, using enough to fill the top of a double boiler. Add the butter to the cheese in the top of the double boiler.

In a bowl, combine some of the milk, the egg, cornstarch, mustard, Worcestershire sauce, and salt. Beat this until well mixed, and pour it over the cheese. Add enough more milk to nearly cover the cubes of cheese. Heat this over moderate heat over water in the double boiler, stirring frequently. When the cheese has almost all melted, use an egg beater to remove any remaining lumps. Continue heating over low heat until the rabbit begins to thicken slightly. Ladle the rabbit over dry toast (and/or crackers) and serve sprinkled with a coloring of paprika.

Let's hope there are not too many guests, because we want a goodly amount of rabbit to be left over. Put this in a jar or crock and, when it has cooled, seal it from moisture and store it in the refrigerator. Here are some ways to use it:

Add a spoonful or more to a cream sauce to make a cheese sauce to serve over fish, hard-boiled eggs, macaroni, asparagus, etc.

Use it cold to spread on crackers.

Spread dry toast with it, and top it with a thin slice of onion and tomato. Broil this until the cheese bubbles and begins to brown. Then top the tomato with a dab of mayonnaise and a sprinkling of paprika, for color.

Use it in a grilled ham and cheese sandwich.

Put a spoonful on a hot hamburg patty, and serve this on toast.

Add a spoonful to a baked potato that has been wedged open.

Use in casseroles whenever cheese sauce is called for, or as a topping whenever a cheese topping is desired.

Use on a toasted bun with whatever else is handy to make a miniature pizza.

Chapter Nineteen

BREADS AND BISCUITS

It's a pity that so many sportsmen and campers reach adult years so dependent on the corner bakery and prepared mixes that they never have learned how delicious (and how amazingly easy) camp-made breads, biscuits, and cakes taste, when cooked outdoors. Make them in the frying pan, in the Dutch oven, or in a pan fashioned from aluminum foil and baked in the reflector baker or in a reasonable facsimile thereof. As they fluff up and turn golden brown they waft a fragrance that helps to make outdoor cooking what outdoor cooking really should be. And when these hot golden nuggets are broken open and slathered with butter or jam, or when they are used to soak up the remnants of gravy or Mulligan Stew, even the greatest gourmet in the crowd will admit that no bakery product could ever approach their deliciousness.

Now of course we can take along prepared mixes and go by what it says on the package, but the old-timers will tell you this is sissy stuff, not to be compared in fun and flavor to starting from scratch and doing the job all by yourself. Give it a dry run at home, if you want to see how quick and easy it is. And, if I may offer a suggestion to wives, daughters, and girl friends, let them learn the easy methods, and have a batch of hot bread or biscuits ready when their heroes come in from fishing. Females with such foresight are the kind men like to take along.

THAT DELICIOUS SOURDOUGH BREAD

In the old days, "sourdough" prospectors and cooks on pack and wagon trains made sourdough breads and biscuits, which of course is why the old sourdoughs got the name. Many woodsmen still do, and modern campers should do so more often. All you need is the "starter pot" and some flour and salt. If you have some milk or milk powder, some eggs or egg powder, some sugar, some shortening, and perhaps some berries or semi-sweet chocolate pieces, so much the better. But all you really need are the essentials of the starter, flour, and salt. The rest are optional embellishments.

We don't have to do our baking by the sourdough method, but let's start with it anyway. No other method gives results more fragrant and delicious.

Making a Sourdough "Starter"

The basis of sourdough baking is the "starter," which is nothing more or less than a culture of yeast in flour and water. You always save about a cup, adding more flour and water so the yeast culture will grow and be ready for use next time. This culture becomes partially dormant when cold, and can be frozen. In normal camping temperatures it can keep going for years, if need be.

Use a glass or earthenware container for the starter, because its acids will attack metal. (In spite of this, some sourdoughs use lard pails.) Use about a 2-quart container, filled less than half full, because the batter expands. For this reason, don't cap it tightly, because gas will want to escape. (An exploded starter can be very messy.)

There are several ways of making starters, but all of them require yeast unless the starter is allowed several days to sour. To do the job quickly, dissolve ½ yeast cake (or 1 package dry yeast) in 1 cup or more of water, milk, sour milk, buttermilk, or potato water. Add 1 cup or more of flour to make a smooth, medium-thick batter. Many cooks also add 1 tablespoon sugar and a pinch of salt, but these are not essential. Let this stand in a warm place (near the fire, or in the sun) until the batter expands and is full of bubbles. It can stand overnight, ready for use in the morning. When the starter has worked sufficiently, it can be kept in a cool place (or can even be frozen, as we have said).

Now, let's make some sourdough breads and biscuits, remembering that when we use some of the starter we always add more flour and water to take the place of what we have used.

Sourdough Biscuits

> *1 cup starter*
> *¼ teaspoon baking soda*
> *1 egg (or egg powder)*
> *1 tablespoon shortening (melted fat)*
> *Flour (enough to make a stiff dough)*

Mix the above ingredients until all are sufficiently blended to make kneadable dough. Roll or pat this flat on a floured strip of aluminum foil, a strip of plastic, a dish towel, or something similar, and cut the dough into biscuit-sized pieces. If these are allowed to raise for an hour or so, so much the better. Set the biscuits in a greased skillet or Dutch oven, or in a pan in the reflector baker, and bake them until golden brown.

If you don't want to bother with fashioning the biscuits, just drop them by spoonfuls onto the greased pan. Remember that in making such breads we need heat on top and bottom. If done in a skillet, put it over the fire until the biscuits are browned on the bottom. Then prop the skillet at an angle against the fire, so heat can brown the tops. Baking should take about 15 minutes, and slow baking will insure golden biscuits properly cooked all the way through.

Sourdough Bread

> *2 cups starter*
> *½ teaspoon baking soda*
> *1 tablespoon shortening*
> *About 1 cup flour*

Mix all ingredients with enough flour to form kneadable dough. Flour the loaf of dough and put it in a greased pan, leaving it in a warm place until it rises to about twice its size. Then bake it in the reflector oven or Dutch oven for about an hour—until the "sliver test" indicates the bread is done clear through. (It is well to start the bread near a fairly hot fire, and then to move it back a bit after 10 minutes or so. Don't let it brown too much too soon.)

Sourdough Pancakes and Waffles

(This is Mrs. Ruth Allman's recipe, whose address is 213 Seventh Street, Juneau, Alaska. Mrs. Allman is an expert at sourdough cookery and sells her Sourdough Starter Mix by mail to people all over the world. Another of her specialties is Wild Rose Hip Preserves, which are a gourmet's treat well worth investigating.)

Mrs. Allman recommends mixing the starter with added flour and warm water the night before, so enough thick, rich, creamy batter will be on hand for next morning's pancakes, plus enough left over to keep the starter going. This of course is necessary if there isn't enough starter on hand to make the quantity of cakes desired. This author's practice is always to keep at least a pint of starter in a wide-mouth glass jar in the refrigerator, or in some other cool place. On the evening before next morning's pancake feast he pours the starter into a large (non-metal) bowl, and stirs in about two cups of flour and enough warm water to make the batter. This rises and works overnight. If it has a slight crust in the morning, this is stirred in. Two cups of the mixture are removed; the rest being stored away for the next starter. The stirring is done with a wooden spoon because the batter's flavor is impaired if the batter comes in contact with metal. Then we proceed as follows:

> *2 cups starter*
> *1 egg*
> *2 tablespoons sugar*
> *4 tablespoons cooking oil*
> *1 teaspoon baking soda*
> *1 jigger water*

Pour the sourdough starter into a mixing bowl and stir in the egg, sugar, and cooking oil. When ready to cook, fold in the soda, which has been mixed with the water, to make a fairly thick liquid batter. Gently mix, and drop by the tablespoonful onto a hot greased griddle. Turn only once when bottoms of cakes are golden brown. (If you can find any blueberries, be sure to add some!) Use the same recipe for waffles.

If it is inconvenient to carry the semi-liquid starter in the non-metal container we have recommended, mix enough flour with it to make a soft ball, and drop this in with the flour (which is handy to carry in a plastic bag). When you reach camp, you can add enough of one or more of the previously mentioned liquids to reliquefy it.

(Alcoa Wrap)

Aluminum foil provides an easy way for reflecting heat onto the top of bread and biscuits. At left, a sheet of foil is propped behind the fire to reflect heat downward. At right, an end of the foil is rolled around a green branch and placed on crotched sticks for support. Bottom of foil is anchored by rocks so the sheet of foil inclines forward over the back of the fire.

Along with these sourdough recipes, the co-feature among woodsmen is bannock, or "camp bread," which was discussed in Chapter Three. Let's look at some of the many ways by which this recipe can be extended to make a wide variety of camp breads.

Bannock (Basic Recipe)

  1 cup flour
  1 teaspoon baking powder
  ¼ teaspoon salt

Mix these dry ingredients together. This can be done before a camping trip by mixing a multiple of this recipe and by carrying the mix in a strong plastic bag, with the opening twisted, folded over, and secured with a rubber band.

When ready to make the bannock, have the skillet greased and fairly hot, because the dough rises quickly and the cake will lose some of its lightness if we don't work fast.

Rub some of the flour on your hands, and quickly mix enough water into the mix to make a stiff dough. Pat this into a cake not over 1 inch thick; flour it well and set it on the hot skillet, which is then placed over a moderate fire. When the cake has firmed and has begun to brown on the bottom, flip the cake over to do the other side. At this point the pan can be propped at an angle in front of the fire, so the heat will reach the top of the cake. Let it bake and brown slowly for 15 minutes or so; then test it with a sliver to be sure it is done. Break it open when hot, and serve it with butter or jam —or with a stew.

Baking Bannock on a Stick

If you have a large bag of the flour mix, roll down the sides of the bag and make a small depression in the flour. Into this pour about 1 cup water or milk, and mix flour and liquid with a clean stick until a stiff dough is formed. This is patted into a cake and cooked as above.

Another variation is to peel a 1-inch-thick green stick of sweet wood (such as birch or maple) and to stir the dough with this. Use only 1 or 2 tablespoons water, which should result in coating the stick with dough about ½ inch thick and 4 or 5 inches upward on the stick. Prop this stick in the heat of the fire until the dough has baked. Then pull the resulting hollow biscuit off the stick. Another way, using a similar stick that has short trimmed branches on its end, is to form the dough into a long cylinder about 1 inch in diameter, and to wind this around the stick. The projections on the stick help to prevent the dough from falling off. Bake this "bread on a stick" as above.

BREAD BAKED ON A STICK   (Boy Scouts of America)

Wrap a thin cake of bannock dough around a peeled green stick and bake it over the coals. This, and a shish kebab, make a tasty lunch, as this Boy Scout demonstrates.

Bannock (Variations)

Now, depending on whether you want your bannock as a bread or a cake, you can add to this recipe to suit yourself. Use milk, or canned or powdered milk mixed in proper proportion, instead of water. Add an egg or equivalent egg powder to double the above recipe. Stir in 1 tablespoon sugar. Add flavorings of any kind, such as cinnamon. Include berries, chopped dates, nuts, raisins, or what have you. Mix 1 tablespoon melted butter or bacon fat in the above recipe. Make a chocolate sauce, and pour it over one of these fancy bannocks for dessert.

Turn the bannock into griddle cakes by adding enough more liquid to make a batter. In this case, stir in an egg and a little shortening, if you have it—and maybe a handful of berries. To make corn bread, use ½ cup corn meal and ½ cup flour instead of the 1 cup flour in the above recipe. In this case, also add an egg. Bannock can be made into biscuits by adding 1 or 2 tablespoons bacon fat or other shortening and by cutting the flattened dough into biscuits. In this case, include nuts, raisins, egg, flavorings, or something else, along with a little sugar, to turn

the bannock, or these biscuits, into very tasty cake. One of our favorites is to stir small pieces of semi-sweet chocolate into the bannock. The little chocolate pieces mixed into the bread make an excellent chocolate cake dessert.

But remember to mix all the dry ingredients first. To make a light and fluffy bannock, it's necessary to work fast after the liquid has been added. Also, don't try to bake any bread or cake too quickly. Give it quick heat at first, but then move it back to slower heat, so it will turn out nicely browned, and baked clear through.

Biscuits

    2 cups flour
    2 teaspoons baking powder
    ½ teaspoon salt
    ¼ cup sugar
    ¼ cup cooking oil or shortening
    1 egg
    Milk (as needed: sweet, sour, or evaporated)

Mix all ingredients, using only enough milk to make a soft dough that can be handled. If solid shortening is used, cut it into the dry ingredients with a fork or two knives. Avoid mixing the shortening for too long a time. When mixed, turn the dough out on a floured surface and knead it slightly, patting it into a cake about ½ inch thick. To insure lightness of biscuits, avoid pressing the dough. Cut it into biscuit-size pieces and bake in fairly hot heat for 12 to 15 minutes. The biscuits can be made in a lightly greased skillet over the open fire if they are turned after about 5 minutes.

To make plain biscuits, omit the egg and sugar. To make baking powder biscuits, use double the amount of baking powder. To make drop biscuits, add enough milk to the baking powder biscuit formula so the dough is soft enough to be dropped from a spoon. If self-rising flour is used, omit the baking powder and salt. For fancy biscuits, include the egg and sugar, and add nutmeg, cinnamon, nuts, berries, cut-up dates, or small chocolate pieces. (In this case, you end up with cakes.) For whole wheat biscuits, substitute for the white flour part or all whole wheat flour. For oatmeal biscuits, add 1½ cups rolled oats. For corn bread, use 1 cup yellow corn meal instead of one of the cups of white flour.

Cheese Bread

>1 can cream-style corn
>¾ cup milk
>⅓ cup shortening
>2 eggs, slightly beaten
>1 cup corn meal
>½ teaspoon baking soda
>1 teaspoon salt
>1½ cups grated cheese

Mix all ingredients except the cheese. Pour half the batter into a 9×9-inch greased pan. Spread with half the cheese. Add rest of batter and sprinkle with remaining cheese. Bake 45 minutes in a 400° oven, or in a Dutch oven or reflector baker for the same time in fairly hot heat.

Corn Bread

>2 cups corn meal
>1 cup flour
>1 cup sour milk (*if not available, add 1 table-spoon vinegar to sweet milk and set it aside until it sours—about 10 minutes*)
>2 cups milk or equivalent mixture of evaporated or powdered milk
>1 teaspoon baking soda
>½ cup molasses
>1 teaspoon salt

Mix all ingredients; pour into a greased pan and bake in a reflector oven or Dutch oven at about 400° for about 45 minutes. Test for doneness by using a wood sliver.

Skillet Bread

>3 strips bacon, halved
>2 cups flour
>½ teaspoon baking soda
>2½ teaspoons baking powder
>1 teaspoon salt
>1½ cups sour milk

Arrange the 6 pieces of bacon like the spokes of a wheel in the bottom of a frying pan. Sift the dry ingredients and mix well. Stir in milk quickly, and pour the dough over the bacon, spreading it evenly. Put lid on skillet and cook slowly about 10 minutes. Pour off any excess fat; turn the bread over, and cook for 10 minutes more.

Doughnuts

Use the Dutch oven, or a similar deep kettle containing a large amount of bacon fat or other shortening. Test the heat of the fat by dropping in a bit of dough. If it bubbles, actively, the fat should be at about the right heat. Don't add more doughnuts unless they keep on bubbling in the fat.

>3 cups flour
>¾ cup milk
>2 eggs
>1 cup sugar
>½ teaspoon salt
>1 teaspoon baking soda
>1 tablespoon cooking oil or fat
>2 teaspoons cream of tartar
>½ teaspoon powdered ginger
>½ teaspoon cinnamon
>½ teaspoon nutmeg

Combine all ingredients into a smooth dough, rolled flat to ½-inch thickness. Using can covers (or what have you), cut dough into doughnut shape, using additional flour to keep dough from sticking. If no suitable doughnut cutters are available, merely cut the dough into 2-inch squares. Fry in hot fat until golden brown. Drain on absorbent paper.

Dumplings

>6 heaping tablespoons flour (*sifted, if possible*)
>2 teaspoons baking powder
>1 teaspoon salt
>1 cup milk or equivalent powdered or canned milk

Mix ingredients, adding only enough milk to make the dough the right thickness to be dropped from a spoon without spreading out in the kettle. Drop by spaced spoonfuls into the kettle of stew. Cover, and cook 10 minutes without removing the cover, since removing the cover before this time will make the dumplings soggy.

Hominy Grits

    4 cups water
    1 teaspoon salt
    1 cup grits
    3 teaspoons butter

Bring water to a boil. Add salt and grits. Cook, stirring, until thick. Turn the grits into a greased pan and dot them with butter. Bake in reflector baker at moderate heat for about 45 minutes, until the grits are brown and crispy.

When cold, grits can be sliced and fried in butter or bacon fat until golden brown. Serve the slices with syrup. (This is an excellent dish to serve with roasted game birds.)

Pancakes I

    2 cups flour
    2 teaspoons double-acting baking powder
    1 teaspoon salt
    2 tablespoons sugar
    6 tablespoons shortening
    3 eggs, beaten
    1½ cups milk or equivalent powdered or canned
       milk

Sift dry ingredients together and blend shortening into flour, working ingredients until they resemble corn meal. (This mixture can be carried in a plastic bag or other container to use on camping trips.) Stir in eggs and add enough milk to bring batter to desired consistency. (If you like thin cakes, the batter should be fairly thin.) Cook on greased griddle, turning once when golden brown on bottom.

Pancakes II

    2 cups flour
    ½ cup corn meal
    2 scant teaspoons baking powder
    1 teaspoon salt
    1 tablespoon molasses or sugar
    ¼ teaspoon baking soda
    2 eggs
    2 cups sour milk or buttermilk (regular milk,
       or even beer may be used)
    6 tablespoons shortening, melted

Stir all ingredients until blended, adding enough liquid to make batter of the right consistency. Cook on greased griddle, turning once when golden brown on bottom.

This recipe is similar to the one above, except that it includes corn meal, and either sour milk, buttermilk, or beer. Try either of these recipes with chopped apple or blueberries.

Potato Pancakes

    1½ cups raw, white potatoes, peeled, grated, and
       with juice squeezed out
    1 teaspoon salt
    1 teaspoon baking powder
    2 tablespoons flour
    1 egg (optional)
    Canned milk

Mix all ingredients, adding only enough milk to bind the mixture. Include ½ cup minced onion, if desired. Drop by spoonfuls onto a well-greased griddle and turn only once when the bottom is golden brown.

Improvised Syrup for Pancakes

Few campers will want to carry syrup. Packaged syrup can be obtained in dry form, which can be prepared merely by boiling it with water. It can also be made by boiling ½ cup brown sugar with just enough water to dissolve it. Another way:

    2 cups sugar
    1 cup water
    ½ teaspoon maple flavoring

Boil the sugar and water together for about 10 minutes, then add the flavoring.

Peanut Butter French Toast

Butter 2 pieces whole wheat (or other) bread. Spread thickly with peanut butter and form a sandwich. Dip in beaten egg. Fry on greased griddle until the bread has browned. Serve with syrup and bacon or sausage.

Polenta

    4 cups water
    1 cup yellow corn meal
    1 teaspoon salt
    2 teaspoons butter
    ¼ cup grated Parmesan cheese
    ¼ teaspoon black pepper
    Dash of cayenne pepper

Bring water to a slow boil and mix in the corn meal and salt. Cook, stirring constantly, until thickened. Put the container in a larger receptacle containing some boiling water, and cook about 45 minutes, until the corn meal tastes done. (Use a double boiler for this, if you have one.) Add remaining ingredients, and cook for a few more minutes. Spoon the polenta around a hot platter and fill the center with wild game and gravy.

PREPARED FLOUR RECIPES

The habit of carrying all-purpose flour, baking powder, and other basic ingredients, rather than prepared mixes, is a wise one, because these simple ingredients can be adapted to a very wide range of recipes, some of which have been given above. However, a container of a prepared biscuit flour, such as "Bisquick," may prove handier on short trips. Packages of prepared flour usually contain several basic recipes, but here are a few others:

Cheese Bread

3¾ cups "Bisquick" or prepared biscuit mix
¾ cup grated sharp cheese
1 egg, beaten
1½ cups milk

Blend ingredients and heat for ½ minute. Pour into a greased pan or aluminum foil dish and bake for about 1 hour in moderate heat. (Leave out the cheese, if you prefer.)

Fried Biscuits

2 cups "Bisquick" or prepared biscuit mix
⅔ cup milk

Stir until the mixture becomes soft dough, beating slightly with a fork. Handling the dough gently, pat it flat on a floured surface. Cut into biscuit-size pieces. Add about 2 tablespoons shortening to a hot skillet and lay the biscuits in the bubbling fat, turning them over after 5 or 10 minutes to fry both sides to a golden brown. (The biscuits will cook faster and lighter if they are covered after they are turned over.)

Tomato Biscuits

2 cups "Bisquick" or prepared biscuit mix
⅔ cup canned tomato juice
1 tablespoon caraway seeds (optional)

Stir with a fork to make a soft dough (which will be slightly sticky). Preheat the Dutch oven, adding some shortening. Pinch off biscuit-size pieces of the dough; mop them in the shortening and line the bottom of the inside of the oven with them. Cover the oven, piling coals on the hot cover. If the fire is right, the biscuits will take 15 to 20 minutes to cook. Inspect them after 5 minutes or so and move the oven to a hotter or cooler place if they seem to be baking too slow or too fast.

They can also be made in a frying pan or a reflector oven. These biscuits are very good when served with wild game.

When preparing breads and biscuits, remember to use a little ingenuity with the recipes, regardless of what they call for. Fruits, raisins, dates, nuts, berries, flavorings, and many other ingredients that may be on hand can transform almost any basic recipe into a wide variety of tasty variations.

Chapter Twenty

WHAT'S FOR DESSERT?

In the preceding chapter we have seen how simple breads and biscuits can be made into very tasty cakelike desserts by adding available items such as sugar, nuts, berries, raisins, flavorings, and chocolate. Now let's explore a few other simple ideas for ending camp meals on a sweet note.

Before doing this, however, let's remember to include in the spice bag discussed in Chapter Sixteen not only such items as cinnamon and nutmeg, but also flavorings such as maple, lemon, and vanilla extracts, plus whatever else our individual tastes prefer for increasing the tastiness of beverages and desserts. These items are compact, light, and inexpensive. They work wonders with foods.

CHOCOLATE: STAPLE ENERGY FOOD FOR SPORTSMEN

And here it also seems appropriate to mention the value of chocolate for campers, because chocolate is a concentrated and delicious energy food, quickly convertible into a wide range of confections, beverages, and desserts. Sportsmen have preferences in selection of chocolate, largely because of food value and convenience. One outstanding item is the semi-sweet chocolate morsels available in transparent bags at any grocer's. These are small, pure chocolate drops that are particularly convenient because they make it unnecessary to break or grate cake chocolate. Being "semi-sweet," they are less sweet than usual bar chocolate, and are ideal for munching on the trail or for inclusion in all desserts and sauces where chocolate is an ingredient.

Also take along plenty of bar chocolate. Select the larger bars because they are less liable to break up or become soft during transportation.

With an apple and a chocolate bar in his pocket, an energetic hunter or fisherman can keep going all day.

RECIPES FOR EASY CAMP DESSERTS

The following desserts have been selected because they are easy to make from ingredients that are normally available:

Apple Betty

Apples are abundant in most areas, especially during the hunting season. Here's a simple dessert that uses them, as well as bread ends, broken crackers, plain cookies, and certain kinds of breakfast foods, even if they are a bit soggy!

1½ *cups cubed bread or broken crackers, or other items, as above*
¼ *cup butter or margarine*
8 *medium-sized apples pared, cored, sliced*
1 *teaspoon cinnamon*
1 *cup brown or white sugar*
¼ *teaspoon salt*
4 *teaspoons lemon juice or equivalent extract*
¼ *cup water*

Toss the bread and melted butter together. Toss apples, cinnamon, sugar, and salt together. Put a third of the buttered bread cubes in a pan. Add a layer of half the apples; a layer of a third bread cubes, the rest of the apples, and the rest of the bread cubes. Sprinkle the lemon juice and water over this. Cover, and bake in moderate heat for about an hour. A short time before the dessert is done, remove cover to brown the crust.

Blanc Mange

2 *cups milk or equivalent processed milk*
3 *tablespoons cornstarch*
4 *tablespoons sugar*
¼ *teaspoon salt*
Flavoring

Mix the cornstarch, sugar, and salt in a little of the milk. Bring the rest of the milk to a boil, and pour in the cornstarch mixture. Cook slowly and stir constantly until the mixture thickens. Cover and cook slowly for about 15 minutes more, stirring occasionally. Stir in flavoring and allow the mixture to cool. Serve with milk, if available. For flavorings, select from these:

Caramel: For this, do not include the sugar in the above recipe. Rub the skillet or pan with butter or margarine and add the sugar, heating it until it melts and becomes light brown. Add just enough water to melt the sugar. Fold this into the above dessert.

Chocolate: Stir in two tablespoons of cocoa, or a handful of semi-sweet chocolate morsels, or equivalent bar chocolate.

Extract: Flavor to taste with a suitable extract such as vanilla, maple, lemon, orange, etc. (Go easy on this. The flavoring may be powerful!)

Fruits: Use drained canned fruits, dried fruits such as raisins, coconut, chopped dates, etc., finely chopped nuts, or fresh berries.

Bread Pudding

This is another recipe for using stale bread, broken cookies or crackers, soggy breakfast foods, or what have you.

> 2 cups bread crumbs (as above)
> 3 cups milk, scalded
> ¼ cup butter, melted
> ½ cup sugar
> 3 eggs, beaten, or equivalent powder
> ½ teaspoon nutmeg or other flavoring
> ½ teaspoon salt
> ¼ cup raisins

Put the bread in a pan or baking dish and pour the scalded milk over it. When cool, stir in all other ingredients. Bake slowly, uncovered, for about an hour. Let the top get crispy.

As in the Blanc Mange recipe, Bread Pudding can be varied by adding chocolate, fruits, nuts, or other flavorings. Also try it with Hard Sauce.

Hard Sauce

> ⅓ cup butter, creamed
> 1 cup sugar (confectioners', preferably)
> 2 tablespoons liquid

The liquid can be cream, milk, coffee, fruit juice, or rum or other liquor. Blend butter and sugar, and beat in the liquid until blended and foamy. If milk or cream is used, add a dash of cinnamon or nutmeg.

Cake

> ½ cup melted butter
> 1 cup sugar
> 2 eggs or ⅓ cup egg powder
> 2 cups flour
> ⅓ teaspoon salt
> 1 heaping tablespoon baking powder
> ¾ cup milk or ⅓ cup milk powder, plus water
> 1½ teaspoons vanilla

For best results, measure proportions accurately. Combine the butter and sugar. If fresh eggs are used, separate yolks and whites. Beat the yolks into the butter and sugar. Sift flour, salt, and baking powder together, and stir this and the milk into the egg-yolk mixture. Beat whites stiff and fold in. Stir in vanilla.

If egg powder is used, mix all dry ingredients (including milk powder, if you use it.) Work in the melted butter. Stir in milk (if used instead of milk powder). If milk powder is used, stir in water to make a stiff pourable batter. Lastly, stir in the vanilla. Beat the batter until it is smooth, and pour into greased pan(s). Bake in moderate (375°) heat in oven or reflector baker for 20 to 30 minutes, until the "sliver test" indicates the cake is done. Let the cake cool in the pan for 5 minutes before turning it out, or frost it in the pan when it has cooled.

For an easy frosting, use the Hard Sauce described above, but make it with almost no liquid, so it will not run. Note that this Hard Sauce can be made in several flavors.

The cake itself can be made in several flavors too. Add maple, lemon, orange flavoring, etc., instead of the vanilla. Add chopped nuts, dates, raisins, or other chopped dried fruit. For chocolate cake, add ½ cup or so of pieces of semi-sweet chocolate or half a cup of cocoa powder. Another tasty idea is to serve pieces of the cake with chocolate sauce poured over them.

Chocolate Sauce

> ½ cup instant cocoa mix
> ½ cup sugar
> ½ cup evaporated milk

Combine above and bring just to a boil, stirring constantly. This sauce can be made with condensed milk by leaving out the sugar. Combine ½ cup cocoa and 1 cup sweetened condensed milk, and bring it just to a boil, stirring constantly.

(Norm Thompson)

A snack in the snow, heated on a single-burner Sterno stove, is enjoyed by this artist while painting Wyoming's Grand Teton Mountains near Jackson Hole.

Excellent chocolate sauce also can be made by melting 1 cup semi-sweet chocolate with ½ cup milk. This is safest when made in a double boiler, but it can be done in a saucepan without burning the chocolate if the mixture is melted slowly and stirred constantly.

Chocolate Pudding

This is another recipe that can utilize almost any kind of cookies, stale cake, or breakfast foods such as corn flakes—even if they are a bit soggy! After it has rained in camp, this is a way to use such foods, which otherwise might be thrown away.

> 1 can (1⅔ cups) evaporated milk
> ¾ cup instant cocoa mix
> ½ cup sugar
> ¾ cup water
> 10 (or so) coarsely broken graham crackers (or the cookies, breakfast foods, etc., mentioned above)

Combine the first four ingredients and bring them to a boil, stirring constantly. Add the graham crackers (or what have you) and cook over low heat for about half an hour, stirring occasionally. Spoon the pudding into dishes.

Coffee Cake

> 4 cups "Bisquick" or other prepared flour
> 1 cup brown sugar
> ½ cup butter
> 1½ cups milk or water
> 1 teaspoon cinnamon powder

Mix ½ cup brown sugar with the flour and combine this with the butter by blending with a fork or two knives, until the mixture resembles a coarse meal. Blend in enough of the liquid to make a soft dough. Pour this into a greased pan, and sprinkle the top of the cake with the rest of the sugar and the cinnamon. Bake in the reflector baker in moderate heat for 20 to 30 minutes, until the "sliver test" indicates the cake is done.

As in several other of these recipes, the formula can be varied by adding raisins, nuts, fruits, or other flavorings.

Dessertwiches

This one is mainly for the young people, but they'll like it!

Combine some sweetened condensed milk with a slightly smaller volume of flaked coconut. Spread both sides of slices of bread with this.

Make sandwiches by sprinkling bits of semi-sweet chocolate liberally between each two slices. Put the sandwiches in a hinged wire broiler and toast them until they are golden brown on both sides.

Energy Bars

This is a favorite chocolate confection that we usually make at home and take along on outdoor trips because it is a compact form of tasty energy that won't break up or melt when carried in the pocket. The proportions are not critical, so let's just use what we have on hand.

Merely combine in a skillet over moderate heat about 2 cups of any one or a combination of ready-to-eat cereals, such as "Grape-Nuts" and "Bran Flakes," plus some raisins, nuts, or coconut, if these are on hand. (The heating serves to make these ingredients crisp and helps to melt the chocolate.) Remove from heat and stir in until melted about 1 cup (a 6-ounce package) of pieces of semi-sweet chocolate. When everything is stirred until well coated with chocolate, drop by spoonfuls onto waxed paper or foil and let stand until firm. (The mixture will be very thick and hard to stir.)

For use on trips, we pat this mixture solidly into a muffin tin and turn out the cakes when they have cooled. Then we wrap them in aluminum foil. They will keep for months in normal climates and are a tasty form of quick energy for outdoor trips as well as an excellent confection in camp or at home. Make them in a double boiler, rather than in a skillet, if possible.

Fritters

  1 cup flour
  1 teaspoon baking powder
  Dash of salt
  ⅓ cup milk or equivalent processed milk
  1 egg or equivalent egg powder

Mix flour, baking powder, and salt thoroughly. Beat milk and egg together, and blend these with the dry ingredients. Drop by spoonfuls into fairly deep fat that is hot enough so that the fritters will bubble vigorously when being fried. Drain on absorbent paper when the fritters are fried to a golden brown. Serve with syrup.

This recipe also is very adaptable in that fruit pieces can be rolled in flour and then dipped in the batter and fried. So can bite-size pieces of cooked vegetables, such as carrots, eggplant, and potato, or clams, scallops, pieces of fish, etc. Corn fritters can be made by draining half a can of whole-kernel corn and mixing it with the batter.

Gingerbread

  1½ cups flour
  1 teaspoon baking soda
  ⅓ teaspoon salt
  ½ teaspoon ginger
  ½ teaspoon cinnamon
  ¼ cup shortening
  ¼ cup sugar
  1 egg, beaten
  ½ cup molasses
  ½ cup hot water

Sift all dry ingredients together. Cream shortening and sugar. Add beaten egg and molasses. Stir in dry ingredients and water. Beat the batter until smooth, and bake in a greased, floured pan about 30 minutes at moderate heat. Test with a sliver to be sure the bread is done. Serve with whipped cream. (Evaporated milk can be whipped if the milk and the bowl are very cold. After the milk is partially whipped, add 1 tablespoon lemon juice to make the cream stiffer, if need be.)

Hot Cake

Combine equal parts (by volume) of cocoa and sweetened condensed milk. Spread this over toast or bread and broil it until it bubbles.

Pies

  2 cups flour (sift before measuring)
  1 teaspoon salt
  ¾ cup shortening
  ¼ cup water

Sift flour and salt together. Mix one third of this flour with the water to form a paste. Cut the shortening into the remainder of the flour until the bits of shortening have been reduced nearly to the size of buckshot. Blend the flour paste into this with a fork until the dough can be shaped into a ball. Divide in halves and roll with a floured rolling pin (or something similar) on a floured surface. Roll from the center out to the edge until the dough is ¼ inch thick. Fold dough in half, and lift it into the pie pan, fitting it carefully to be sure there are no air spaces between dough and pan. Fill the pie; crimp on the top crust, and trim edges. Slit the top crust, so steam can escape.

(Boy Scouts of America)

Berry pies, cooked in a reflector baker.

Time for a beverage break!
Left: The author (left) and Joe Novick pause for a snack while bow-hunting for deer in Maine. Right: Captain "Honk"
Clarke (left) and the author enjoy a beverage break while fishing for striped bass off the Connecticut shore.

A single-crust pie is made by using the bottom crust only, with edges crimped. Prick the bottom crust in several places with a fork, so it will not bubble up. Bake in fairly hot heat (425°) for about 15 minutes, until properly browned.

Here are a few fillings (and remember that you can take along excellent canned or dehydrated fillings):

Apple Pie Filling

    6 to 8 tart apples
    4 tablespoons flour
    1¼ cups sugar
    1 teaspoon cinnamon
    2 tablespoons butter or margarine

Peel, core, and slice apples thickly. Combine dry ingredients. Spread half of dry ingredients over bottom of crust. Add apples evenly to fill the shell. Sprinkle the rest of the dry ingredients over the top of the apples and dot with butter. Put on top crust and bake for approximately 45 minutes in fairly hot (425°) heat.

Berry Pie Filling

    4 cups fresh berries
    3 tablespoons flour
    1 cup sugar
    ¼ teaspoon salt
    2 tablespoons butter or margarine

Mix dry ingredients, and carefully mix these with the berries. Add filling to the pie shell; dot with butter; put on top crust and bake for approximately 45 minutes in fairly hot (425°) heat. (In making a blueberry pie, try sprinkling about 2 tablespoons of lemon juice over the berries when they have been added to the pie.)

In using canned berries, omit the salt and use a little less butter. Use a whole No. 2 can of berries, juice and all. Mix all ingredients, and cook over medium heat until the juices have thickened. Cool the filling; add to pie shell and complete the pie as above.

Custard Pie Filling

   4 eggs or equivalent processed eggs
   ½ cup sugar
   ½ teaspoon salt
   2½ cups milk or equivalent processed milk
   1 teaspoon vanilla
   Dash of nutmeg

Beat eggs. Add sugar and salt. Add milk and vanilla. Pour liquid into a baked pie shell and sprinkle with nutmeg. Bake 10 minutes in fairly hot heat (450°) and then move pie to slower heat (325°) for about 30 minutes. (Reducing the heat should keep the pie from curdling.)

Drained fruit can be added to this pie. Make a coconut pie by spreading coconut over the top before baking.

Shortcake

   2 cups flour (sift before measuring)
   4 teaspoons baking powder
   1 teaspoon salt
   ½ cup shortening
   ⅔ cup milk or equivalent processed milk

Sift dry ingredients together and cut in the shortening until blended like coarse meal. Stir in milk. Turn the dough out on a floured surface and knead it slightly, then roll it to ½ inch thick. Bake as one cake or cut into individual cakes. Baking time will be about 15 minutes in fairly hot (450°) heat. Separate the cake(s) into upper and lower halves, serving while they are hot. Dot the lower half with plenty of butter, and pour over it fresh or canned berries or fruit, adding sugar to the fruit if it needs to be sweetened. Put on top half of the cake and add more fruit. Serve with whipped cream, remembering that canned milk (or milk crystals) can be whipped if everything has been thoroughly chilled.

Spoon Cakes in Chocolate Sauce

   1 cup brown sugar
   4 tablespoons cornstarch or ½ cup flour
   Dash of salt
   3 cups water
   1 cup (6-ounce package) semi-sweet chocolate
      morsels
   1 cup "Bisquick" or other prepared flour
   2 tablespoons sugar
   ⅛ teaspoon cinnamon
   6 tablespoons milk

Combine brown sugar, cornstarch, and salt in a skillet and stir in the water gradually. Cook over low heat until it thickens. Then stir in the chocolate until the mixture is smooth. Meanwhile, make a spoon cake mix by combining the flour, sugar, cinnamon, and milk, mixing them together lightly with a fork. When the chocolate sauce is bubbling gently over a slow fire, drop the spoon cake batter into the sauce, ½ teaspoonful at a time. Cook uncovered for 10 minutes, then cover tightly and cook 10 minutes more. Serve at once, with plenty of sauce.

OUR OUTDOORS—A PRICELESS HERITAGE TO PRESERVE

When this great country of ours was young, its lakes and rivers teemed with fish and waterfowl; its forests and plains with game animals and birds. The abundance of Nature's bounty seemed inexhaustible, but for many generations it was woefully abused. We stripped our forests, polluted our rivers, and we slaughtered our fish and game to the extent that some species now are extinct—while others are in danger of becoming so.

Today, through the co-operation of sportsmen's clubs, the Izaak Walton League, outdoor writers, and other conservation-minded groups, this disastrous trend in many areas is being checked—and in some places is being reversed. Landowners who once closed their acres to campers and sportsmen whose predecessors had abused their privileges now gradually are welcoming them again. In return, they rightfully expect that visitors will ask permission to enter private lands, and that guests will neither harm fences and other property nor be careless with guns, matches, and litter.

In the abuse of our heritage of the great out of doors, unfortunately all must suffer for the thoughtlessness of a relative few. Whenever one of the few is known, it may be proper to let him know his actions are decidedly unpopular.

Since we outdoor cooks and campers now number in the tens of millions, united and singly we can have a powerful effect on the conservation and restoration of our natural resources. We can become active members in conservation and education groups such as the Izaak Walton League. We must make our elected representatives realize that the restoration of our forests, our rivers, and our wild life is of primary importance, and that further abuses will not be tolerated. Each of us can set an example of appreciative co-operation with landowners; of taking no more fish and game than we really need; and of keeping our camp sites as clean and neat as we would like to find them. If there is no receptacle for the disposal of refuse, we can burn it, bury it—or even carry it home. Used cans, wet papers, and crumpled foil never did add to the view!

America is one of the most beautiful lands on earth. It provides us with fish and game, gorgeous scenery—and abundant facilities for outdoor fun. As good sportsmen, let's all join together to keep it that way!

CREDITS
AND REFERENCES

In addition to credits mentioned elsewhere, the author expresses appreciation to the following organizations for photographs (identified by trade names) and information submitted for use in this book. Readers who desire additional information on the outdoor products referred to may obtain it by writing to the addresses listed below:

"ABERCROMBIE": (Outfitters) David T. Abercrombie Company, 97 Chambers St., New York 7, N.Y.

"ALCOA WRAP": (aluminum foil) Aluminum Company of America, 1661 Alcoa Building, Pittsburgh 19, Penna.

"ANDROCK": (Outdoor cooking equipment) The Washburn Company, 28 Union Street, Worcester 8, Mass.

"BARRIER": (insect repellent) Sterno, Inc., 300 Park Avenue, New York 22, N.Y.

"BETHANY": (picnic griddle) Bethany Fellowship, Inc., 6820 Auto Club Road, Minneapolis 20, Minn.

"BLU-BURN-R": (bottled gas coffee percolators) Blue-Burn-R Products, Inc., Highway 69 South, Monroe, Wis.

"BOY SCOUTS OF AMERICA": National Director of Program Resources, Boy Scouts of America, New Brunswick, N.J.

"CAMPERS KITCHEN": (portable kitchens) Campers Kitchen Company, P. O. Box 6062, San Antonio 9, Tex.

"CARRY-LITE": (plastic water cans, refrigerators, etc.) Molded Carry-Lite Products Co., 3000 West Clarke Street, Milwaukee 45, Wis.

"CHAR-BROIL": (portable grills) Columbus Iron Works Company, Columbus, Ga.

"CHARCOAL KING": (broilers and grills) Berten Products, West Cornwall, Conn.

"CHUCK WAGON": (emergency food kits) Chuck Wagon Foods, 176 Oak Street, Newton 64, Mass.

"COLEMAN": (portable stoves, refrigerators, etc.) The Coleman Company, Inc., 250 North St. Francis Ave., Wichita 1, Kan.

"COVERED WAGON": (charcoal grills) Covered Wagon Products, Inc., 8605 Lincoln Avenue, Morton Grove, Ill.

"CRONCO": (portable refrigerators) Cronstroms Manufacturing, Inc., 4225 Hiawatha Avenue, Minneapolis 6, Minn.

"CURTIS COOKER": (portable grill) Curtis Cooker Corporation, 45-B Exchange Street, Rochester 14, N.Y.

"DEXTER": (cutlery) Russell-Harrington Cutlery Company, Southbridge, Mass.

"DISPOSA-PAN": (disposable aluminum frying pan) Sterno, Inc., 300 Park Avenue, New York 22, N.Y.

"ECLIPSE": (portable grills) Eclipse Metal Manufacturing Corporation, Eden, N.Y.

"EVINRUDE": (outboard motors) Evinrude Motors, 4143 North 27th Street, Milwaukee 16, Wis.

"FORD TIMES": (magazine) Ford Motor Company, *The American Road,* Dearborn, Mich.

"HANDY TABLE": (folding tables with chairs) Milwaukee Stamping Company, 800 South 72nd St., Milwaukee 14, Wis.

HIBACHIS: (charcoal stoves) Cutlers International, Ltd., 1776 Broadway, New York 19, N.Y.

"HI-LO": (portable grills) Union Steel Products Company, Albion, Mich.

"INSTA-LITE": (camp stoves, vacuum jugs, etc.) Metalcraft Manufacturing Corporation, Bent & Potomac Streets, St. Louis 16, Mo.

"JET CHEF": (black-on-one-side aluminum foil) B. F. Gladding & Co., Inc., South Otselic, N.Y.

"JOHNSON": (outboard motors) Johnson Motors, Waukegan, Ill.

"J-T FLAMELESS GRILL": (grill) J-T Flameless Grill Company, 312 Wyndhurst Ave., Baltimore 10, Md.

"KAMP PACK": (freeze-dried foods) Bernard Food Industries, Inc., 217 North Jefferson Street, Chicago 6, Ill.

MAINE: (State of) Department of Recreation, State Office Building, Augusta, Me.

"MERCURY": (outboard motors) Kiekhaefer Corporation, Fond du Lac, Wis.

"MUSTANG": (cooking kits) Mustang Manufacturing Company, 602 Elliott Avenue West, Seattle, Wash.

"NESCO": (portable grills) Nesco Industries, Inc. (Division of Knapp-Monarch Co.), Bent & Potomac Sts., St. Louis 16, Mo.

"NESTLÉ": (cocoa and chocolate products) The Nestlé Company, Inc., 100 Bloomingdale Road, White Plains, N.Y.

"NORM THOMPSON": (outfitters) Norm Thompson — Outfitters, Jackson Hole, Wyo.

"NUTRAMENT": (meal-in-a-can) Edward Dalton Company (Division of Mead Johnson & Co.), Evansville 12, Ind.

"OUTDOOR NEBRASKA": (magazine) Nebraska Game, Forestation and Parks Commission, Lincoln 9, Neb.

"PALCO": (cooking kits) Worcester Pressed Aluminum Corporation, 13–15 Hope Avenue, Worcester 3, Mass.

"PEAVEY": (axes and hatchets) The Peavey Manufacturing Company, Brewer, Me.

"POP-TENT": (tents) American Thermos Products Company, Norwich, Conn.

"PRIMUS": (cook stoves) Therm'x Company of California, Ferry Building, San Francisco 11, Calif.

"RAEMCO": (camp stoves) Raemco, Inc., P. O. Box 482, Somerville, N.J.

"REYNOLDS WRAP": (aluminum foil) Reynolds Metals Company, 19 East 47th Street, New York 17, N.Y.

"SKOTCH KOOLER": (portable refrigerators, water jugs, etc.) The Hamilton-Skotch Corporation, 11 East 36th St., New York 16, N.Y.

"STAR-LITE": (freeze-dried foods) Armour & Company, P. O. Box 9222, Chicago 90, Ill.

"STERNO": (solidified alcohol fuels, camp stoves, etc.) Sterno, Inc., 300 Park Avenue, New York 22, N.Y.

"TAYKIT": (cook stoves) Progressive Merchandising, Inc., 35 East Wacker Drive, Chicago 1, Ill.

"THERMOS": (vacuum bottles, lanterns, cook stoves, refrigerators, etc.) American Thermos Products Company, Norwich, Conn.

"TRAIL PACKET": (dehydrated foods) Ad. Seidel & Son, Inc., 2323 Pratt Boulevard, Elk Grove Village, Ill.

"WEAR-EVER": (aluminum cooking utensils) Wear-Ever Aluminum, Inc., New Kensington, Penna.

OTHER BOOKS ON OUTDOOR LIVING

The Outdoor Guide, by Louis M. Henderson (1950), Stackpole and Heck, Inc., Harrisburg, Penna. ($4.50). How to live in the woods, including simple cooking methods and recipes.

The Outdoorsman's Cookbook, by Arthur H. Carhart (1955), The Macmillan Company, New York ($2.95). A very complete book of simple outdoor cooking recipes and methods.

Living off the Country, by Bradford Angier (1956), The Stackpole Company, Harrisburg, Penna. ($5.00). An authoritative book on how to stay alive in the woods in emergencies.

On Your Own in the Wilderness, by Colonel Townsend Whelen and Bradford Angier (1958), The Stackpole Company, Harrisburg, Penna. ($5.00). A complete and authoritative text on outdoor living.

The New Way of the Wilderness, by Calvin Rutstrum (1958), The Macmillan Company, New York ($4.50). A guide to wilderness travel featuring equipment and methods.

Guide to Cooking Fish and Game, by Werner O. Nagel (1960), The Missouri Conservation Commission (75¢). An excellent compilation of fish and game recipes.

Wilderness Cookery, by Bradford Angier (1961), The Stackpole Company, Harrisburg, Penna. ($3.95). An excellent cookbook for the wilderness camper.

INDEX